Business, Charity and Sentiment

Part Two

Business, Charity and Sentiment

Part Two

The South Australian Housing Trust 1987–2011

Susan Marsden

Wakefield
Press

Wakefield Press
1 The Parade West
Kent Town
South Australia 5067
www.wakefieldpress.com.au

First published 2011

Designed and typeset by Paul Wallace
Printed in China by the Opus Group

National Library of Australia Cataloguing-in-Publication entry:

Author:	Marsden, Susan, 1952– .
Title:	Business, charity and sentiment. Part two: the South Australian Housing Trust 1987–2011 / Susan Marsden.
ISBN:	978 1 86254 970 8 (hbk.).
	978 1 86254 971 5 (pbk.).
Notes:	Includes bibliographical references and index.
Subjects:	South Australian Housing Trust – History.
	Public housing – South Australia – History.
Dewey Number:	363.58099423

Contents

Introduction and acknowledgements

Business, Charity and Sentiment: the South Australian Housing Trust 1936–1986 was launched by Premier John Bannon in the Housing Trust's old headquarters at 17 Angas Street, Adelaide, on 26 September 1986. As I wrote later to a newspaper, 'It is my earnest wish that readers will learn a greater understanding of the Trust's role in the social and economic history of the State, and gain a sympathetic concern for those who must suffer and wait during the most recent of a series of housing crises which have afflicted South Australia'. That wish also animates this new history of the Housing Trust for the twenty-five years following 1986.

I also hoped that *Business, Charity and Sentiment* would be put to practical use in informing new ministers, boards, employees and customers of the Trust. And so it was. I hope this modern history will be put to similar good use by the South Australian Housing Trust (SAHT) and Housing SA.

Contemporary history is a fraught business, especially when it involves controversial events, and the historian cannot write as critically or as comprehensively as for more distant times. Public records are closed, and most informants are still employed or in official positions, limiting their ability to offer frank reminiscence. In these circumstances, it is the more remarkable that I was allowed access by the Department for Families and Communities to SAHT and Housing SA records, their Intranet, and to many informants. Amidst the alarms and uncertainties of radical organisational change, staff kept their long commitment to public housing, and a willingness to share the Trust's achievements in a new history.

This updated history draws not only on SAHT and other official records, as well as on secondary sources, but also on tenant and staff recollections, including responses to my questionnaires, and recordings or writings from the Minister and former Board members. All of these informants are listed by name in the bibliography.

I am grateful to the South Australian Housing Trust Board for commissioning this work in 2006, and to the SAHT and Housing SA for providing access to records and staff, as well as encouraging people to contribute recollections. I would especially like to thank executives Malcolm Downie, Helen Fulcher and Phil Fagan-Schmidt; successive history project managers Beverley Morris, Mignon Schneider and Shirley Trebilcock; as well as Alison Bogdanowicz, Wendy Hackel and Rosie Mangan. Thanks also to work-experience student Anne Lord, especially for her help in collecting tenant and staff memoirs.

Most of the illustrations in the book are from Housing SA, as explained in the note below. Alison Bogdanowicz and Shirley Trebilcock, together with (it seemed) half the staff on level 5 at Riverside, also gave welcome help in locating, copying and providing information on illustrations. In particular I appreciate the contributions of Josie Pastore, Brenton Herringe, Eleftherios (Lefty) Morias, Michael Findlay and Tasnim Morium. I am also grateful to those who have created the invaluable SAHT Memorabilia Collection, including Wendy Hackel, Jan Mudge (History South Australia) and the collection's volunteers.

I would like to thank Paul Wallace for his patient and professional editing and indexing of this later history as well as for the book's design which is intended to match the first volume (designed by Erica Fairbanks in 1986).

Finally I thank my friends Maria Dam and Russ Lamb for sharing their peaceful house near Maleny where I wrote the main draft of this book.

I wish to dedicate this new history of the South Australian Housing Trust to the memory of another historian, Averil Holt, who became a dear friend after working with me as a researcher and oral history interviewer for the original *Business, Charity and Sentiment*.

Susan Marsden
Adelaide 2011

A note on the illustrations and abbreviations

Most of the images in the book are reproduced from those held by Housing SA (HSA) at the Riverside headquarters in Adelaide. Many SAHT photographs and drawings have been scanned and digitised by HSA, and are stored in the DIMS database. Other illustrations are reproduced from pictures, posters, plans and documents held at HSA in the SAHT Memorabilia Collection. Most of the remaining illustrations have been copied from those in current HSA offices.

Illustrations provided by the author (S Marsden) and by other people are acknowledged individually.

A list of abbreviations used in the book is supplied with the glossary in the Appendices.

CHAPTER ONE

Greater than ever before, 1986–1995

The State Jubilee 150 year, coupled as it is with the Trust Golden Anniversary, will live in my memory all my life. All the more so when the Premier presented Mr and Mrs Peacock with the keys to the 100,000th dwelling on 5 December. They were ecstatic, and that is what the Trust is all about. (Ray Paley 1986)[1]

Almost on the eve of ... the International Year of Shelter, the SA Housing Trust is celebrating its 50th anniversary ... the Trust has performed a remarkable role in providing shelter for South Australians, including the neediest. About 20 p.c. of South Australians live in houses built by this energetic body. The Trust is the second largest landlord in the nation ...

[T]he need for shelter by people on low incomes, especially single parent families, who have little hope of buying houses or renting privately, is greater than ever before ... In an age in which welfare tends to be impersonal, the Trust maintains a caring attitude and friendly image. But the waiting lists grow longer and the Trust's deficit grows bigger, and the challenges ahead are formidable. They call for all the skills and flexibility for which the Trust has been notable for half a century. (*The Advertiser* 1986)[2]

Introduction

The year 1986 was a carnival of commemoration. A crowd of guests at the Angas Street headquarters celebrated the Housing Trust's 50th and the state's 150th anniversaries when Premier John Bannon launched the book, *Business, charity and sentiment: the South Australian Housing Trust 1936–1986*.[3] Another ceremony marked completion of the 100,000th house. The international standing of this productive public enterprise was commended at the World Planning and Housing Congress held in Adelaide in the same year.

The Trust was astute in celebrating state events in practical ways. The Jubilee 150 Homes Scheme completed 1,850 flats for the aged during 1986, a joint venture program described by the Chairman as 'a striking example of the spirit of innovation and community concern which characterised the Trust'.[4] *The Advertiser* praised these many accomplishments, but warned also that the demands were 'greater than ever before'. The Trust was dealing with great responsibilities and unprecedented challenges. The phrase 'greater than ever before' has thus a double meaning and this chapter explores both of them.

In the decade 1986–95, the Housing Trust was one of South Australia's principal public authorities. Its responsibilities reached their greatest variety and extent, even going offshore, when in 1993 the World Bank selected the Trust, with Price Waterhouse Urwick, as its preferred consultant to develop property management systems for social housing in six cities in China.[5]

Construction was the Trust's main activity. By 1989 more than 110,000 homes had been built; a remarkable 20% of dwellings in South Australia. While the high point of public housing construction was in the period 1956–86 when the government constructed an average of 22% of the new dwellings built each year, in the years of the Bannon government (1982–91) the share was almost as high at 20%.[6]

This last great burst of construction augmented an already large stock and, with generous allocation policies, it was not surprising that the Trust had the second longest waiting list of applicants in Australia, after New South Wales. In 1986 there were 156,200 people on waiting lists in Australia, with 57,437 of them in NSW, 39,600 in SA, 28,722 in Victoria and 9,323 in Queensland. But the South Australian authority's energetic program bucked the national trend by containing and even shortening waiting lists. By 1992 the list had grown to 216,339 in Australia, but the state ranking had changed, with NSW (71,458) now followed by Victoria (45,791) and then SA (41,892). There were 39,600 applications to the Housing Trust in 1986, compared to 36,574 in 1995.[7]

Melva Wallace, one of those applicants, was on the Trust's waiting list for 13 years. Another was Joanne Holmes: 'Everyone put their name down so I went and put in an application. I waited 15 years'.[8] By contrast, Mrs Daphne Pettman had to wait only three months after applying in 1970. As in that earlier period, waiting times could vary according to location, as 'KM' found. She was single, working full-time in an unskilled job and sharing private rental housing when she applied in about 1981. She waited five years, contacting the Trust every six months, but the 'waiting list [for her preferred area] was moving very slowly. Spoke to the Trust about my problem and was informed of areas that were moving faster. Changed location preference and was housed within 6 months. All other needs answered'.

In each year during the period 1988–96 the Trust owned more than 60,000 dwellings, but this large number disguised the beginnings of a steady reduction as rental stock was sold or redeveloped. Land development also continued, but involved more complex arrangements and intentions, mixing public and private capital, rental and sales houses, fringe subdivision and metropolitan redevelopment. The Trust gained new functions, including support for community housing, private rent assistance and Aboriginal housing, but by 1995 several of these were hived off to separate agencies. Land banking and development roles were transferred, although urban redevelopment gained momentum. (These are discussed further in Chapter 3.)

Top: Eleanor Witcombe (an Ericksen descendant) opens 'Ericksen Estate' Cottage Flats, a Jubilee 150 project at Yorketown, in 1986, applauded by District Council Chairman George Sherrif and SAHT Central Regional Manager Tom Pears (far left).

Above left: Plaque at Gladstone marking one of many SAHT joint venture building projects for South Australia's sesquicentenary.

Above right: Premier John Bannon opens the door for the new tenants of the 100,000th Trust house at Parafield Gardens in 1986, photographed by Milton Wordley.

This chapter explores the effects of 1980s growth and 1990s curtailment, not only on the housing authority, but also on the South Australians who paid the rent or sought help. Public critiques of public housing and shifting state policy, in combination with the rising number of high-need tenants and diminishing funds all had an effect. The Trust began to narrow its ambit to providing direct housing services, and faced pressure to restrict them further to welfare or 'social' housing. Commercial activities – such as managing shopping centres, building factories and land banking – were maintained throughout the decade, but were halted at its end.[9]

Board members and staff grappled with serious new challenges. They had faced earlier tests to meet urgent housing demand with constrained resources, but this time there was a fundamental difference in government response, which reduced public services, including house building, and repositioned the Trust itself. Many of the ensuing changes were anticipated from within. The Annual Report of 1989–90 warned that the 1990s were 'likely to see a substantial reduction in the volume of the Trust's work because of external financial constraints', but gave 'a positive assurance it is committed to continued improvement in the quality of the service'. Because of a dramatic reduction in the housing program, General Manager Paul Edwards asked senior staff in 1990, 'can we justify pretending that we are still a public housing authority. Should we not face facts and accept that if we are administering a scarce commodity in the form of affordable housing we are morally obliged to seek to ensure it goes to those in greatest need'.[10] The institutional repositioning of the Trust extended over the full 25 years after 1986 and is an important theme of this updated history.[11]

Institutional transformation was reflected by frequent changes in personnel, with a succession of ministers, department heads, Housing Trust managers and chairmen. Minister Terry Hemmings introduced a new set of housing advisors when he established the Office of Housing, a policy unit run by Greg Black. The unit was absorbed into the Department of Housing and Urban Development under Michael Lennon in 1993. The stability of the Australian Labor Party government under John Bannon, premier from 1982, was shattered when the State Bank collapsed in 1991. Bannon's successor, Lynn Arnold, was premier only until 1993 when a Liberal government, elected under the leadership of Dean Brown, ended 11 years of Labor rule.

Hemmings was Minister of Housing from 1982–89, far longer than any other minister who served over the 25 years following 1986. Subsequent ministers and their portfolios changed frequently, illustrating a continual redefining of the Trust's position in supplying state services. Hemmings and his successor Kym Mayes (1989–92) were titled Minister of Housing and Construction; Greg Crafter (1992–93) was Minister for Housing, Urban Development and Local Government Relations, as were his Liberal successors John Oswald (1993–95) and Scott Ashenden (1995–96).

Ministerial Liaison Officer Tina Lloyd noted that despite the change of government, John Oswald had formed a close working relationship with the general

Ray Paley (centre left) and Housing Minister Terry Hemmings (centre right) attend the opening of 'Ngapala Court' at Eudunda in 1986.

managers. 'He made several visits to city and country regional offices to meet staff and discuss local issues as well as tour the housing stock.' After him, Minister Ashenden 'held the position for a relatively short time and worked closely with the CE of the Department of Housing and Urban Development, Bob Solly'. Next, Stephen Baker was Minister for Housing and Urban Development (1996–97). 'Housing' disappeared entirely from the title when Dean Brown was Minister for Human Services (1997–2002). The portfolio re-emerged as Minister for Housing with Labor's return to government in 2002.[12]

Within the Trust, Paul Edwards was General Manager for 12 years (1978–90), but his successor, Richard Parker, was there for less than four (1991–94), followed by a short-lived two-person administration. Ray Paley's eight-year chairmanship of the Board (1980–88) was also succeeded by briefer appointments: Leon Sykes, Peter Humphries and, from 1993, Professor Rod Oxenberry from the University of South Australia.

The minister's budget outline in 1993 indicated the wide range of activities still carried out by the Trust. Programs included 'areas as diverse as housing finance, land supply, management of the 63,000 strong stock of rental accommodation, housing supply, urban consolidation initiatives, assistance to private renters, cooperative and community housing programs and others'.[13] It is also evident that there was competition in the budget between public housing and community housing. More fundamentally, with the government's attention focused on reducing state debt, the borrow and build philosophy of the 1980s had been replaced with its opposite.[14] The mid-1990s were pivotal, and the change of state government at the end of 1993 confirmed the shift from broadly interpreted public housing to more narrowly focused social housing, with the result that activity was significantly curtailed.

All of these changes were cemented by new legislation. Through the decade 1986–95 the Trust's housing role was based on the original 1936 Act, the 1940 *Housing Improvement Act*, and the 1958 *Country Housing Act*. The new *South Australian Housing Trust Act 1995*, which came into operation on 1 January 1996, had profound implications, bringing the Trust's broad land development, industrial and commercial activities to an end. The new Act was a clear expression of the institutional repositioning at both state and national government levels in Australia.

Trends

In 1986 an editorial in *The Advertiser* described the demands on the Housing Trust as greater than ever before because of long waiting lists, the complex needs of applicants, withdrawal of Commonwealth funding, and rising debt. The economic context was crucial. The Trust had suffered from recessions in 1973 and 1983 that reduced rental income due to the high unemployment of the factory workers and labourers who were their traditional tenants. Unemployment in metropolitan Adelaide in 1976 was 3.9%, but reached 10.01% in 1986. De-industrialisation contributed to that rise. Economic restructuring reduced manufacturing's share of South Australian employment from 35% of the workforce in 1971 to 25% in 1990.[15] The decline also weakened the customary role played by public housing in supporting the state's industrial economy. The eighties decade was a boom–bust time for Australia. Rapid economic growth in the late 1980s was followed by recession in 1991–92. Both left their mark on the Trust.

The years 1973–95 have been described as the 'last throes of public housing' in Australia.[16] The first signs were evident in South Australia in the 1970s. Generous support for public housing under Sir Thomas Playford did not survive the defeat of his Liberal and Country League government in 1965. The new Australian Labor Party government under Don Dunstan was suspicious of well entrenched statutory authorities.[17] The Trust was criticised as not being accountable to ministers or communities, an argument that influenced state housing policies, and continued to do so under later ALP administrations. The Dunstan government reined in funding and, more importantly for the Trust's long-term survival, amended the Act to bring the Trust under ministerial control and created a housing portfolio. Works supervisor Keith Rothe, who was employed by the Trust through successive Liberal and Labor governments, offered his own pithy conclusion: 'Bring back the *Tom Playford era* and just erase the *Dunstan era completely*, from then on everything went haywire and completely bureaucratic (what a disaster)'.

From the 1980s rising costs, falling incomes and a transformation of the political context wrought permanent change on Australia's public housing sector. As Hayward wrote,

> The post-War Keynesian consensus which emphasised market failure and the need for remedial government action was replaced by a new ideology, popularly known as economic rationalism ... Governments of all political persuasions became enticed by the notion that competitive markets with minimal government regulations offered the best solution to Australia's economic woes.

As a result, at state and federal level, 'social spending has been pared back, and strongly targeted to those on low incomes ... the financial system has been deregulated; many public sector businesses have been privatised ... [or] required to emulate private business practices'. State housing authorities (SHAs) were subjected to many reviews, and changes to the Commonwealth State Housing Agreement required them to reform. 'Almost all aspects of their operations have been under review, from allocations policies and rent setting, through to funding mechanisms, tenancy relations and construction policies. The SHAs have not fared well in this period of review and restructure'.[18]

In the first decade after 1986 the Trust retained most of its powers as a statutory authority, although funding was run down. The Commonwealth State Housing Agreement (CSHA), under which the federal government provided cheap loans, was no longer a major source of funds. Commonwealth support was markedly reduced during the years of the Fraser Liberal government (1976–81) which acted to limit public housing to welfare provision. The Dunstan government reinforced that role, setting the Trust firmly on the path of housing the poorest people, heralding a contraction of its broader economic role. These events influenced a long transformation over the 1980s and 1990s.

As the authors of a review of American public housing observed, 'Public housing can ... be defined not so much by a static set of terms but by the process of negotiation between sponsor and beneficiary, between obligation and right'.[19] In his analysis of housing policy in South Australia, David Kilner described 'an uneasy and unresolved compromise in the 1980s' over public housing policy, which was 'struggling to be comprehensive but did not quite make it'. There was strong support for home ownership and public housing. The trend to welfare housing encompassed new groups in need, but housing was still not considered to be a universal social service. Kilner concluded, 'There had probably never before been a time when public housing had been in so much disrepute and faced so much resistance. This is ironic in view of the great strides it made in diversifying and improving its designs, land use and locational choice'.[20]

Above: Trust meeting at Port Pirie c1986. Standing from left: Neil Griffin, Jim Messner, Bob Fairweather, Doug Price, Elizabeth Johnston, Sheila Hall, Ian Halkett, Terry Bywaters, Graeme Bethune. Seated from left: Paul Edwards, Ray Paley, Marilyn Sard, Hugh Stretton.

Left: Steph Key, when a Trust member (between 1984 and 1996); she was later Housing Minister.

Housing activists also looked for progress in developing client oriented services; tenant participation; diversified housing, including support for cooperatives and an independent appeals system for tenants; a greater representation of women as senior managers and more lateral recruitment of staff. The Trust did take action in those areas, for example, encouraging tenant participation for the first time. Indeed, the Trust was probably at its most innovative and accommodating during this decade.

As Marsden and Parkin concluded in 1989, some criticisms reflected a 'divide between the more conventional, masculine, internally-recruited, organisationally-loyal managers of the Housing Trust and the more socially unconventional, locality-oriented, tertiary-educated, politicised activists in the community housing sector'.[21] Some activists later joined the Trust, helping to effect cultural change within it, as well as implementing significant new services.

Demographic trends also influenced housing policy. South Australia's distinctive demography was shaped by sharply contrasting phases of growth since World War II. There was a very rapid increase in the 30 years after 1945 when the state had one of the fastest-growing populations due to a high rate of immigration. In the following three decades South Australia had the nation's lowest rate of growth. By 2001 it shared only 1.4% of Australia's population growth and had 7% of the people, who were the oldest in the country with 14.5% aged 65 and over, compared to the national average of 12.6%.[22] A particular need for housing for aged people in country towns encouraged the Trust to approach local councils and charitable organisations to form joint ventures to build housing so that elderly people could remain in their communities.[23]

An ageing population also contributed to an increase in the number of single people wanting to rent. In 1991 nearly half (46%) of the applicants on the Trust's waiting list were single with no dependants. Leith MacGillivray, who applied in that year, was a single woman in her sixties, renting student share houses, who wanted to live independently. She wrote, 'Because of my age, volunteer work and return to University, I could not afford to even consider a mortgage. Because Public Service employment was frozen, I was employed on two-year contracts but this also meant uncertainty of income. Housing Trust seemed the answer'. She was a tenant from 1992 to 1998. In her group of 60 units there was only one married couple. Few other residents were employed. 'There was quite a turnover, with newcomers often followed by the Salvation Army with a load of furniture'.[24]

South Australia did not share the general improvements in the Australian economy during the 1990s, and suffered from a narrowing economic base and rising unemployment. The economy was focused on debt management, and a limited ability to generate revenue reduced the government's capacity to fund public housing. The collapse of the State Bank in 1991 catastrophically damaged state services. The bank had merged with the Savings Bank of South Australia in 1984, following national deregulation of banking, and embarked on unrestrained corporate lending. When the bank collapsed with debts of $3.1 billion, the whole state was thrown into debt as the bank's deposits were underwritten by the government.[25] The collapse affected state finances throughout the 1990s. Spending was drastically reduced. Helen Ottaway spoke for many colleagues in recalling that 'with the State Bank saga, there seemed to be more interest in the financial viability of the Housing Trust than in the past and we had to tighten our purse strings'.[26]

A phase of political uncertainty was another consequence of the crash. ALP Premier Bannon resigned in 1992. Greg Crafter, an experienced Cabinet member, set up a new department while he was Minister of Housing and Urban Development (1992–93), but his final ministry was short-lived, as the ALP government was resoundingly defeated in the 1993 election. The incoming Liberal government established an audit commission to consider public finances, aiming to cut costs and reduce the failed bank's debt. Public service cutbacks and the sale of state assets followed. These actions soon affected the Trust, although alterations to housing policy specifically took longer to implement.

Finances

Hugh Stretton argued that the Housing Trust's first 40 years cost the taxpayers nothing, as everything was paid for by tenants, home buyers and industrial investors. The main link to government was a credit guarantee, enabling the Trust to borrow at low interest and service loans from earnings.[27] In addition, between 1982 and 1986, South Australia was unique in nominating its entire federal Loan Council allocation for housing, taking full advantage of the generous low interest rate of 4.5%. However, from 1987 all states were limited to an allocation of 60%.

By then, Housing Trust funds came from a wide range of sources, from more expensive commercial borrowings as well as state and Commonwealth loans and grants, rents, mortgage repayments, and the proceeds from selling houses, factories and land. In that year the Trust reported an operating deficit of $7.165 million, and an income increase of only 6.9%, compared to a 20.3% rise in expenditure. The Auditor-General criticised the high deficit and recommended raising rents and reducing operating expenditure. But the government had frozen rents for two years – full rent increases were subject to Cabinet approval – and in 1986 permitted only an 8% increase.

Although politically unpopular, rents were progressively raised to market (private rental) levels. By 1991 such 'market rents' were approximately 75% of the level of private rents, and a metropolitan double unit rented for an average $4,000 annually. Rent rises brought less financial relief than might have been expected, because an increasing proportion of tenants were granted rent rebates, an increase accelerated by the move to market rents. In Stretton's words, after 1970 'technological change, small government, privatisation and other causes ... ended the full employment that financed the tenants to pay their rents'. Nine per cent of tenants received rebates in 1974; by 1987 nearly two-thirds of them (64.34% or 36,910) were on reduced rents – losing the Trust $945,219 a week. By 1990 rebates were provided to 73% of new tenants.[28] Catherine McLaughlin became one of them: she was retired, on a pension, and needed to move to Adelaide. She applied to the Trust in 1990 and was allocated a unit at Renown Park 12 months later. 'I have had no problems with Housing Trust. They have always been very helpful'.

The 1994 Triennial Review classified rebates as community service obligations (CSOs), that is, non-commercial services supporting tenants. Other CSOs, costed at $131.8 million, were social services such as priority housing assessments and referrals to support agencies, excess water subsidies and modifying houses for disabled tenants. The cost of CSOs was not the only financial challenge. Compared to the earlier era, there was also much greater expenditure on maintenance, itself a direct consequence of the large post-war program that had used cheap building materials.

The maintenance costs of post-war housing are illustrated in Bernadette Kuhar's recollection of taking up residence in the Plympton Park estate in 1994. Her Trust dwelling was 'Very small. Poor design. Massive back yard'. She thought that a concession or compensation should have been provided for maintaining the yard. At the same time, the house had been 'comprehensively repaired/renovated which was nice and helped me to feel like a real human being'. In 1993–94, the Trust budgeted over $50 million for the maintenance of 61,000 dwellings. Half were first generation homes built before 1968 that required extra maintenance and upgrading, as most had, in the words of the review, '1950/60 standard amenity levels in key areas, such as the kitchen and bathroom'.[29] As Hayward asked: would policy makers in the 1950s and 1960s have placed such emphasis on 'the quantity of public housing units built at the expense of quality considerations had they been aware of the longer term consequences that this posed for maintenance expenditure?'[30] There was, as the Board noted, competition between 'the objectives of housing to those in need and the need to improve the asset base'.[31] In 1997, for example, when the Trust managed 58,077 rental properties, $59.7 million was spent on their maintenance. As the minister pointed out ten years later, 'We've got the oldest public housing stock in the nation'.[32]

This large stock was also the Trust's greatest asset, and a considerable one for the state as a whole. That asset had been augmented by the large 1980s building program, but in the 1990s emphasis shifted from newbuild to realising asset value through upgrading, replacement and sale. The 'strategic management of its assets [was] to ensure that Trust houses contribute to the best possible provision of service to customers at the same time as safeguarding public assets'.[33]Asset management became a high art, combining strategic planning and the assessment of the viability and usefulness of individual assets. David Kilner, who managed the Trust's Housing Strategy Unit, observed, 'Whether particular dwellings were retained, redeveloped or disposed of could then be a complex function of age, design, type, location, condition, standard of amenity, maintenance requirements and suitability for changing client needs'.[34]

As there was little scope to increase rents to control the Trust's deficit, the alternative was 'control of expenditure'. This was canvassed in a report by Assistant General Manager Jim Messner in 1987: 'Rents are now ... being raised as far and as fast as feasible and Government's capacity to maintain even the present

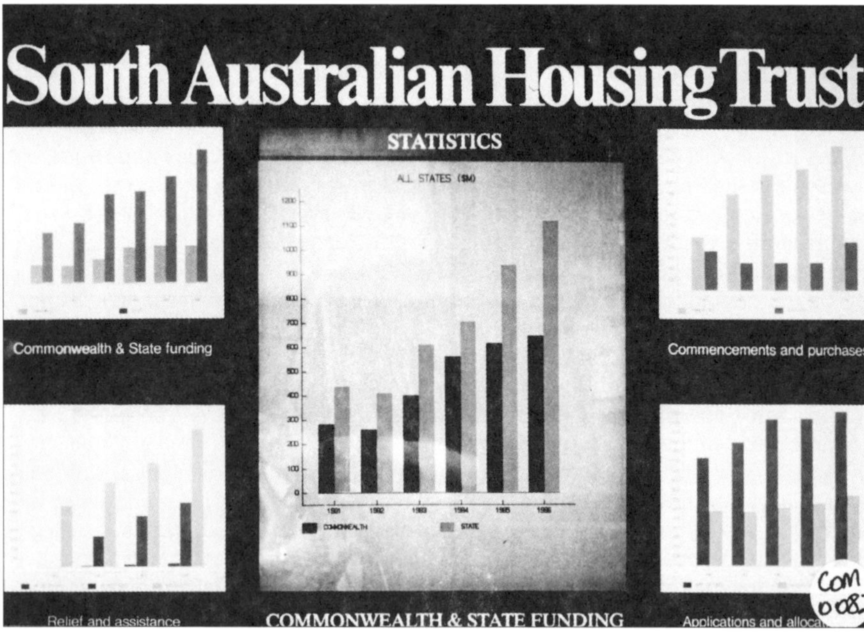

Poster prepared for Commonwealth/State housing ministers' conference with almost all indicators showing steady rises between 1981 and 1986 – except for Commonwealth funding.

level of funds is substantially reduced'. There was no option but to critically review all fund flows and activities. His recommendations covered staffing, work practices – some of them dating from the Trust's earliest years – and property. He suggested a 10% cut in employees, including nine who still collected rents door to door, despite police warning of the dangers of this practice.[35] Door to door collection was discontinued a month later. The Trust experimented with a variety of methods of rental payment. A Pensioner Warrant Scheme allowed tenants to have their social security pensions forwarded to deduct rent, but this was withdrawn in 1988, except for Aboriginal tenants. Australia Post was contracted to collect all rents in 1991.

Messner also recommended closing the transport depot at Elizabeth West, and a non-viable timber mill at Torrensville Depot, and selling the under-utilised part of the 2.6 hectare site. He urged retaining other activities at Torrensville: the nursery (relocated from Marden in 1982), which was the Trust's sole source of plants; the merchandise depot, which saved money by bulk buying; and the soils laboratory – especially useful as testing of contaminated development sites was now compulsory. Sales of other vacant land should continue: they had raised $86.46 million in 1986, releasing capital for construction and relieving the rate burden. Messner concluded, 'the savings to be achieved will not resolve the inherent contradictions between the social purposes of the CSHA and the financial structure of that Agreement. They will, however, provide a breathing space during which these issues can be resolved on the political level'.[36]

They never were and never did. South Australia's funding through the CSHA declined in monetary terms and as a percentage of the national total. Each renegotiated agreement – with one exception – was smaller than before. The state compensated by nominating Federal Loan Council funding to public housing, but in 1989 the Commonwealth ceased funding via this source entirely, partially compensating by increasing CSHA grants. State governments then sought alternative sources with higher interest rates.

House prices in Australia leaped during the late 1980s, increasing by almost 20% each year, long-term interest rates rose to 8–10%, and home mortgage rates peaked at 17% – a post-war record. Even when rates dropped again, the Trust was still paying off commercial loans negotiated at 16%. This had far reaching effects, as housing loans were set at interest rates equal to, rather than below, the long-term bond rate, forcing the Trust to pay higher rates and run up debt.[37]

The Trust's 'Common Public Sector Interest', that is, borrowings at commercial interest rates, reached a staggering $372.035 million in 1988, and the Board embarked on a debt retirement strategy involving sales of its biggest asset: housing stock. That stock's value was $3.27 billion in 1993.[38] The Trust also ceased borrowing for capital works, cut staff, outsourced maintenance and rent collection, and upgraded financial reporting systems. Non-concessional debt was reduced to $263.491 million by 1994. The Trust recorded the highest ever surplus of $20.134 million in 1988–89, but funding had been reduced by 51%. These major financial anxieties are reflected in the small tale of a lost $50 note. Carmel Hallion joined the Trust in 1986 as Front Counter Clerk and Relief Cashier. 'Come my first Christmas, I was extremely concerned that my money may not balance ... It didn't, it was the worst moment – I was $50 down – we found the $50, it had slipped over the back of the drawer. You can imagine my relief'.[39]

The decline in Commonwealth support was temporarily reversed in the early years of Bob Hawke's Labor government that came into power in 1983. Grants were increased in a plan to double Australia's public housing stock and assist economic recovery by stimulating the housing industry (as historically done through the Trust). CSHA funding reached $203.445 million nationally in the mid-1980s, but a decade later the Trust's 1992 Annual Report recorded a drop to $146 million, the lowest level in 20 years.[40] The reduction greatly decreased the Trust's ability to buy or build houses, or to improve them. The 1989 CSHA included grants in recognition that public tenants could not afford to pay market interest rates on the capital cost of their houses, but did not cover rental rebates provided by the Trust. The 50th anniversary of the CSHA (signed on 19 November 1945) came around in 1995. Since 1953, when South Australia joined, each agreement had provided 'the financial glue binding together our State based public housing system'.[41] This was the last period for which that could be said.

Torrensville Depot during the 1980s: (clockwise from top left) Ross Manning in the office; staff Christmas party (Peter Jackson is leaning on the ice cream trailer facing front); stacks of timber used during the Trust's big building years; and garden work. 'The timber was for roof trusses. That was the biggest thing we did there. We would supply TBS (to be supplied) items to builders to get economies of scale.' (Brenton Herringe)

Another unprecedented financial challenge involved the diversion of both state and federal funding to alternative forms of housing support. When the Minister outlined the state's housing budget in 1993, he described not only additions to Housing Trust stock, but also 'a 3 per cent increase in funds to help people find private rental accommodation, and in 1993/94 this brings the allocation for private rental and support services to $14 million'. These funds were provided through the Trust, but another 200 houses were to be built through cooperative programs, and a further 100 provided by community housing associations. 'In addition, rent relief for 1993–94 will be $8.4 million, compared with $6.1 million from both the South Australian and Commonwealth Governments, and an additional $2.25 million by the State Government'.[42]

Restructuring

The first steps to transform the Trust were taken when Paul Edwards succeeded Alex Ramsay as general manager in 1978. Former staff member Fred Foord said that Ramsay's sudden death 'left us all in a state of shock. I had not felt a need for major changes, but that is what happened'.[43] Foord found Edwards 'a pleasant enough man personally but absolutely ruthless in his new job. Undoubtedly Paul made some very substantial changes as G.M. some of which ruffled feathers'.[44] Edwards swiftly formalised workplace processes, creating resentment among older staff that was often expressed during research for the 1986 anniversary history *Business, charity and sentiment*.

Malcolm Downie was one of the 'change agents' appointed in Edwards' time. An Arts graduate who had majored in urban geography and demography, Downie joined Corporate Development in 1981. His early impression was of 'a large family that had suffered a significant loss through the death of Alex Ramsay in 1978 and was adjusting to changing circumstances'. In 'the musty old head office building at Angas Street', time seemed to have stood still. Placed on the 'Golden Mile' near Edwards' office, Downie watched much coming and going. His arrival coincided with the loss of 250 staff through the first voluntary early retirement scheme, 'which hit sections such as Architects and Engineers particularly hard', although many (including Foord) were re-engaged as consultants 'to enable a proper handover and recording of their collective wisdom and expertise'.[45] Downie continued,

> I vividly remember Jim Crichton, then Deputy GM on the warpath – which seemed to happen most days, as Jim took the brunt of the Ministerial enquiries and chased down answers through his trusted managers. Ian Halkett was never too far away from the action ... in charge of the operational policy area. Jim was certainly a fearsome sight having been called up there myself on one occasion and reminded that just because I had a university degree, I shouldn't profess to know anything about Trust operations until I had served my time. How much time one had to serve could be gauged by the balance of the conversation, which was a trip through Jim's career commencing as a

junior aged 16 years responsible for filling the ink wells on the clerks' tables some 40 years earlier.[46]

Edwards was slowly gaining respect for his 'style and new directions'. Downie helped research his speeches in a 'very busy diary' and was promoted in 1986 after preparing a report on outstanding maintenance of rental property, following a three month state-wide survey. The findings also informed a Public Accounts Committee Inquiry into future maintenance costs of all state assets. Downie moved to the Office of Housing as Acting Manager in 1987, 'working closely with the Trust and other ... housing providers in aligning state housing policies and practice'. He contributed to a major inquiry chaired by Harrison Anderson, published as *Beyond Tent City: A report on findings into youth homelessness*. Downie moved to Tasmania in 1988, where like other former Trust staff, he gained further senior positions, culminating in his appointment as Director of Housing Tasmania in 2001.

As Edwards told Trust staff in 1990, 'Cartledge, Ramsay and Crichton ... were great men in their day and they did not hesitate to change things. But their day is gone and we face the need to change some of the things they helped create'.[47] Ramsay had once declared himself the last 'great centraliser' in conversation with Ian Cox, Director General of the Department for Community Welfare, who was famed for decentralising the state's welfare services.[48] Cox also emphasised the importance of community participation. His philosophy was echoed by Edwards, who regionalised Trust services in the late 1970s and encouraged tenant participation and self-managed community housing.

These changes were strongly backed by the Board. Chairman Paley and Deputy Chairman Stretton personally marked the 50th anniversary by commissioning Robert Hannaford to paint a portrait of Edwards, who 'had successfully orchestrated the Trust's achievements in recent years'.[49] They presented the portrait in 1987 to hang with those of revered Housing Trust men. The paintings soon found a new home. A physical relocation that symbolised and cemented workplace modernisation took place in 1989.

After 30 years in the rundown Angas Street building, head office was moved into the high-rise Riverside Centre on North Terrace, built in 1987 as part of the Adelaide Convention Centre complex. Angas Street remained a liability, as the first purchaser went into receivership and another buyer could not readily be found. Although the terms offered on Riverside were 'very attractive', the new building imposed its own cost burdens, the Minister reporting the Trust's payment of $14.187 million in rent and other charges between 1989 and 1993.[50]

Hugh Stretton, a Board member since 1971, retired in 1989. Stretton had published highly esteemed books that described the Housing Trust as a successful experiment in public–private sector cooperation.

As he describes it, he spent 20 years on the Housing Trust board, 17 of them as deputy chair and, working with able executives, 'learned how to get

Robert Hannaford's portrait of Paul Edwards, 1987. This was the last in the Trust's tradition of displaying portraits of significant men.

Jim Crichton (centre), on his farewell in 1989 with colleagues (from left): Kevin Burgemeister, Terry Bywaters, Chris Hoffmann, Joy Reynolds, Peter Wilson, Tom Pears, John Girardi, Trevor Deacon, Brian Phillips and Frank Schultz.

2000 or 3000 houses a year built well and economically, at widespread city and country town locations, by private contractors competing for the work and getting most of it done by independent tradesmen in strong unions'.[51]

But Stretton was well aware of the contraction of that work. At his last Board meeting in 1989, members debated a new corporate plan that noted suggestions for abandoning the traditional concept of public housing for welfare. The plan described this as 'a significant change in philosophy', but acknowledged that in practice the Trust was 'now carrying out a "welfare" role', because it had 'responded to the needs of those coming to it for assistance and adjusted its programmes so that it is responsive to those people, the overwhelming majority of whom are people in real housing need'.[52]

The change in philosophy was to a large extent a political decision beyond the control of Board members or managers. Edwards described ALP Minister Terry Hemmings as 'personally supportive of the Housing Trust', getting on well also 'because we are both migrants of the same age, and I knew him as Mayor of Elizabeth when I first arrived ... but ... there is a problem which exists now ... and that is the role of advisors to Ministers'. Hemmings set up an independent avenue for advice through an Office of Housing. Edwards argued that this approach was destroying public housing authorities in NSW and Victoria because ministers were 'advised by enthusiasts' with limited experience, who thought up 'compelling notions ... on the fringe of the real issues that need to be addressed'. Discounting the contribution of housing bureaucrats also damaged morale. Labor governments tended to have 'more of these enthusiasts telling them what should happen', and were more suspicious than Liberal governments of existing authorities. The recent CSHA (under a federal Labor government) also owes less to the contributions of public housing managers, such as Ramsay in the past, 'and a lot more to the ministerial advisors'.[53]

In 1989 the Trust made another break with the past by actively recruiting a larger intake of tertiary graduates than it had in the past. Sixty applied for the first 10 positions. The newcomers enjoyed a special induction program, followed by placements in different offices that, in the words of one graduate, gave them 'an opportunity to experience working in a wide cross section of areas ranging from tenants to finance in both country and metropolitan regions'.[54] The following year a new graduate selection process was tested. It included a written paper, psychological tests, observed discussions and an interview. Mignon Schneider, who started in 1991, was one of eight graduates selected for employment. She recalled the graduates benefiting during their first year as they were moved to a different section every three months, giving them an overview of activities, getting them widely known, and helping them gain new positions. Some existing staff considered the graduates to be a threat to their job security, an antipathy reinforced by an anti-intellectual culture in the Trust. Schneider described 'a long history of nepotism and cronyism within the SAHT, which was evidenced by the close family and personal relationships between employees'. As an independent statutory authority, the Trust had not been obliged to follow public service recruitment policies. One result was that some of the staff were not competent to meet the demands of the positions they held. Schneider observed that, 'The restructure exposed the lack of competent skill levels in some staff'.[55]

Edwards instigated a comprehensive restructure of the Trust in 1990, his last year as manager. He engaged Jan Connolly and Helen Hardwicke from the Public Sector Management Board to review regional services. They proposed a model, similar to Homes West in Western Australia, with housing managers having a broader range of management functions placed in an expanded number of regional offices working in teams and responsible for all services to tenants. The model was adopted. Edwards explained to staff, 'Where 10 years ago we took the management and coordination of service from Angas Street to regional offices we are now taking it still closer to the consumer with a fully empowered manager for about every 500 homes'.

The regional restructure extended to the whole organisation, Edwards aiming to 'clearly distinguish between line activities (in housing supply, in industrial and commercial and in what used to be regional and community services) and central staff activities – corporate policy and finance and management services'. He emphasised the role of managers as stewards 'of the human and financial resources entrusted to them'. 'The staff are going to be fully involved in fleshing out the detail of the implementation process of organisational change. Tenants are going to be as fully involved as possible in the management of the housing they occupy'.[56]

Many employees recall 'The Restructure' of 1990. In Tina Lloyd's words,

> An unprecedented program of staff training commenced. All service delivery staff were required to apply for positions in the new structure ... there was considerable anxiety amongst staff. Many found the training programs and interview processes stressful. Most staff applied for multiple positions, hoping to be successful in at least one and many staff were required to relocate to the new regions from their former workplaces.[57]

The new graduates feared they would not be kept on as permanent employees and, although they were retained, Schneider remembers the restructure resulting in 'widespread redeployment and redundancy of long-term staff and disaffection among a number of those who remained'. However, in recognition of Edwards' management and the work of Training Manager Judy Hood, the Trust won a national 'employer award for leadership in achieving excellence in human resource development' from the Australian Institute of Training and Development at the end of 1990. The Trust accepted Edwards' final change in September 1990, the month he departed 'to pursue other career options in the United Kingdom', his country of origin.[58]

Corporate Services, headed by Ian Halkett, was the first new division created in a decade. It was formed to 'assemble information, carry out both practical and

Riverside headquarters (centre building) from across the River Torrens, 1990.

theoretical research ... and provide advice on the performance of service delivery units'. Halkett explained that a multitude of skills in the Trust would combine in 'an exceptional housing policy unit' to answer the challenges of changing needs in an environment of fiscal constraint.

Housing Trust News also reported Jan Connolly's appointment to the new position of Director, Housing Operations, to oversee the restructure of regional offices. She combined 'a detailed knowledge of the operations of regional and community services while retaining the objectivity of someone external to the Trust'.[59] Connolly in turn engaged Helen Fulcher to review implementation of the restructure, using her experience at HomesWest in Western Australia, which had adopted a similar model under the management of Greg Black. Fulcher described the model as a 'very flat structure of service delivery ... moving away from specialist roles to the generalist housing manager who took on all of the functions of tenancy management from vacancy, debt collection, through to disruption'.[60] There were 'more delegations to the regional officers to respond to the community in the way that they thought fit, so less central control essentially'. One of Black's criticisms when Emergency Housing Officer in South Australia had been that the Trust's regional offices were really the central office in disguise. In Fulcher's experience since then, the alternative movement has gained momentum with managers informed, 'In each region you can have it structured as fits your region and your local communities'.

Richard Parker followed Edwards as General Manager from 1991 until 1994. Parker, like Edwards, had not worked previously for the Trust, but had a solid background in housing and industrial development, and project management, with qualifications in economics, town planning and business. He had worked in the Papua New Guinea Housing Commission, in the Victorian government's Major Projects Unit and, since 1990, as general manager of SA Urban Land Trust (SAULT). He extolled the Housing Trust's 'excellent reputation', and through its work with SAULT at Seaford was familiar with 'the Trust's ability to work with a variety of organisations'. Parker also stressed his personal experience as 'a husband, a father, a sailor and a traveller', and told staff, 'I want to be seen as energetic, with a breadth of experience professionally and personally and above all as a human being'.[61]

Parker hoped to build on the Trust's reputation and 'broaden its scope and emphasis', and succeeded at first in doing so. In 1991 the Trust took on a new set of responsibilities by absorbing the Office of Housing (formerly part of the Department of Housing and Construction) and assumed a primary role in managing urban development.[62] Development, Policy and Planning, and Major Projects divisions were formed to improve coordination of policy advice. The Emergency Housing Office was again combined with the Trust, allowing private rental services to be delivered from regional offices.

Parker accelerated the 'Restructure' of the Regional and Community Services Division. This was also completed in 1991. Managers were appointed to the Adelaide, Elizabeth, Salisbury, The Parks, Gawler, Hillcrest, Noarlunga, Warradale, Port Adelaide, Modbury, Whyalla, Murray Bridge, Port Augusta, Port Pirie, Port Lincoln and Mount Gambier regions, in which last a new building was opened for 18 staff. Stephen Penglase (Port Lincoln) described the restructure as 'a major event in the Trust's history and one which should change many aspects of the way in which we do business'. His colleagues spoke the mantras of 'new efficiencies', staff teamwork, and 'client satisfaction ... through tenant management and decision making'.[63] Housing managers were appointed to manage groups of 400–500 dwellings, and client service advisers helped people with private housing. Anne Gale was one of two women appointed regional manager – in the new Modbury region. This was combined with Hillcrest in 1994 to create the third largest Trust region, responsible for 6,000 tenants.[64]

Regional and Community Services implemented customer service standards in 1993. Other changes included an independent Public Housing Appeals Unit (as required in the CSHA); formation of the Community Housing Authority and the Aboriginal Housing Authority; a bond guarantee scheme; customer satisfaction surveys; a student housing pilot and the On-Arrival Accommodation program for migrants.[65] Parker made his own views clear on these changes. For example, he considered that cooperatives complemented other public housing. Giving evidence on the Housing Co-operatives Bill, he said that the Trust could not take on that

Above: staff at a 'Customer Contact' Session, 1987.

Below: staff meeting with Paul Edwards seated front right.

complex responsibility, whereas the new South Australian Community Housing Authority could give it proper attention. There would be 'ample opportunity for intermeshing and networking of personnel and services', and he anticipated his own appointment to the board.[66] His view of the housing portfolio was one in which 'member agencies can carry out its unique mission within a unified policy framework'. Agencies would work to a common purpose with interlocking board membership and sharing of staff and facilities. 'The Housing Trust will have a central role as the key employing body. The ultimate aim of these developments is to deliver a coherent set of housing and land development services to the community, at an affordable price and in an economical manner'.[67]

General Manager Edwards had opposed turning the Trust into a government department. He argued that its position as Australia's most highly regarded housing authority was due mainly to being a statutory authority with some autonomy and the influence of Alex Ramsay's 'humane, sensitive approach to people'. If the Trust became a department, 'it would cease to have its ear primarily attuned to

Trust members and staff at the new Mount Gambier office c1991. They include (seated from left) Leon Sykes (Chairman), Richard Parker, Kym Mayes (Minister), Jan Connolly, Terry Bywaters (South East regional manager) and Pat Jordan (Office Administrator; (middle row) Jill Sporer, Irene Hart, Liz Hodgman, Deb Moore, Valerie Finnis, Samantha Clift, Cherie Knott, Donna Higgins; (back row) Lindsay Manuel, Witold Shentall (now deceased), Kevin Howell, Geoff Foy, David Mulshine.

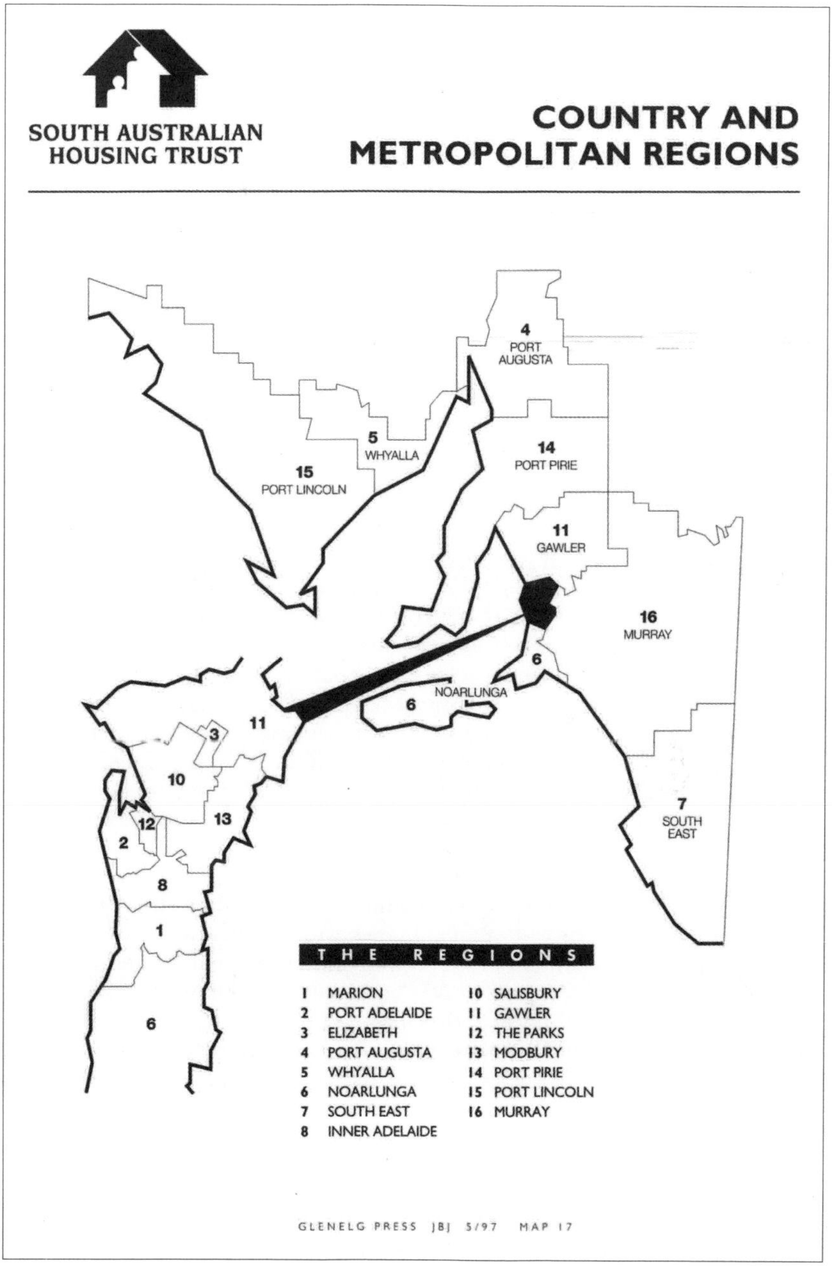
SOUTH AUSTRALIAN
HOUSING TRUST
COUNTRY AND
METROPOLITAN REGIONS
4
PORT
AUGUSTA
5
WHYALLA
15
PORT LINCOLN
14
PORT PIRIE
11
GAWLER
16
MURRAY
6
NOARLUNGA
6
7
SOUTH
EAST
11
3
10
12
13
2
8
1
6
THE REGIONS
1 MARION
2 PORT ADELAIDE
3 ELIZABETH
4 PORT AUGUSTA
5 WHYALLA
6 NOARLUNGA
7 SOUTH EAST
8 INNER ADELAIDE
10 SALISBURY
11 GAWLER
12 THE PARKS
13 MODBURY
14 PORT PIRIE
15 PORT LINCOLN
16 MURRAY
GLENELG PRESS JBJ 5/97 MAP 17

the people coming in, and have to have its ear primarily attuned to the dictates on high, and that would destroy the essential ingredient'.[68] Soon after his departure, steps were taken to reposition the Trust as an agency subject to departmental control. 'Departmentalising' began later in South Australia and took longer to implement fully than in other states and territories. For example, in NSW the *Housing Act 1986* replaced both the Housing Commission and the Land Commission with a new Department of Housing. Four major reviews were completed in 1993, which helped to effect similar changes to the Housing Trust. There was a national Industry Commission of Inquiry into the effectiveness of public housing. In South Australia there were a ministerial review of the Housing and Urban Development portfolio; a Commission of Audit that examined the Trust's financial and policy positions; and the customary Triennial Review to assess its longer-term financial status. There was also the South Australian *Development Act 1993* that set new constraints and challenges for the Trust.

The powerful Industry Commission review proposed that the roles of housing authorities as private developers and public housing providers be separated – disregarding the success of developmental authorities, such as South Australia's Trust, in combining both functions, and that redevelopment of public housing estates required both roles. The Industry Commission would separate welfare functions from housing and landlord functions, and from the revenue generating functions that had subsidised the welfare roles. These proposals were soon reflected in the management structure of the Housing Trust.

South Australia's Labor government established the Department of Housing, Urban Development and Local Government Relations in July 1993. It was managed by Michael Lennon. Housing Minister Greg Crafter aimed to 'unite land, housing and recreational needs to assist in the expansion of the South Australian economy'.[69] The change was also motivated by 'debt management, economic rationalisation and greater coordination between related spheres of activity'.[70] Crafter 'confirmed the ongoing role of statutory authorities', but the Trust Board was uncertain about the implications. Opinion soon hardened. In August 1993 the General Manager told Lennon that the department's budget imposed significant extra costs on the Trust for establishing and operating the department.[71] The Minister said that integration of activities was planned mainly in corporate services, information technology and support functions, inadvertently confirming the Trust's suspicions when he told Parliament's Estimates Committee what had already occurred, including: 'utilisation of the Housing Trust maintenance system involving private contractors across the department to reduce costs and take advantage of the Housing Trust's buying power; utilisation of the Housing Trust purchasing and supply unit for major purchase contracting'. He said that full functional integration would not be completed until mid-1994.[72]

Nor were legislative changes for incorporating the Trust into a departmental structure resolved at the change of government in December 1993. JKG (John) Oswald, the new Liberal Housing Minister, set up yet another review to examine all agencies in his portfolio and to 're-examine proposals for organisational change'.[73] In an 'open letter to staff', Oswald emphasised the importance of redeveloping old estates and dealing with the lengthening waiting list, stressing the 'extreme importance' of involving the private sector. The same issue of *Housing Trust News* in 1994 headlined the 'Elizabeth North redevelopment deal signed' by the Minister with private sector project managers Delfin Property Group.[74]

When Richard Parker left the Trust, the institutional change mooted by the new government, and which he had set in train (effectively doing himself out of a job), was implemented. When the review of the Housing Portfolio was completed in September 1994, the Trust's corporate support services were transferred to the department and a radically new organisational structure divided the Trust into two separate business units. Housing Services provided customer services to tenants. Property Management was responsible for building acquisition, construction, sales and redevelopment. The general manager was replaced with a two-person administration: Peter Jackson (Property Management) and Jan Connolly (Housing Services). Bob Solly (from Victoria) was appointed CEO of the Department of Housing and Urban Development.

The Trust's Board restated familiar purposes, a 'mix of social and commercial activities sustaining economic viability', but the restructure would 'make the two functions of providing [housing] assistance and managing the assets quite separate and discreet ... The separation defines those two distinctive functions'.[75] This change aroused disquiet. National Shelter forum participants argued that separating property from tenancy management could create 'a conflict of interest between social values ... and the pressure to make a commercial return on properties', and make the 'qualitative aspects of housing management' second priority.[76] Helen Fulcher confirmed the ensuing 'time of tension between the social and the commercial objectives' in the Trust, and recalled 'locking heads often with one of the more colourful characters in Assets'. When having to modify houses for people with physical disabilities, Assets, 'driven by a commercial agenda, wanted to charge us internally a much more significant rent than we would usually pay in order to cover the costs of ... modifications, but also they were anticipating that when they sold that property its capital value would be less'.

The Trust's two-entity structure also presented administrative difficulties, soon voiced by Board members themselves. 'The absence of a single General Manager meant that the task of co-ordinating the Trust's diverse activities now fell even more heavily on the Board. No matter how well the two General Managers were performing their roles, achieving that balance is not their primary job'.[77] Many within the Trust had been surprised by the appointment of Connolly, an outsider, and were placed under pressure as she strove to meet demanding deadlines and to follow up the Board's instructions.

Nineteen ninety-five was a hinge year in the history of the Housing Trust because its broad economic and urban roles were halted, and a new Act was passed. Until 1995 functions were based upon the founding *South Australian Housing Trust Act 1936*, and the Housing Improvement Act. The latter Act was updated in the *Housing Improvement (Standards) Regulations 1992*. The Trust's Charter and code of practice was also tabled in Parliament and incorporated the tenants' charter developed in 1993. The most important event was passage of the new South Australian Housing Trust Act. As a result, two major urban development functions were permanently transferred to the South Australian Urban Projects Authority, established under the *Housing and Urban Development (Administrative Arrangements) Act 1995*. The Trust's broad-acre land development was terminated with the transfer of all vacant land not required for public housing to the new authority.

The new legislation was a clear reflection of institutional repositioning in governments. The department responsible for the Trust explained that the new Housing Trust Act reflected the National Housing Ministers' conference of 1995 and the state government's consideration of the Hilmer Report on National Competition Policy.[78] The *Residential Tenancies Act 1995* was also passed in 1995. Residential tenancy legislation had been introduced in South Australia in 1978, but did not apply to Trust tenancies until 1995.[79]

Staffing reflected these changes. The number of staff hovered at just over 1,000 through the 1980s, the 1987 Annual Report recording 1,189, an increase of only 97 (8.9%) over nine years. This was described as a productivity achievement, because over the same time the number of tenants rose by 41.7%, applications by 84.7% and housing completions by 39.1%. Staff were also handling new services, including rent and mortgage relief, housing cooperatives and joint ventures.[80]

Technology driven workplace change helped to improve productivity and services. Elizabeth Anderson described using the first computers in the 1980s: 'First there was the Wang – a monster of a machine ... The trainer from IBM was almost as much a novice as we were, and we all learnt from each other'. Then they had to learn how to use the next generation of machines: word processors.[81] In 1989 a total of 62,000 manual rent ledgers were replaced with computerised rent applications and management and accounts receivable systems. *Housing Trust News* reported that the new rental applicant system took 12 months to develop, gained a silver award in the Australian Government Technology Productivity Awards and improved service to clients. All applications could now be handled by computer, with 250 terminals linked to a system that gave regional offices instant access. 'So, at the touch of a button the computer can describe the client's situation. For example, Trust staff can tell a person looking for a three bedroom home in the southern suburbs exactly what the availability is'. The system was expected to save $500,000 annually.[82]

The Board commended the Trust's own chairman, Ray Paley, for bringing 'special financial expertise to bear on the accounting, computing and corporate planning revolutions which had been accomplished during his years of office'. Just as importantly, Paley had cultivated 'a wide personal acquaintance within the Trust and given individual recognition and encouragement to a great many Trust staff that had never previously had such links with Chairman or Board'.[83]

A different approach to productivity was taken in the 1990s to reach 'optimum workforce levels in line with the government's overall workforce reduction strategy', in other words, cutting down. In 1993 staff were reduced by 18% despite an increase of 10% in the demand for services. In three short years, staff were cut by one-third. By 1996 there were 614 – half as many as in 1986. The biggest reduction followed the Trust's division into Housing Services and Property Management. Restructuring in Property Management resulted in a one-third reduction of the construction and maintenance workforce, 'and the traditional skill base shifting away from its technical nature'.[84] Many staff remained for the long term: committed, loyal and industrious, as Mignon Schneider and Malcolm Downie fondly recalled. Helen Fulcher observed more movement of staff in the Western Australian agency HomesWest than in the Trust, and 'that probably still holds, in that say the majority of the leaders of our regional offices are people who've been there for a very long period of time'.

Public households

> It is November 1987 and I'm driving up Albert Road, Mt Barker. I'm on my way to look at a house that the Trust has offered me ... I did wonder how I'd come to be in the position of tenant in a trust home but marriage breakup and divorce can really affect future choices. (Elizabeth Ostermann)

Mrs Dot Whelan, who had shifted in 1984 from her old Rosewater double unit to a smaller place, moved in her 90th year into a nursing home in 1990. Trust staff brought flowers, honouring her as one of their oldest tenants. 'So ends a tenancy that spanned fifty three years and witnessed a depression, a world war and many social changes'.[85] Housing circumstances for South Australians on low incomes had worsened during Mrs Whelan's last years as a tenant and over the following decade, as the costs of buying or renting privately rose beyond reach.[86] An analysis by *Australian Society* in 1989 concluded 'that the housing crisis has become a chronic condition for many members of the community irrespective of rises and falls in interest rates and house prices'.[87] They were not helped by the privatisation of government owned banks and reduced Commonwealth support for public housing, despite the many applications from people unable to get or carry out paid work. As William Pegram recalled, 'After losing jobs also lost our house'. Then followed private rental and a five year wait for a Trust unit at Plympton.

The trend was not inevitably upwards – in 1989 the Trust reported a 4.5% decrease in rental applications since the previous year – but an ever-increasing proportion was from 'people experiencing a combination of financial hardship and social disadvantages'.[88] 'Zoi W', whose employment as a nurse ended after suffering clinical depression, applied to the Trust soon afterwards in 1988 when her mother died and the friend she was sharing a house with also became ill and was moved. 'I had to leave and I would, literally, have been homeless. I was absolutely frantic, still suffering depression and with no other family help I was extremely lucky that I had a HT person who worked her heart out for me'.

Above: rebuilding the computer room at Angas Street, c1980s. New wiring is being placed in walls and under the old building's high ceiling.

Right: Mrs Dot Whelan celebrating her 90th birthday with Trust staff Sue Daw (left) and Tricia Brand (right), photographed for Housing Trust News October 1990.

Allotted accommodation at Ashford, where she has remained, she described her happiest experience as a tenant was 'initially getting a place of my own – a roof over my head – not being homeless. (If *that* had happened I often wonder if I would have needed to go into hospital)'.

The Annual Report of 1986 confirmed the Trust's shift in emphasis from economic development to providing housing and related services 'for those in need and within their capacity to pay', effecting a change from 'a total development authority' to these main objectives:

> [M]eet as much housing need as possible through an integrated range of programs ... targeted to both lift people out of housing related poverty and to prevent them from falling into it; ensure that the limited resources available are allocated to ... priorities of need; ensure that the quality of housing and ... services is driven by the needs of customers and takes account of community expectations.[89]

Andrew Parkin, who chaired the South Australian Housing Advisory Council, noted in 1987 that the Trust's traditional open eligibility and diverse clientele had changed in response to the need to house 'an avalanche of needy cases', resulting in new public tenants resembling those elsewhere in Australia: 'mainly the non-working poor. The change is regretted even as the necessity for it is

understood'.[90] The change in emphasis was also reflected in staffing, with new job titles and responsibilities. Janet Combridge, who started with the Letting Section at Angas Street in 1985 and became a housing advisor, explained that 'before we were advisors we were the allocations officers and did offers. Much simpler in those days'.[91] Staff also offered more welfare oriented and diverse services, encompassing Trust tenancies and assistance to private renters and purchasers.

There were other consequences of the change. In 1987 a report on difficult tenancies was presented to the Board, which agreed to ask for a Cabinet paper from housing, law enforcement, health and welfare officers 'dealing with responses to neighbourhood disruption and violence', advising how to coordinate agency responses to 'individual situations', and ensure support for tenants with special health and welfare needs. At the same time, the Board agreed on 'a more rigorous enforcement of the Conditions of Tenancy', up to eviction, formerly a rare event.[92] Ellen Greenslade recalled the Trust removing tenants living next door at Parafield Gardens 'because of their abusive, loud, destructive nocturnal activities. The whole street was up in arms about them'.

Leith MacGillivray, who had expected the Trust to be as she'd known from visiting friends who were tenants, had not realised how 'unemployment, homelessness and poor living conditions had become so widespread'. The 'heterogeneous group' of tenants in her block of city units 'had "fault lines" in abundance'. Quiet elderly and middle-aged residents such as her were alarmed by the rowdiness and petty crimes of other tenants. 'Younger ones, many of them caught in a generational unemployment trap, wanted lots of loud noise, and often alcohol, day and night, within a very resonant quadrangle. Several were addicted to drugs'.

The pressure to house people with special needs was intensified by the government adopting policies of de-institutionalisation; the practice of moving mentally ill people out of state psychiatric institutions. Earlier movements in Britain and the USA were based on concern for human rights and driven also by the desire to reduce public expenditure. De-institutionalisation followed a similar course in Australia. It began in the 1960s and accelerated in the 1980s. Psychiatric hospitals were closed and the number of psychiatric beds was reduced, and mental health services were 'mainstreamed'. The change from institutional to community care (or simply to community life) had serious consequences for mentally ill or disabled people

> across the spectrum of health care provision, community welfare agencies, and housing agencies ... Demands upon community welfare and housing agencies increased, as people newly discharged from institutions needed these services to help them survive in the community. In addition, pressure upon families and carers rose as people with mental illness called upon them for assistance in community living.[93]

As the provider of public housing with secure tenure, affordable rents and a capacity to modify houses, the Trust was the best, and often only, option for tenants with disabilities. Although costly, the easiest task involved physically modifying houses for disabled tenants and supplying homes for assisted living that were run by community organisations. By 1991 the Trust reported having built or modified 4,528 such dwellings with a further 138 leased to other organisations.[94] The Trust had not only to provide homes, but also deal with difficult and sometimes violent tenants struggling to cope with independent living. As one officer noted, 'The transition from street homelessness or long-term hospitalisation to public housing can be traumatic'.[95]

It could also be traumatic for other Trust residents. Peter Chigwidden, himself on a disability pension and a Trust tenant since 1990, described his group of flats as a good place to live, but within 12 months 'it went down hill dramatically and soon became a very dangerous place to live'. The large complex had a big transient population and many tenants 'had little or no social skills and were not prepared for the close community living and sharing of common areas'. High-needs tenants were placed in complexes of walk-up flats without considering their effects on other tenants. 'For a period of 18 months we had the neighbours from hell.' The phrase was repeated in many other tenant contributions to this history.

One of Leith MacGillivray's neighbours needed five skips to cart off his rubbish when he left. 'I was told he had lived on the streets since he was nine because in this way he was safer than at home.' She also recalled that

> Mental health problems were a further concern. Some wards at Northfield Hospital had been closed and the theory, policy, was for people to live as independently as possible with the help of carers and counsellors who paid regular visits ... There was a very lonely woman who ... when not taking her medication ... often became violent. On one occasion she threatened to set fire to all cars. On that occasion she was taken to Glenside, handcuffed, in a paddy wagon. I did not see visitors or counsellors come ... Another elderly woman persisted in walking out on the street scantily clad ... One man, each Friday night, walked up and down the length of his balcony, yelling and hollering indecipherably.

Many mentally ill people moved out of institutions into boarding houses in the city, mainly in the West End, but business and support agencies found it 'inappropriate to refer people who exhibit obviously challenging behaviours and those who are mentally ill to the Hindley Street precinct', and in any case those rooming house beds were closing down as premises were sold and redeveloped.[96]

De-institutionalisation also contributed to youth homelessness, although this was less remarked on than for the mentally ill. A similar shift from state institutional care began during the 1970s, influenced by changing views of children's welfare and the rising costs of running orphanages. Most of the large state children's homes were closed down.[97] By 1990 more than 30% of the Trust's new tenants were young. The supply of special housing was increased, and Direct Lease Youth joint ventures (begun in 1981) were expanded with houses leased to groups of young people, or run with partial supervision by community organisations. Joint ventures included the Cities of Elizabeth and Noarlunga.[98]

In 1993 the Trust introduced the Stretton Award for staff to undertake research, study or travel. The first recipient, Paul Smith, visited the British government's pilot scheme, Single Homeless in London, which coordinated policy on homelessness across sectors. Projects were intended to fast track housing and coordinate support to help new residents live in the community. As Smith explained on his return, the Trust had tenancies failing, especially those of people with a mental illness, who formed as much as half of the homeless population, and young people affected by the state's restructure of youth accommodation services. A South Australian adaptation of the British scheme could mean that 'we can approach the broad issues of homelessness in a joint way with other agencies'. The key to success was extensive liaison between agencies, and South Australia could build on existing partnerships between the Trust and the Department of Family and Community Services and the restructure of Mental Health Services.[99]

Aboriginal housing

Aborigines make up the single poorest group of South Australians, and proportionately the greatest number of them live in public housing. A symbolic representation of Indigenous people in a newly developed Housing Trust area was

the Shedley sculpture placed at Christies Beach in 1965. Later research found that this was the first major public artwork to represent Aboriginal people or their culture in Adelaide.[100]

The Trust managed rental housing for Aboriginal tenants through the Aboriginal Housing Unit and the South Australian Aboriginal Housing Advisory Committee from 1973 until 2000. At the 1996 census more than two-thirds (71.7%) of Aboriginal households were renting (public or private housing), compared to less than one-third (27.6%) of non-Indigenous households. Close to half of Aboriginal households were in public rental or community association housing (39.6% and 6.7% respectively). The census indicated that the overall rate of poverty in South Australia's Aboriginal households was increasing.[101]

The census also revealed a high level of overcrowding in Aboriginal family and group households, most commonly in rural areas.[102] Pitjantjatjara Elder, Yami Lester, suggested that poor housing worsened his people's health; and the company Healthhabitat, working over several years in remote areas, found that wear and tear due to overcrowding caused the most damage to houses.[103] Many Aboriginal families lived in the city, but patterns of occupation were wider than for non-Indigenous people. Port Augusta, for example, was one of the most important localities as a permanent place of residence, as well as a major regional centre, and a regular meeting place for many people travelling from remote areas, homelands and other towns. The Trust supplied Aboriginal housing throughout South Australia, including to the remote Anangu Pitjantjatjara Lands (AP Lands). The Anangu people (Pitjantjatjara, Yankunytjatjara and Ngaanyatjarra) gained title to over 100,000 square kilometres of their traditional lands in the far north-west of the state with passage of the *Pitjantjatjara Land Rights Act 1981*.

The complication of community control in the AP Lands as well as remoteness created difficulties and expense in supplying houses.[104] A select committee of Parliament reported that the design and allocation of houses was determined by the AP Development Committee, with representatives from each community, but there were complaints about inadequate or uneven allocations to the different homelands. By the 1990s state and Commonwealth agencies were spending $4.9 million annually for housing on the AP Lands (the average cost of a new house was $200,000), and 'the designs and standards developed for Anangu housing have been recognised nationally for their cultural appropriateness and for the ease with which the finished product can be maintained'. However, as the select committee concluded, 'houses delivered to the AP Lands fall short of community expectations. Research conducted in 1998 noted that the identification of "strategies for improving living conditions for Anangu" had resulted in minimal changes for the better in terms of housing'.[105]

By the mid-1980s in-migration of Aboriginal people from the West Coast and Flinders Ranges had swollen rental applications for public housing, especially in Adelaide's north-western suburbs. A history of Port Adelaide Central Mission describes its 'involvement with this deeply disadvantaged group of Port residents' whose rate of unemployment had reached 70% among the young. Neighbours complained about overcrowding and offensive behaviour; 40 people were found living in a double unit at Taperoo. The Mission asked Aboriginal residents who they preferred as landlord. Most favoured the Trust because 'you knew where you stood with them and they were pretty good with repairs'. Mission staff sent their report to Parliament. 'More housing was later allocated for Aboriginal people in the northwest region, and management was moved from the Aboriginal Affairs Department to the Housing Trust.' The writers concluded that this 'was a long-term positive outcome for the Mission's advocacy'.[106] The Trust also supported housing cooperatives in Adelaide, including the South Australian Aboriginal Housing Association, and an Aboriginal women's shelter was established in Trust accommodation in 1988. (Nunga Mi:Minar later provided houses for up to 11 families.)

The Aboriginal Rental Housing Program had been moved from the Minister of Housing to the Minister of Aboriginal Affairs, but the Trust resumed delivery of the program in 1993, continuing when it was transferred back to Housing in 1995. The Trust's role was not long-term, however. A review in 1992 recommended a separate housing authority, and an Aboriginal Housing Advisory Council was formed in 1993 to help set this up. The Aboriginal Housing Authority was duly established in 1998 in the hope of gaining 'efficiencies, less duplication and better planning' by directing state and Commonwealth funding through one agency.[107] Housing Trust dwellings and services were transferred to the new authority in 2000.

Tenant participation

'An organisation housing tens of thousands of households cannot be run democratically, although its management can be run more openly and with greater tenant participation as the SAHT set out to prove.'[108] The Trust had a reputation as a humane organisation, but it was also a paternalistic one. Paul Edwards challenged this tradition. For the first time in its history, the Trust made a serious effort to encourage tenant participation and promote tenants' rights. Four tenant liaison officers were appointed in 1987.

Representatives from local tenant and resident groups joined the first Regional Advisory Board at Marion in 1985 and worked with staff to develop policies. Mrs Glenice Bennett remembered that Shirleen Davis, the 'LO' for her group of flats at Glenside, 'was instrumental in setting up our Barwell Tenant Committee in 1988. I was Secretary for 3 years before becoming Chairperson which I still am. In 1990 the Adelaide Regional Advisory Board [RAB] was set up and I have been in the chair since'. Other RABs were established in Elizabeth-Gawler, Modbury and The Parks, and in the Southern and Riverland regions. Benefits flowed in both directions, for example, Gilberton tenant Alison Murchie recorded 'very good' relations with the Trust. 'Have improved as I have become involved through RAB and learned how it operates'. RABs were still going strong 20 years after they began, although longstanding members would agree with Glenice Bennett: 'I enjoy the group, but getting younger tenants involved is hard'. Alison Murchie

Aboriginal workers help build in a remote area. The sign reads, 'This house is being erected by the SA Housing Trust for the Aboriginal Housing Board of SA with the aid of Aboriginal trainees and with funds made available under the Federal Government's grants in aid scheme'.

tried to organise a formal committee to represent the Elliott Lodge complex, 'but no-one was interested so I organise informal morning teas and lunches every two months or so'.

Direct communication with all tenants was started with the first statewide issue of the Trust's *Tenant Newsletter* in 1989, in which Edwards wrote of 'a responsibility to make sure that you, as a tenant, are kept informed about developments which might affect you and your household'.[109] *Focus 2000*, a magazine by and for tenants, began publication, followed in 1995 by *Trust Talk Tenant Link* (later *Customer Chat*), which combined the tenants' newsletter with the Trust's own. This was an initiative of the Gawler RAB. A member, Mrs Betty Alberton, was on the first editorial committee and described *Trust Talk Tenant Link* as going from strength to strength.

John Strang of Modbury RAB recalled, 'This RAB was the cause of all SAHT housing being given "Sulo" bins for rubbish collection'. Apart from the RAB, from 1994 he was active in the Operational Policy Advisory Committee (OPAC), Customer Forum, Home and Community Care Committee, forums on difficult and disruptive tenants, drug actions, parliamentary reviews, Community Grants Committee, and newsletter committees of *Tenants' Link* and *Trust Talk Tenant Link*.

In 1989 a statewide tenant conference was held and a Trust Tenants Advisory Council was formed. The Council aimed to convey tenants' views on policies and practices to the Trust; promote understanding of the Trust's roles; support tenant participation and make representations to governments on legislative and resource changes. As Parker told the Council's AGM in 1991, 'If tenant participation is to be meaningful, we need to be a partnership not only in dealing with local tenancy issues but also trying to share the big picture challenges that are facing the Trust today', including the cost of rental rebates, and whether the Trust should allocate housing 'only to those in greatest need'.[110]

The CSHA of 1990 required that social housing providers set up formal appeal systems, and Housing Advice and Support SA was formed.[111] In 1992 the Public Housing Appeals Unit was established for appeals against Trust decisions and, in 1993, a charter of rights for tenants – the first in Australia – was developed by a committee of staff, tenants and consumer advocates. The Charter of Rights for Public Housing Tenants illustrates the profound historical changes in the Trust. It affirmed that public housing was 'available to all South Australian residents who are not homeowners, and who are in receipt of an independent income, irrespective of race or ethnic origin, disability, marital status, age, religious or political opinion, sex or sexuality'. Eleven rights were specified. They were the right to: security of tenure; access to records; confidentiality of personal information; be treated with respect; a decent standard of housing; form a cooperative; form tenant groups; appropriately modified housing if disabled; participate in managing their dwellings and estates, and in developing policies; housing at rents based on size, type and location, and income; appeal against decisions. The charter was an essential step in codifying policies and procedures which the

Trust recognised as 'fundamental to a sound relationship with its clients'. The charter was added to the tenants' handbook and published in *Focus 2000*.[112] In 1995 the first customer satisfaction survey of public and private rental services was undertaken and renters were invited to seminars on customer involvement.

Betty Alberton joined her local participation group in 1991, later the Elizabeth/ Gawler Regional Advisory Board, which runs the Tenant Information Centre at Davoren Park. She also became secretary of the Trust's Public Housing Customer Forum. Looking back on her days as a tenant at Elizabeth from 1962, she said that relations with the Trust were much harder then. 'I think you were more in awe of the Trust and too frightened to say or do anything that might lead to you losing your house.'

Sandra Chapple, who has rented a Trust home at Port Pirie since 1989, has always enjoyed good relations with staff *except* when she tried to set up a tenants' group. She talked with the regional manager about starting up a regional tenancy group. 'I had never been a part of anything like it in my life, so had to do a lot of learning ... about how they run.' She proposed that the 'RTG' set up a community house with volunteers offering arts, fitness and computer classes and counselling. 'JPs were willing to come and help ... Other organizations and groups were willing to join in and make this a place for everyone.' They would run play groups, plant a community garden, and form a 'Drop in Centre, just for a cuppa and a chat for people who needed just a bit of company'.

The regional manager was impressed with Chapple's plan and said 'somebody from Adelaide was coming to look it over'. But the visiting officer told Chapple 'she was closing any avenues open to me to open up a Regional Tenancy Group'. She thought that Chapple 'was some big time professional'. Chapple had 'put 12 months of really hard work into getting this up and running for the tenants of Port Pirie and also to help the Workers of the Trust in Pirie'. She 'had organized so many people ... and they were all so keen to get something like this up and running here in Pirie, then in one minute this woman came and stopped everything'. Without Housing Trust backing the local council wouldn't support it either. 'I don't think the word crushed is really strong enough about how I felt.' Her work as a tenant activist 'came to a screaming halt', and she became suspicious of the Trust's own efforts. 'I just didn't believe that the people running these focus groups were being honest, they seemed to want tenants' participation, but not for them to ... be a part of the outcome, they only wanted them so they could say they had tenant participation with this decision.'[113]

Private households

In the interests of creating stable and self-sufficient communities – and supporting the building industry – for 50 years from 1946 South Australian governments made persistent efforts to foster home ownership, using the Trust to supply houses or help to purchase them. Half of the 100,000 houses built by the Trust up until 1987 were sold to homeowners, and although the Trust no longer built houses for sale, it sold allotments in new subdivisions to private purchasers, encouraged sales to sitting tenants and offered rental purchase. There were many, however, like Josephine Elphick, a tenant at Findon since 1963, who would have liked to buy their Trust home, but could not: 'I did ask about twenty years [ago] but not enough money'.

New schemes were rapidly introduced and replaced. These included a low deposit home purchase scheme, another rental purchase scheme and a mortgage relief scheme. There were also new hindrances. Melva Wallace, who considered buying her Trust unit, wrote that 'changes in HT policy and the event of [state] stamp duty changed my mind'. In 1986, H.O.M.E., a progressive purchase scheme, was introduced to encourage tenants who could not afford to purchase on their own, to buy a minimum 25% share. H.O.M.E. guaranteed interest rate protection, which helped buyers struggling to meet high mortgage repayments driven up by record interest rates in the 1980s. On an overseas visit in 1987, Edwards followed up contacts in his native UK on joint ventures and shared ownership, and sales to tenants.[114]

The Trust's rental purchase scheme was replaced in 1989 by a capital-indexed loan program administered by HomeStart Finance Ltd. HomeStart was established as a government-owned corporation and became a statutory authority in 1995 – in the same year the State Bank's housing loans portfolio was privatised and sold to St George Bank for $730 million. As was once done by the State Bank, HomeStart financed low- to moderate-income earners buying or building homes. At HomeStart's launch the government promised $1 billion in loans over the next four years, and in that time approved $922 million in loans to more than 14,000 households. Demand eased as interest rates fell. In 1993 a purchaser on average weekly male earnings required 31% of his income to service a new loan. The minister described this as the best result since 1983 when only 28% of earnings were required. He stressed the important relationship between HomeStart and the Housing Trust. In 1991 an ABS survey found that 80% of all rental householders would prefer to be home buyers, and a majority of Trust tenants had stated in their applications that home ownership was their goal.[115]

The Trust itself continued to help buyers, and from 1990 administered HomeSure mortgage assistance to provide monthly grants to eligible owners. The new scheme was not very effective – Kenny described it as 'an electioneering stunt' by the Bannon government – and failed to help the promised 35,000 families. 'In reality the scheme helped fewer than 2,000 families, with administration costs outstripping the pay-outs (which failed to top even one million dollars).'[116] A more determined effort was also made to encourage tenants to buy their Trust homes, and 25 real estate firms were appointed across the state in 1992 as selling agents. The drawback was that recently built homes were usually the ones sold, leaving older public housing stock that was increasingly costly to repair and upgrade.

These schemes maintained the Trust's longstanding role in helping purchasers. By contrast, until the 1980s it gave only limited help to private renters. This was mainly through the Housing Improvement Act (Control of Rentals of Sub-Standard Houses), with inspection and rent controls encouraging private landlords to improve dwellings, in Stretton's words, 'disciplining the State's private landlords in an unusual way'. A highlight of the induction course for new Trust staff in 1989 was Housing Improvement and Rent Control's 'guide to great South Australian dunneys'.[117] The sanctions did have good effect: 30% of privately rented houses were found to be substandard in the 1940s, compared to 2% by the 1990s.[118]

A total of $55.86 million was spent by private landlords on upgrading substandard dwellings between 1979 and 1993.[119] The impact of these regulations was extended when they were also applied to owner-occupied houses in the 1980s, but the change, purely administrative, was short-lived. Murray Hutchesson, who was employed by the Trust from 1973 as a design engineer, remembered 'political fallout' when 'aggressive' Trust inspectors imposed controls on too many owner-occupied houses, and controls were again restricted to rental housing.[120]

Housing Improvement's very success also 'prompted some thoughtless cost-cutting'.[121] This was one of several Trust functions marked for removal, sparking public condemnation from Geoff Francis, one of the inspectors who had recently taken a redundancy package, reducing their number from 14 to 2. Francis told *City Messenger* that 'the hamstrung section' would not be able to pressure landlords into repairing houses and flats. By placing rent control, 'if the landlord is charging $150 a week and the roof gutters are falling down, the ceiling has collapsed, the electrics are faulty, the walls have been eaten away by white ants, the rent can be reduced to, say, $30 a week'. In an echo of the 1930s Inquiry that led to the original Act, the ex-inspector reeled off 'horror stories' about privately rented houses. He'd found 10 tenants paying $50 each to rent a timber-framed, galvanised iron lined house in Kilburn with one toilet; he'd seen brooms turned on their ends holding up ceilings in a Mile End house; and many places with huge cracks and dangerous plumbing and electrics. 'It used to be the ones built at the turn of the century. But people are buying these and doing them up. Now, it's homes that were built just before or just after the war.'[122]

Francis pointed out that rent control had also saved the government money, as once rent was reduced, rent relief was stopped, but now 'they're throwing all that money away'. He also regretted the loss of expertise in letting go highly qualified inspectors.

> And the fact that they have let us all go, speaks for itself.
>
> The Liberals don't like it. It's the people 'in the know' who own these houses: doctors, solicitors, ex-mayors ...
>
> The argument will be that people should be more aware of what they are renting, but some people will just fall through the net ... Where are they going to turn to? Things are going to deteriorate now that the landlord is going to get his own way.[123]

Richard Parker, quoted by *City Messenger* in response, said that inspectors had left because of public service cutbacks, but the Trust would still respond to

LOOKING TO BUY?
HAVING PROBLEMS MEETING REPAYMENTS?
REAL ESTATE
MORTGAGE
H.O.M.E.
COULD HELP YOU
• Low interest loans
• Rental purchase: minimum deposit and extra security
• Mortgage relief: to help some buyers in difficulty.
StateBank
H.O.M.E.
State Bank Loans:
See your local branch or call the bank on 210 4799
Rental Purchase:
Call the Housing Trust 210 0209 or the State Bank 210 4799 or see your local office.
Mortgage Relief:
See your local Trust office or call 210 0216
HOUSING TRUST
HOME OWNERSHIP MADE EASIER.

'An example of substandard housing', Drayton Street, Bowden, Annual Report 2002–03.

complaints from private tenants. That approach halved the number of houses found to be substandard each year. Mary Yeates, the Trust's Housing Improvement Manager, noted also that making tenants responsible for identifying substandard houses placed them at risk of eviction by aggrieved landlords and 'made the tenant the focus of the issue, rather than the condition of the house'. The Housing Improvement Act's wider intention was lost, 'risking the loss of a very good model for State intervention in housing'.[124] Standards were upgraded in the Housing Improvement (Standards) Regulations 1992. Both the Act and the regulation were placed under review in 2004, but the Housing Improvement Act was retained. As the list of houses submitted for Board review in late 2005 indicates, controls in some cases lasted for decades: a house in Newman Street, Semaphore, was first listed as substandard in 1967, and one in Daly Street, Gawler in 1969.[125]

Retaining even a restricted housing improvement role was fortunate, as the Trust's own rental stock was cut, adding to the number of private renters. Fifty years of large-scale public housing provision had markedly reduced the proportion of South Australians in private rental. In 1986 the private sector was only three-quarters the size of those in other states. But that trend was reversed in the 1990s. By 2001 the proportion of private tenants had risen to the same level as in 1976 and their number was now the highest in South Australia's history.[126]

By then the Trust itself was assisting many private tenants. The problem of housing for young people, highlighted in International Youth Year (1985), led to the Direct Lease Youth Scheme for those having 'severe difficulty accessing private rental accommodation or a history of failed private rental'.[127] Special housing was later offered also to tertiary students. The Emergency Housing Office (EHO) gave more liberal help to private applicants and tenants, including advice, advocacy, money and emergency accommodation. The office integrated housing justice and welfare for private households in crisis. Although financially linked, the EHO was physically and ideologically separate from the Trust and operated independently for a decade.

Both Edwards and Parker sought to re-integrate the EHO with the Trust and to streamline administration. There were conflicts in dual reporting to the minister by EHO and Trust managers. They argued that a single organisation should deliver comprehensive housing services, as most households moved though a lifecycle from private to public rental, ending in home ownership. Some analysts questioned that assumption, as welfare needs went beyond housing and required professional skills. Victory argued that failing to understand this complexity and to intervene properly in a crisis 'inevitably impairs the achievement of housing objectives and undermines the socially just accommodation outcomes', and that the Trust had neither the resources nor the authority to address all of the problems of private renters.[128]

The Auditor General recommended a merger in 1987, and Hemmings moved the EHO back into the Trust in 1988. Full integration and regionalisation followed with the restructure of 1990–91. Downie remembers 'lots of interesting discussions over the different culture of the EHO – the lounge furniture and rugs in the waiting area, free coffee and telephone facilities for clients and the casual clothing worn by the staff'. The EHO was replaced by PRESS – Private Rental Establishment and Support Services. The social justice and welfare functions were administered by Community Service staff following a one-week induction, and without requiring a welfare-based professional background. The EHO had employed skilled staff and had been able to increase their number quickly, unlike the Trust. Other than emergency financial help with bonds, rents and removals, PRESS provided fewer services than had the EHO. Victory argued that in making PRESS assessments, staff needed to take into account housing needs and resources, income and expenditure, household characteristics, previous assistance and the nature of the accommodation crisis. The Trust's traditional focus on housing outcomes alone, limited the focus to providing or not providing financial assistance.[129] However, integration did widen geographical access to former EHO services, including the rental listings service 'Whereabouts', delivered from regional offices from 1993.

By then the Trust administered three support programs for private low-income renters: Housing Improvement and Rent Control, PRESS, and (the state's) Rent Relief. The Commonwealth downgraded support for public housing, while extending it for private renters, by introducing its own rent relief scheme.[130] The number of assisted private renters soon approached that of public tenants. In 1992 financial assistance and advice were given to 56,665 privately renting households. Victory argued that although the Trust had undertaken the private rental programs by default, they were changing it into 'a de facto income support organisation for both public and private tenants'.[131]

A 1994 review justified PRESS 'on the grounds of tenure equity, the depth of housing need, the insecurity inherent in the rental market, the likely effects of not providing assistance, and the stresses placed on public housing'. One in four private tenants in South Australia was receiving a rental bond. Although strictly targeted, that assistance had grown by two-thirds since the Trust's restructure in 1991 and was more generous than in other states: South Australia assisted 28% of all private renters in Australia but had only 8% of the population. The main change suggested by the review was that, instead of paying millions to the Residential Tenancies Tribunal for renters' bonds, the Trust should offer bond guarantees, paying out only when required. The guarantee system was introduced in 1995, and helped free money for the Trust's own housing, although more than half of bond monies was lost annually.[132]

The policy trend to favour private rather than public rental did not necessarily reflect the preferences of renters. In 1991, the Australian Bureau of Statistics (ABS) asked renters which tenure they preferred. Most favoured home ownership, but for those who wanted to rent, 27% would prefer to be public tenants, compared to 9% wishing to rent privately. A decade later another survey found that 79% of poor private renters were under stress, paying more than a quarter of their income in rent. Of these households 23% were paying more than half their income in rent.[133]

The questionnaire sent to Trust tenants for this history asked them to compare their experiences as public and private renters. Peter Chigwidden found that 'The private renters had a house inspection every six weeks and responded much quicker to maintenance issues'. Many other responses emphasised security of tenure and lower rents in Trust homes. Miss Mary Cusack wrote: 'Much more stable existence and generally cheaper as SAHT tenant. Landlords can decide they need property or to sell property which leaves [private] tenant out in cold'. Most private rental dwellings were located in Adelaide's old, inner suburbs with landlords letting properties that would eventually move out of the rental market to owner occupation.[134]

Paul Burger, who moved into a Trust flat at Brooklyn Park in the mid-1990s, saw the advantages as the good location near public transport and shops, and getting a rent subsidy, although that was lost if his income rose to the point where he had to pay full market rent. Nor could he reduce rent by sharing his flat as many private tenants do, because his own rent would instead be raised. 'Zoi W' was annoyed by not being allowed to run a business or earn money from a Trust property, again unlike private renters.

> WHY NOT??? Does the HT think we're all going to run Brothels??? What if like myself with no car, family support, chronic illness, exhaustion etc [this

> could be] the best and/or maybe the ONLY way one can start to help oneself out of the poverty trap and thus (A) Pay taxes (B) Afford increased rental.[135]

Burger also identified as a disadvantage the social stigma because he was lumped with the 'hoons' housed by the Trust.

> I am a second-class citizen; two laws apply; one to welfare tenants; the other to ordinary tenants. In private rental, estate agents evict troublesome tenants with greater ease and frequency. Nobody grants the value of a good welfare tenant and bad welfare tenants 'rule the roost'. Instead of receiving eviction notices, troublesome tenants receive messages they interpret as them doing nothing wrong because under the social equity policy Housing SA cannot make someone homeless.

Trust property

'The Trust's main asset, and hence major tool for achieving its mission and the Government[']s objectives, is the stock of dwellings available for rent.'[136] House building was the main activity in this decade and created a valuable asset, soon drawn upon. The number of rental dwellings bought and built during 1986 reached 3,107, a record matched only in the boom 1960s. (Strata titled units were included in purchased housing from 1988.) In the decade 1980–90 stock increased by more than 20,000 units, a 50% increase. Additional homes were supplied to community housing.[137] When the Trust's 100,000th house was completed in 1986, the Trust had supplied more than any other state except NSW, where 150,000 were built by the Housing Commission between 1942 and 1986.[138]

Malcolm Downie described sitting at Board meetings as section directors gave answers for the monthly Performance Report. A highlight was hearing 'Dean Lambert explaining away the delays in the capital works program'. Downie recalled 'timber framed kits being lost off boats in stormy crossings to Kangaroo Island and ... how wet weather had delayed jobs in rural and remote regions of the State'. He was puzzled by that excuse but 'finally understood the impact on a construction site when it rained when I travelled to those more remote areas as General Manager 25 years later and realised what Dean had meant all those years ago!'

Some of this construction was funded by high interest rather than the traditional low interest loans. The Trust began a debt retirement strategy to pay off high interest commercial loans funded by sales.[139] The Trust had been the only state authority that had 'steadfastly refused ... to engage in large-scale asset stripping through discounted sales' to tenants, but as a result, housing stock had 'attained a considerably higher level of maturation than in the other states'.[140] The Trust's 1994 Triennial Review found that 37% of homes were the old double units, with 76% of them being over 30 years old. Only 30% of housing was less than 30 years old. 'The quantity of aging stock indicates that the Trust will need to invest substantial funds in redevelopment or amenity'.[141] The three approaches taken:

to upgrade, replace and realise the value of stock by sale, had a marked impact on housing design and amenities, as well as on suburban character.

Sandra Chapple listed the work done to upgrade her Port Pirie double unit:

> They have replaced my hot water system, the roof, put insulation into the ceiling, replaced the stove, upgraded the kitchen, upgraded the bathroom, put new tiles into the laundry and toilet, replaced the toilet, put in new aluminium windows, cemented the drive way, put up a new fence, and last but not least given me paint to paint the place out several times.
>
> I can't speak highly enough of their efforts to make my life easier and happier here, odd jobs are done by professionals, they are quick and do an excellent job, and if any don't do a good job I only have to tell the Housing Trust and things are changed to make sure it is done properly the next time.

Clear eyed about the costs of upgrading, she added, 'I have never wanted to buy this property, it is too old and they are asking way too much for it ... it has a lot wrong with it ... that would cost a small fortune to fix up'. Murray Hutchesson suggested that maintenance problems could also develop in medium density developments built after the 1970s, as from then rental houses were constructed only by private contractors.

Public tendering for maintenance work was implemented in 1989. A 24-hour telephone-based maintenance service was introduced in 1991. Improvements in managing housing stock included the introduction in 1993 of 'Check It', a statewide asset condition database. A self-audit maintenance process and quality assurance for contractors were also introduced. Chapple described being able to report bad work as 'a good thing'. She often had had work done earlier, 'and the people they sent were terrible ... when I contacted the staff they fobbed me off ... and so you finally just stopped bothering to report shoddy work ... The staff they have on maintenance now are very helpful and give you their full attention ... respect given, respect received ... goes a long way to a healthy and happy relationship between tenants and Trust'.

From the 1990s new housing designs were assessed for five star design energy rating. Design and construction concentrated on smaller houses to cater for the many applications from one and two person households, as well as for the shrinking households of ageing tenants – although Melva Wallace spoke for many in liking the spaciousness of her older unit: 'I have a large family and the younger ones like to stay with Nan occasionally'.

All dwellings continued to be built by private contractors to Trust designs, except for design and construct projects where private builders constructed houses of their design on their own or the Trust's land. This scheme had ended by 1988, but was picked up again in the early 1990s.

Over the decade 1986–96, the Trust owned its largest number and variety of rental dwellings, reaching an all-time peak of 63,022 in 1992. (See also Appendix 1.) In 1988 the International Year of the Homeless funded the Heffernan

Trust homes (1986–95). Top: upgraded and converted double units,

Above: Port Augusta, low energy and accessible single unit with stepless entry, solar panels, pergolas and trees,

Top right: medium density housing, Mitchell Park redevelopment.

report, which confirmed a long decline – as much as 90% since the mid-1950s – in commercial boarding and lodging houses in metropolitan Adelaide. Proprietors sold up when boarding houses became less profitable, although public and private sector alternatives had expanded. To ensure that this form of accommodation survived, the Trust assessed every boarding house offered for sale in Adelaide, and between 1976 and 1993 purchased or built 12, with a total 290 beds. Seven boarding houses were in central Adelaide, and five were leased to welfare agencies. The seven in the city represented 23% of the 920 boarding house beds within Adelaide City Council and, as the housing minister pointed out, 'one can see that quite a large percentage of city residents form this category of tenants'.[142]

The enthusiasm for diversifying housing stock extended to the restoration and adaptive reuse of houses and other buildings of historical significance. For example, work commenced on Barton Vale House at Enfield and Mornington House in Unley in 1988.

Redevelopment and urban renewal

Declining funds and policy changes curtailed the Trust's building program and encouraged new partnerships with private firms in greenfield projects and in redeveloping rental estates. The change dovetailed with the view that public housing should be integrated with, rather than separated from, private housing – a change in thinking prompted by the social stigma and concentrated disadvantage associated with the old estates. The provision of public rental houses was altered from building clusters and segregated estates to mixing them with private dwellings in an attempt at social mix. Such partnerships with private firms began at West Lakes in the 1970s but, in the new ventures, Trust housing was scattered throughout the development. The new approach was adopted in partnerships formed initially in fringe areas, at Golden Grove and Seaford, and on large areas of undeveloped public land, as at Regent Gardens (Northfield Project).[143]

Australia's first National Urban Renewal seminar was co-hosted by the Trust in 1998. Organising chair, Peter Jackson, said that authorities 'were facing similar challenges in determining the best strategies for renewing post-war, large-scale public housing estates'.[144] Urban redevelopment (called also renewal or regeneration) was carried out in established suburbs at Mitchell Park, The Parks (renamed Westwood), Elizabeth (Rosewood), Hillcrest, Windsor Gardens, and at Whyalla, Port Pirie and Port Lincoln. (See also Chapter Three.) The sale and redevelopment of Trust houses and estates was also a sign of the privatisation of public assets. This was yet another instance of institutional repositioning of the Housing Trust in relation to the private sector.[145]

Industrial and commercial

There had been enduring bipartisan acceptance of the Trust supplying buildings for expanding industries. Factories were built in 1986 for SABCO at Albert Park, and for Firmadoor at Regency Park. In 1993 Premier Lynn Arnold opened a 4,500 square metre factory for Air International at Golden Grove but, as another MP remarked, other businesses had failed, leaving vacant factories on the Trust's hands. The Minister responded that the Trust was 'a useful arm to economic development ... particularly job creation', offering facilities on attractive terms to industries the government was trying to draw into the state. On the negative side, he said 'during a period of steep economic decline and restructuring of the manufacturing industry', there was 'some fallout ... and we have been left with premises which are hard to use for other purposes – indeed, we have incurred some debts'. Parker said that the Trust had incurred a loss on the leased Pulkra property in Torrensville, but that there had been no other liquidation that had left it owning a vacant building. The Trust was continuing the program. One factory was 'an extension of the solar optical plant in the southern suburbs, which ... is one of South Australia's success stories in ... export and a very labour-intensive, high technology outfit in that area'.[146]

Good progress was reported in 1995 on factory work for SOLA International at Lonsdale, and the Trust also managed the Regency International Accommodation Project that provided accommodation for 120 students, a manager and administration for the International College of Hotel Management at Regency Park.[147] But 1995 was the Trust's last as an industrial builder, and commercial activities had already been scaled down. In 1987 the sale of a set of five shops and a clinic at Hillcrest had ended the Trust's ownership of neighbourhood shopping centres.

The AMP Society told the Premier in 1987 that it planned a large extension to the Colonnades at Noarlunga Regional Centre, and would prefer to build on

Barton Vale at Enfield, under restoration by the Trust and private developers, 1986.

freehold land rather than continue the leasehold arrangement with the Trust. The General Manager advised keeping the arrangement which supplied funds 'beneficial both to the Trust income and the State budget'.[148] However, both Elizabeth and Noarlunga Centres were readied for sale in 1994. The Industrial and Commercial Property Division had one of its busiest years in 1995, completing the Lonsdale research and development facility, a factory for Gerard Industries at Strathalbyn, and facilities for the Australis and Motorola projects at the new MFP Technology Park.[149] The South Australian Housing Trust Act passed in 1995 brought both industrial and commercial development roles to an end. Effective from 1 January 1996, the division was sundered from the Trust lock, stock and barrel, and staff, functions, assets and liabilities were vested in the Urban Projects Authority (UPA). The UPA assumed that industrial and commercial property would make a loss for the next 15 years.[150]

Housing by other means

Joint ventures

Tapping into alternative funding sources – housing by other means – informed partnerships with other organisations. A joint venture was launched in 1986 with the Jubilee 150 Homes Scheme to build cottage flats in cooperation with other groups, most of them in partnership with local councils in country locations. Chairman Ray Paley travelled to 17 openings from as far afield as Port Pirie and Mount Gambier, and reported:

> Wherever I went I was able to experience the excellent relationship the Trust has with the community. The groups of cottage flats were all well built with attractive landscaping. The developments represent the high standard of our work ... 39 Trust developments have received Awards or Commendations from the Civic Trust ... The Scheme has engendered so much community spirit, co–operation by local Government and organisations that I hope we can build on that foundation and develop an ongoing joint venture program.[151]

Most early joint ventures were with councils and drew on Commonwealth funds through the Local Government and Community Housing Program. Tying in with the push to increase the population of central Adelaide, several projects involved Adelaide City Council; for example, a group of walk-up flats designed for the corner of Gilbert and Vinrace Streets.[152] 'Crichton Court' (after former Assistant General Manager Jim Crichton), in association with Western Community Hospital, provided 20 units for the aged at Henley Beach, a project heralded as 'a forerunner to similar ventures', both in South Australia and Australia.[153] Commercial joint ventures were also contemplated, and the General Manager told the Housing Industry Association in 1987 that the Trust was 'looking into a scheme in Western Australia whereby HOMESWEST joined with private developers in housing projects'. HIA 'expressed real interest', and public–private ventures became a major feature of the Trust's development work.[154]

Cooperative housing

The Trust also helped to establish a parallel social housing sector. Cooperative, or community housing offered another way to gain housing. As the Trust observed, 'A major feature of the scheme is the channelling of private lending institution funds into the low income housing area'.[155] Untied funds were provided for community housing within the CSHA from 1978. The Henderson Inquiry into Poverty (1975) and lobbying by community groups for crisis accommodation also led to the Supported Accommodation Assistance Program (SAAP) for homeless people, jointly funded by Commonwealth and state governments. In contrast to welfare responses that typified most other government responses to de-institutionalisation and homelessness, community housing grew out of a commitment to the tenant group taking a participatory role.

Cooperatives were part of a general trend to broaden choices for social housing. State housing authorities were, however, involved by way of funding and supplying houses. Alongside Australia's eight housing authorities, thousands of small non-profit providers emerged, supported by special government programs. They came to include supported housing, crisis accommodation, transitional housing for mentally ill people, cooperative housing, community managed rental housing, Indigenous housing and independent living units for the aged.

In South Australia, Greg Smith of the Department of Housing, and Greg Black of the Emergency Housing Office, raised the idea of cooperative housing in 1979. They were backed by Paul Edwards. A community group could form to borrow

The last phase of factory building by the Trust. Top: SOLA International factory at Lonsdale. Above: newly-completed Clipsal factory.

A resident (centre) holds the key to newly-completed Carrington Mews in 1994 with (left to right) Graeme Cowan (Chair, Multi Agency Community Housing Association), Richard Parker, Bill Taylor (DHS) and John Haren (MACHA). Carrington Mews was built on the former Menzels Plastics site in Adelaide for lease to community organisations to shelter people in difficulty.

money from a bank or building society and house people on low incomes. The loans would be guaranteed by the Trust and repayments subsidised by the government.[156] The Trust responded warmly to the idea, as a cooperative could gain access to private funds and supplement its work. Community housing was also 'seen as an opportunity to develop effective community participation in the management of social housing, whilst at the same time offering an option for tenants with special needs'.[157]

The Trust held a seminar in 1980 in which Edwards explained that 'we need to develop a variety of housing forms and a variety of housing tenures to match the varying needs'. Dawn McMahon led the Women's Shelters Housing Association, incorporated in 1980 as the state's first rental co-operative, which negotiated a loan with the Co-operative Building Society. Women's Shelters was followed by the Hindmarsh Housing Association (1980) and the Northern Suburbs Aged Housing Association (1981). By 1987 Women's Shelters and Northern Suburbs had each opened 100 dwellings.[158]

Port Adelaide Central Mission, run by the Uniting Church, also opened discussions with the Trust in 1980. The Mission proposed to supply management skills for a housing association which would provide an opportunity for low-cost purchase by local tenant members. The Portway Housing Association was in place by 1984, and was managing 13 dwellings purchased from the Trust by 1986. As other housing associations would find, 'There were difficulties with inexperienced tenants ... With so many single-parent families it was difficult for most to participate actively in managing the project'. The Mission maintained support until Portway became self-sustaining. The Trust also acted as 'midwife' and maintenance manager for the Mission's other housing programs for homeless youth and Aboriginal students. By 1999 Portway managed 80 properties, and was one of more than 120 such co-operatives housing around 5,100 people in urban and rural areas around Adelaide'.[159]

After a review of cooperative housing, two new replacement programs were introduced in 1989: the Community Housing Association Program and the Co-operative Housing Program. Cooperatives were member run organisations that managed houses for members' benefit, while community housing associations were for people disadvantaged by low income, poor circumstances or disability. Community housing associations were non-profit and responsible for management, such as tenant selection, rent collection and maintenance. Associations were managed on behalf of tenants by voluntary committees, supported by sponsor organisations.[160] The *South Australian Co-operative and Community Housing Act 1991* established the South Australian Cooperative Housing Authority (SACHA) in 1992 to administer tenant managed cooperatives. SACHA in its early years was staffed by the Trust, operated from the same building and had the Trust's general manager on the board. Responsibility for community housing was transferred from the Trust to SACHA in 1995, but there was a continuing overlap as the Trust operated the Crisis Accommodation Program, Supported Tenancies Scheme, Disability Housing Program and boarding houses. SACHA member organisations participated in the Trust's community housing ventures or leased Trust property, and there was also interaction through client referrals, in a constant 'two-way traffic'.[161]

Bernadette Kuhar's recollections illustrate other interactions. She first applied for Trust housing as she was a sole parent in an abusive relationship 'with little real prospect of purchasing a house', and needed 'subsidised rent and security of tenure'. She waited six years until 1994, and believed that she was 'only housed ... that soon as I was a member of a Housing Co-operative and was making legitimate, legal, non-violent, non aggressive, non destructive waves for the Housing Trust. I would be less of a problem for the Housing Trust as a tenant'.

By 1994, although community housing accounted for only 4% of South Australia's social housing, its effects were widely evident. Building societies were lending money for rental housing; local planning by-laws had been challenged and urban consolidation and infill promoted; tenant–landlord relationships were redefined, and there had been a change in language from public to social housing.[162] There was, however, a sense that the cooperative sector had lost the 'fire in the belly' of the 1980s. Community housing gained greater attention under the Liberal government after 1993, but this support was mainly for housing associations rather than cooperatives, because of the need to shelter de-institutionalised people with disabilities.[163] As had once been the case with the Trust, government action both contributed to, and helped to ameliorate, housing problems and shaped housing organisations.

Unlike alternative housing sectors in other countries, South Australian organisations managed government owned or private housing rather than develop their own. 'Consequently, their policies are closely controlled or regulated by government and their capacity for independent growth and innovation is limited'. Growth was partly at the expense of public housing, as Trust stock was reduced through transfers to community organisations, as well as by sale and redevelopment. Community organisations gained around 1,500 dwellings between 1992 and 2000, but there was a net loss of 6,700 dwellings available for public and community housing.[164]

As a housing researcher Chris Paris concluded, 'Most of the supposed advantages of new forms of social rental housing provision (diversity, flexibility, responsiveness to tenants' needs) can be met in an enlarged, improved and modernised public housing sector'.[165] Formerly paternalistic authorities such as the South Australian Housing Trust were developing more flexible responses to customers, and Paris described the Trust as one of the world's successful public housing models:

> [These] large, semi-autonomous housing agencies ... had four things in common: strong government financial support; relative independence from the vagaries of party policy or changes in government; size to enable economies of scale; and determination to improve ... overall quality and supply of social rental housing.

By the time these words were published in 1993, all four characteristics were under threat in South Australia.[166]

Notes

Quotations from people named in the text are usually from those who supplied information to this update history, in questionnaires, letters, interviews and emails (also listed in the Bibliography). Sources referred to only once or twice are included in these chapter notes with full publication details. Most Internet references are listed only in these notes. Titles given in brief have full details provided in the Bibliography. Where possible, sources of information for a whole paragraph are grouped into one note at its end. Unattributed facts are usually drawn from the 'Chronological history of the South Australian Housing Trust', updated in 2006 by Marsden. Months are abbreviated, and other abbreviations are listed in the Glossary.

1 Ray Paley, Chairman's message, *Housing Trust News* (*HTN*), 11, Dec 1986, p. 3.

2 *The Advertiser*, Editorial, 8 Dec 1986.

3 S. Marsden, *Business, charity and sentiment: the South Australian Housing Trust 1936–1986*, Wakefield Press, Kent Town, 1986.

4 SAHT, Board Minutes, 24 Feb 1987 (quoting Chairman Ray Paley).

5 SAHT, Board Minutes, 26 Jan 1993; 24 Jan 1995. Australia's Deputy Prime Minister Brian Howe had asked SA to drive the Australian part of the project. SAHT officer J. Chan provided accounting and property management services during a four month assignment in 1995.

6 D. Kilner, *Housing policy in South Australia since white settlement*, Digitalprintaustralia.com, Adelaide, 2005, p. 287.

7 D. Hayward, 'The Reluctant Landlords? A History of Public Housing in Australia', *Urban Policy and Research* 14 (1), 1996: 'The last throes of public housing? 1973–1995 The Economic, Political and Housing Context' (Table: Public housing waiting lists by State, 1986–1992), <www.infoxchange.net.au/rhchome/iurhc/s0501.htm> viewed July 2007; SAHT, 'Housing Trust in focus 1988–89' (supplement to Annual Report), p. 6. Hayward: Western Australia, with the most closely comparable housing authority and population, had 11,190 on the list in 1986. By 1992 WA and Tasmania, like SA, had kept increases modest, but there had been a decided lengthening of waiting lists in Queensland (24,498) and the territories.

8 As explained above, this information attributed to tenants and other people associated with the SAHT was provided in questionnaire responses, respectively from Melva Wallace (6 Dec 2006) and Joanne Holmes (30 Nov 2006).

9 S. Marsden and A. Parkin, 'Hugh Stretton and the South Australian Housing Trust', in *Markets, morals and public policy*, 1989, p. 210 (quotation); Kilner, *Housing policy*, p. 210; SAHT, Annual Reports.

10 Edwards, in *South Australian Housing Trust* [Newsletter], 5, March 1990, p. 3.

11 The phrase is from Brennan and Castles: 'Something significant has been happening in Australian institutional life over the last two decades or so – a kind of institutional repositioning, a move to a more competitive institutional order'. G. Brennan and F. Castles, eds, *Australia reshaped: 200 years of institutional transformation*, Cambridge University Press, Cambridge, 2002, Introduction, p. 1.

12 Parliament of South Australia, 2007, *Statistical Record*, p. 179. Hemmings was Housing Minister for the longest duration of any minister from 1965 (when the ALP reintroduced the portfolio) until 2006. Throughout the Trust's history, governments could never quite decide where public housing should fit. Liberal governments tended to prefer other arrangements. There was no housing portfolio of any kind from 1927–65, including during Playford's entire term as premier (effectively keeping the Trust as a flexible agency of state development) and housing was subsumed in 'human services' under a later Liberal government in 1997–2002.

13 SA Parliament, House of Assembly, G. J. Crafter, address to Estimates Committee, 16 Sept 1993.

14 D. Kilner, *From dream to reality: a history of The Northern Suburbs Housing Co-operative Inc 1981–2002*, Northern Suburbs Housing Co-operative Inc., Adelaide, 2002, p. 170.

15 Both sets of statistics, Scott Baum & Riaz Hassan, 'Economic restructuring and spatial equity: a case study of Adelaide' *Journal of Sociology* 1993; pp. 29, 151, 156, 157.

16 Hayward, 'The Reluctant Landlords?'

17 B. Badcock, 'Land and housing provision', in K. Sheridan, ed., *The state as developer: public enterprise in South Australia*, Royal Australian Institute of Public Administration, Adelaide, 1986, p. 174.
18 Hayward, 'The Reluctant Landlords?'
19 S. Purdy and N. Kwak, 'Introduction: new perspectives on public housing histories in the Americas', *Journal of Urban History*, 33 (3), March 2007, p. 361.
20 Kilner, *Housing policy* (both quotations), p. 211. Kilner has had a long career in housing, including at the SAHT, in community housing, as an advocate and a consultant, and his PhD thesis forms the main part of this book.
21 Marsden and Parkin, p. 211.
22 G. Hugo, 'SA's population policy', *Independent Weekly*, 9–15 Feb 2008.
23 Description of Joint Ventures Scheme by Dennis Hawkins, *HTN*, **1**, 1, June 1989, p. 4.
24 Dr Leith MacGillivray, (E) (response to questionnaire), 14 Jan 2007.
25 See: C. Kenny, *State of denial*, Wakefield Press, Kent Town, 1993; Greg McCarthy, *Things fall apart: a history of the State Bank of South Australia*, Australian Scholarly Publishing, Melbourne, 2002. Two of Australia's four state banks (the other was the State Bank of Victoria) collapsed for similar reasons.
26 Helen Ottaway, (E), 24 Feb 2007.
27 H. Stretton, *Australia Fair*, UNSW Press, Sydney, 2005, p. 120.
28 SAHT, Annual Report 1986, p. 31; SAHT, Board Minutes, 28 April 1987; Chronology; Stretton, *Australia Fair*, p. 120 (quotation); J. Kemeny, *From public housing to the social market. Rental policy strategies in comparative perspective*, Routledge, London & New York, 1995, pp. 92, 93.
29 SAHT, Triennial Review 1994, pp. 2.6, 6.7 (statistics and quotation).
30 D. Hayward, 'The Reluctant Landlords?' conclusion,
31 SAHT, Board minutes, 22 Feb 2000.
32 Interview with Hon Jay Weatherill 11 Jan 2007 (SLSA OH 807/1) (unless indicated, other quotations from him are from the same interview).
33 SAHT, *Housing Trust in Focus*, 2002, p. 34.
34 Kilner, *Housing policy*, pp. 334 (quotation), 357.
35 SAHT, Board Minutes, 28 April 1987.
36 SAHT, Board Minutes, 28 April 1987.
37 Government Management Board, SAHT, Triennial Review 1994, p. ii; Hayward, 'The Reluctant Landlords?
38 SAHT, Triennial Review 1994, p. iii.
39 Carmel Hallion, (E) (E) to S. Marsden, 22 Jan 2007.
40 'Blackchat', no 2, 11 Feb 2002: intranet staff newsletter, from Greg Black, who also noted that this amount was 'twice what we get now'; V. Hasan, 'A critical review of the evolution of approaches to public housing provision in South Australia' B Planning thesis, University of South Australia, 1997, p. 20.
41 Hayward, 'The Reluctant Landlords?'
42 SA Parliament, G. J. Crafter, address to Estimates Committee, 16 Sept 1993.
43 See also S. Marsden, 'Ramsay, Alexander Maurice (1914–1978)', *Australian Dictionary of Biography*, 16, Melbourne University Press, Carlton, 2002, pp. 52–54.
44 Fred Foord, (E), 10 Sept 2007.
45 Malcolm Downie, (E), 23 Oct 2007.
46 Downie, 23 Oct 2007.
47 Paul Edwards, in *South Australian Housing Trust* [Newsletter], 5, March 1990, p. 1.
48 See B. Dickey, *Rations, Residence, Resources: A History of Social Welfare in South Australia since 1836*, Wakefield Press, Adelaide, 1986, pp. 293–294.
49 SAHT, Board Minutes 24 Feb 1987.
50 *HTN*, 1, 2, Dec 1989, p. 2 (quotation); Crafter, 16 Sept 1993.
51 *Adelaide Review*, archives 2004–05: on Hugh Stretton, <www.adelaidereview.com.au/archives> viewed Oct 2007.
52 SAHT, Corporate Strategy 1989–1993 (1989), quoted in Marsden & Parkin, p. 211.
53 SLSA, SRG 660/1/40, Paul Edwards, interviewed by S. Marsden, for *B.C & S*, 11 Sept 1984 (transcript, pp 32–34).

54 *HTN*, 1, 3, Feb 1990, pp. 4–5 (including quotation).
55 Mignon Schneider, interview by Anne Lord, 7 Feb 2007. Schneider noted that the Trust's graduate selection process has since been simplified, and that staff selection processes are now strictly in accordance with public service policy.
56 Edwards, in *South Australian Housing Trust* [Newsletter], 5, March 1990, p. 4 (both quotations); SAHT, Annual Report 1989–90, p. 14; Hutchesson interview.
57 Tina Lloyd, 'SAHT history' (memoir), 13 Sept 2007.
58 *HTN*, 1, 7, Oct 1990, p. 6.
59 ibid., pp. 1 (including quotations), 2.
60 Helen Fulcher, interview by Susan Marsden, 11 January 2007.
61 *HTN*, 2, 1, Feb 1991, pp. 1-2.
62 *HTN*, 2, 5, Dec 1991, p. 2.
63 *HTN*, 2, 3, July 1991, pp. 8–12 (including quotations); *HTN*, 2, 5, Dec 1991, p. 1.
64 *HTN* (new series), 1, Sept 1997, p. 1.
65 SAHT, *Our history* <www.housingtrust.sa.gov.au/text/text.asp?swId=1&pgId=11>.
66 *HTN*, 2, 3, July 1991, p. 4.
67 *HTN*, 2, 5, Dec 1991, pp. 1, 3.
68 Edwards interview, 11 Sept 1984 (transcript, p. 35).
69 Crafter, address to Estimates Committee, 16 Sept 1993.
70 J. Victory, 'Social justice in the market place and the South Australian Housing Trust' B Social Work thesis, University of South Australia, 1993, p. 24.
71 SAHT, Board minutes, 18 May and 17 Aug, 1993.
72 Crafter, address to Estimates Committee, 16 Sept 1993.
73 SAHT, Annual Report 1993–94, p. 2.
74 *HTN*, 5, 1, Mar 1994, pp. 1, 2 (quotation).
75 SAHT, Annual Report 1994–95, p. 2.
76 National Shelter (Australia), *Public housing in Australia: issues and directions for change*, Canberra, 1994, pp. 109, 111.
77 SAHT, Board Minutes, 23 May 1995.
78 SA Dept of Human Services, SAHT Act 1995: National Competition Policy Review report, [?2000].
79 M. Slatter & A. Beer, 'Housing evictions in South Australia: a study of bailiff–assisted evictions', Flinders University and SAHT, Adelaide, 2003, p. 3. See also Kilner, *Housing policy*, pp. 325–330.
80 SAHT, Annual Report 1987, p. 17.
81 SAHT, Memorabilia Collection Volunteers' Newsletter, 1, Aug 2006, p. 3. Marsden had her own experience with the Wang: she wrote *BC&S* by hand and Trust staff 'wanged' it, printing the first draft on a continuous run of paper which she laid out along the hall at home, chapter by chapter, and edited by written insertions and by cutting, moving and sticky taping sections. Meanwhile Deputy Chairman Hugh Stretton edited another printout with the use of whiteout, and Trust staff also made suggestions. Marsden's final draft, cut-and-pasted and written-over, was returned to the Wang operators.
82 *HTN*, 1, 1, June 1989, p. 1.
83 SAHT, Board Minutes, 8 Dec 1987.
84 SAHT, Annual Report 1993–94, p. 3; 1995–96, p. 21.
85 *HTN*, 1, 7, Oct 1990, p. 3.
86 One non-government sector response was the *Dunstan Fellows Affordable Housing for Australian Families Program*, led by Julian Disney, launched by the Don Dunstan Foundation in 2005 (Annual Report 2004–05), <www.dunstan.org.au/docs/DDFAnnualReport_20042005.pdf> viewed Dec 2007.
87 '¼ acre quandry', *Australian Society* supplement, March 1989.
88 *South Australian Year Book 1990*, ABS, Adelaide, 1990, p. 171.
89 SAHT, Annual Report 1986, p. 1; *South Australian Year Book 1990*, p. 170.
90 *Australian Society*, Aug 1987.
91 Janet Combridge, (E), 29 Jan 2007.
92 SAHT, Board Minutes, 24 Feb 1987.

93 C. Wilding, 'Improving quality of life after deinstitutionalisation through "Ordinary Adventure" ...', *Journal of Leisurability*, 27 (1), 2000, <www.lin.ca/resource/html/Vol27/V27N1A3.htm> viewed Dec 2006.
94 SAHT, Annual Report 1991, p. 6.
95 Paul Smith, in *HTN*, 5, 1, Mar 1994, p. 10.
96 Gael Fraser & Associates, 'West End boarding and rooming house strategy', Report prepared for Adelaide City Council, 1997, pp. 6, 19 (quotation).
97 S. Marsden, R. Carrigan, A. Romanic & R. Whitten, *An overview of past and current practice. A brief history of State involvement in the care of children and young people in South Australia*, Report for DFC, 2006.
98 SAHT chronology; *Housing Trust in Focus, 1999–90*, p. 11.
99 *HTN*, 4, 3, Oct 1993, p. 7; for Smith's report, see *HTN*, 5, 1, Mar 1994, pp. 10–14.
100 Verbal information provided by Gavin Malone (in preparation for his PhD thesis), 28 Feb 2007.
101 DHS, South Australian Housing Trust Triennial Review 1997–98, 1999–2000, 2001, pp. 16–17. The overall rates of poverty in SA were 27% in 1991 and 32.2% in 1996, compared to national proportions of 27.5% and 29.6%.
102 SAHT, Triennial Review 1997–98, 1999–2000, p. 17: the proportions in 1996 were respectively 20.5% of rural Aboriginal households, compared to 14% in other urban areas, and 9% in Adelaide.
103 D. Schwartz, 'Housing shame needs more interest', *Eastern Courier*, 21 Nov 2007 (Lester's observation was reported in 1985).
104 Parliament of SA, Select Committee on Pitjantjatjara Land Rights, Final Report: presented by Chris Larkin, General Manager, Aboriginal Housing Authority, 29 October 2002, Q913.
105 Select Committee on Pitjantjatjara Land Rights, Final Report, 2004, p. 52.
106 B. Dickey & E. Martin, *Building community: a history of the Port Adelaide Central Mission*, Port Adelaide Wesley Centre, Adelaide, 1999, pp. 215 (including quotations), 216.
107 Select Committee on Pitjantjatjara Land Rights, 2004: evidence presented by C. Larkin, 29 Oct 2002 (Q910).
108 Kilner, *Housing policy*, p. 210. (See also p. 297.)
109 *South Australian Housing Trust* [Newsletter] 1 [May 1989], p. 1.
110 *HTN*, 2, 5, Dec 1991, p. 4.
111 Kilner, *Housing policy*, p. 297.
112 *HTN*, 4, 3, Oct 1993, pp. 12, 13 (quotation).
113 Sandra Chapple, (Q) and (E), 30 Nov 2006.
114 SAHT, Annual Report 1986, p. 3; SAHT, Board Minutes, 24 Mar 1987.
115 Kilner, *Housing policy*, pp. 304, 309; Crafter, 16 Sept 1993. The HomeStart Finance Board reported directly to this Minister, and was from 2002 a member of the government's Housing Management Council, one of SA's four housing agencies, together with SAHT, SACHA and the AHA. From 2002 HomeStart Finance also began to provide loans to not-for-profit aged care facilities. State Records of SA, RDS 2008/07, 2009: HomeStart Finance, p 12.
116 Kenny, p. 23.
117 *HTN*, 1, 1, June 1989, p. 3.
118 Stretton, *Australia Fair*, p. 119.
119 Kilner, *Housing policy*, p. 250.
120 Murray Hutchesson interview, 16 Oct 2007.
121 Stretton, *Australia Fair*, p. 119.
122 Megan Lloyd, 'Tenants left prey to greedy landlords', front page article, *City Messenger*, 29 June 1994.
123 *City Messenger*, 29 June 1994.
124 Stretton, p. 119 (including statistic and quotation).
125 SAHT, Board Minutes, 13 Dec 2005.
126 Kilner, *Housing policy*, pp. 324–325.
127 Housing SA, SAHT services, *Direct Lease*, viewed Dec 2006 <www.housingtrust.sa.gov.au/text/text.asp?swId=1&pgId=220>.
128 Victory, 'Social Justice', pp. 33–34 (quotation), p. 35.
129 ibid., pp. 45–50.

130 The SAHT did not administer Commonwealth Rent Assistance and this was not available to public housing tenants who received rent subsidies (reduced rent) based on household income in Trust dwellings.
131 Victory, 'Social Justice', pp. 4, 29.
132 SAHT, Annual reports; Kilner, *Housing policy*, p. 328 (including quotation); information from Tina Lloyd (April 2010), who explains that lost bond money was raised as a Housing Trust debt against the private tenant and had to be repaid. Further bond assistance (or an offer of Trust housing) was not given until the debt was repaid or in some urgent/priority cases until a repayment schedule was agreed.
133 Kilner, *Housing policy*, pp. 296–7, 324.
134 Victory, p. 16.
135 'Zoi' requested the use of this pseudonym (Q and additional notes, 13 Dec 2006).
136 SAHT, Triennial Review – 1994, Adelaide, 1994, p. ii.
137 Kilner, *From dream to reality*, p. 67.
138 NSW Department of Housing, *The History of Public Housing in New South Wales*, <www.housing.nsw.gov.au/history.htm> viewed Aug 2006.
139 B. Badcock, 'Thirty years on: gentrification and class changeover in Adelaide's inner suburbs, 1966–96', *Urban Studies*, 38 (9), 2001, pp. 1569–1570.
140 Kemeny, *From public housing to the social market*, p. 104.
141 SAHT, Triennial Review – 1994, p. iii.
142 Crafter, 16 Sept 1993.
143 Hasan, pp. 22–24.
144 *HTN*, 5, June 1998, p. 1.
145 V. Milligan & B. Randolph, 'Privatising public housing: cases from Australia', Paper presented at ENHR conference, Slovenia, 2006, viewed August 2007 <http://enhr2006-ljubljana.uirs.si/publish/W17_Milligan_Randolph.pdf> p. 3.
146 *HTN*, 4, 2, 1993, p. 5; Estimates Committee, 16 Sept 1993 (quotations). SOLA International, founded in Adelaide in 1960, became a large global manufacturer and supplier of plastic spectacle lenses.
147 SAHT, Board Minutes, 23 May 1995.
148 SAHT, Board Minutes, 22 Sept 1987.
149 SAHT, Board Minutes, 24 Jan 1995.
150 SAHT, Board Minutes, 19 Dec 1995.
151 Palcy, *HTN*, v 11, Dec 1980, p. 3.
152 SAHT, Board Minutes, 24 Feb 1987 (plan approved).
153 SAHT, Board Minutes, 8 Dec 1987.
154 SAHT, Board Minutes, 10 Mar 1987.
155 *Housing Trust in focus 1988-89*, p. 21.
156 The Trust also provided bridging finance until the cooperative could obtain a private loan, but this practice was ended by 1987. SAHT, Board Minutes, 28 April 1987.
157 SA, Office for Community Housing, <www.communityhousing.sa.gov.au/site/page.cfm?u=155> viewed June 2007.
158 Kilner, *From dream to reality*, pp. 3, 32 (including Edwards' quotation), 33, 40–42, 214; SAHT, Board Minutes, 24 Mar 1987; G. Fraser, 'Community housing and urban renewal', Master of Regional and Urban Planning, University of SA, 1999, p. 117. When the South Australian Co-operative and Community Housing Act was introduced, the names of the first three associations were changed to Northern Suburbs Housing Co-operative, Hindmarsh Housing Co-operative, and Women's Housing Association (Fraser, 'Community housing and urban renewal', p. 117).
159 Dickey & Martin, *Building Community*', pp. 211, 212 (both quotations), 213; Fraser, 'Community housing and urban renewal', p. 117 (1999 figures).
160 Office for Community Housing, <www.communityhousing.sa.gov.au/site/page.cfm?u=155> viewed June 2007. Many existing cooperatives changed their names to make this distinction clear, for example, Prospect/Enfield Association for Community Housing became PEACH Housing Co-operative Inc. (Brenda Graham, *PEACH Housing Co-operative Inc, 1983–2005: our story*, PEACH, Adelaide, 2nd ed, 2005, p. 15.)
161 Kilner, *Housing policy*, p. 352.

162 Kilner, *From dream to reality*, p. 40.
163 Fraser, 'Community housing and urban renewal', pp. 14–15.
164 Kilner, *From dream to reality*, p. 170.
165 C. Paris, *Housing Australia* Macmillan Australia, South Melbourne, 1993, pp. 241–2 (his italics).
166 ibid., p. 243.

CHAPTER TWO

A reform agenda, 1996–2005

> My happiest SAHT experience was the day I received a letter advising me that SAHT had a vacancy at last! (Michael Elijah, 29 November 2006)

> We have won national and State awards in everything from ecologically sustainable house and sub-division design, disability accommodation and community participation to urban regeneration, reporting to Parliament and customer service ... [P]robationary tenancies, housing visits and maintenance changes have all been introduced. 1999 looks to be another significant year highlighted by implementation of government housing reforms ... (Greg Black, 1998)[1]

Introduction

The years 1996–2005 were among the most difficult and demanding in the history of the South Australian Housing Trust. The Trust had to respond flexibly to established trends – rising demand for social housing combined with reduced funding – and make comprehensive internal changes due to new legislation and the creation of new agencies.

The new Housing Trust Act took effect on 1 January 1996 and abruptly ended the Trust's industrial and commercial, land banking and joint venture development roles.[2] A report published nine years later suggested that 'social evolution rather than policy evolution' was the main reason for the transformation of the Trust. Changes in housing demand and in South Australia's general social and economic character, followed by new public policy, 'meant that the Housing Trust's distinctive formative mission largely dissipated', and it 'became effectively a welfare housing agency'.[3] An explicit statement of that welfare role was set out in the Board's report to the minister in 2000:

> The Trust continues to assist vulnerable population groups through the development and implementation of policies that redistribute resources to those in need ... The majority of the Trust's customers (approximately 95%) are individuals and families on low incomes.[4]

This chapter charts the final steps involved in changing an exceptional public housing authority into a standard welfare service provider. The Trust had been an indispensable agency of a uniquely South Australian approach to development. Eleven per cent of homes in SA were public dwellings in 1997, nearly double the national average of six per cent.[5] In 2001 the Trust's total asset base of $3.2 billion included $3 billion in rental houses.[6] But South Australian governments now sought to bring housing policy into line with other states and national standards. By 2006 only 7% of the state's houses were rented from the Trust.

Public service cutbacks and privatisation of state assets, in combination with departmental changes, curtailed the Trust's independence and range of functions, and hastened stock and staff losses. The change consolidated developments already in train, but also 'marked a fundamental shift in philosophy and implementation involving a substantial winding back of public sector responsibility for housing finance and supply'.[7] The shift marked the abandonment of South Australia's Liberal tradition, illustrated by the expansion of the Trust under earlier Premiers Playford and Hall. For the new Liberal government of 1993, 'being similar rather than different ... seized the agenda. This is the key to understanding South Australian housing policy in this period'.[8]

Institutional repositioning included a move into mainstream public service and a further narrowing of functions. Momentous change occurred in 1997 when the Trust became a subordinate public agency in the new Department of Human Services (DHS), bringing it closer to the standard housing agencies of the other states. Most other housing commissions had been replaced by departments during the 1970s. The most decisive act in bringing the Trust into line with them followed a national meeting of ministers in 1997, which discussed income-based eligibility tests for public housing. South Australia was the only state without one, and in 1998 the minister announced its introduction, together with changes to the management of the waiting list and limitations on conditions of tenure.[9] This critical shift was cemented by national policy change, effected in the 2000 Commonwealth-State Housing Agreement which required housing assistance to be based on need rather than the earlier concept of security of tenure.

The Housing Trust was also repositioned in relation to the private sector, with the sale of houses being described as the 'privatisation of public housing'.[10] Privatisation included transfer of houses to community housing organisations whose growth contrasted with the decline of public housing.[11] A similar commitment to private ownership and privatised services, and tight control of finances, characterised the incoming Labor government under Premier Mike Rann in 2002. Despite having promised during the election to stop selling public housing unless matched by new development, the government continued to do so, perpetuating a 'delivery mix of home ownership, an expanding private rental sector and a residual public sector'.[12] Hayward's prediction was borne out: 'The twentieth century will end in much the same way as it began, with Australian Governments ... reluctant, rather than willing, landlords'.[13] Kilner concluded his history of housing policy in a similar vein. Changes since 1990 had pushed Adelaide 'back to a nineteenth century model of land and housing markets – an unregulated market with high urban density and a substantial private rental

SOUTH AUSTRALIAN HOUSING TRUST

MAKING THE MOST OF OUR KNOW-HOW

The SA Housing Trust is the principal property and tenancy manager of public housing in South Australia, on behalf of the State Government.

For over 60 years, the Trust has proudly helped South Australians to enjoy secure and affordable housing:

> it has built or purchased more than 120,000 homes, or about 20% of all existing South Australian houses

> it manages 60,000 rental properties, reflecting an asset base of around A$ 3.7 billion

> its annual turnover exceeds A$ 375 million.

The Housing Trust offers a range of services and capabilities to its business customers.

Asset management

- Financial and customer needs analysis to maximise the economic performance of public housing assets

Managing rental housing

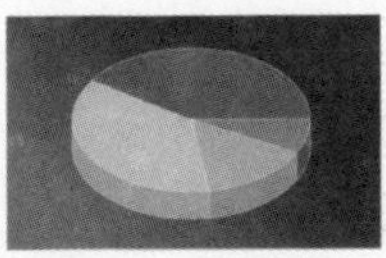

Institutional strengthening

- Change management and strategic planning skills for the effective administration of public housing

Tenancy and rent management

- Strategies and systems for managing demand for rental accomodation, setting rents, and for timely and cost-efficient rent collection

New technologies for affordable housing

Construction engineering

- Innovative building design and construction methods for problem sites

Environmental engineering

- Energy and waste water management for housing developments, and land reclamation in contaminated areas

Creating homes for individuals

Remote communities

- Innovative planning and technology for housing in remote communities

Older people

- Accommodation designed for people whose physical capacities, financial circumstances and service needs may change in old age

People with disabilities

- Housing design to support independent living in the community

Master planning

- Concept planning and documentation for urban projects to meet today's lifestyle needs

Urban renewal

Project management

- Delivery of quality urban renewal and building construction projects within agreed budgets and timelines

Housing Trust poster c1997

market, with the twin dreams of mass home ownership and substantial social housing being progressively abandoned'.[14]

In *Australia Fair* (2004) Stretton described the Trust's 'present role ... as a provider of a reduced stock of welfare housing [as] ... a sad end to an inspired and productive bit of unorthodoxy'.[15] However, other activities introduced over the past 20 years were flourishing. In the view of Board member Don Lee,

> This last decade might be characterised as a period of decline for the Trust, which it was if measured by housing stock reduction and the health of its recurrent accounts. However it was also a time of many achievements, of which management and staff can be rightly proud.

A changing environment

> The culture of the Trust in getting the job done and caring about things was a strength which would be built upon. There would be challenges to confront and changes to be made. (R. B. Oxenberry, 1998)[16]

By the mid-1990s public housing had, for the first time in Australia, formally become welfare housing. As construction shifted from mass-produced estates to scattered smaller projects, housing authorities also came under financial pressure. With a high proportion of tenants on low incomes, it was difficult to run surpluses on operations. Rental rebates, interest payments and high maintenance spending forced authorities into operating deficits.[17] Static Commonwealth funding and changing policy were other factors. The new Coalition of Australian Governments (COAG) agreed in 1995 on a national competition policy to end the monopoly status of public utilities, aiming to make them more efficient. State governments would gain a windfall by privatising gas, electricity and water utilities, but retained responsibility for social services. The 1995 agreement locked them into a competition ethos which, coupled with pressures for small government, downplayed social policy. Competition added to the demand for public housing and at the same time reduced revenue, soon restricting the funds available for such services.[18]

In 1996 a Liberal-National Party coalition under Prime Minister John Howard replaced the Keating Labor government. The new conservative government abolished the Department of Housing and Regional Development, replacing national co-ordination with bilateral state agreements, and ran down direct grants. The Howard government maintained a commitment to national competition, including enterprise bargaining for workers. Casual and part-time employment rose and those workers – many of them female – did not do as well as permanent and unionised workers at gaining wage rises. The disparity also reinforced differences between prosperous regions of economic growth and those with few employment opportunities, with obvious impacts on areas with many low-income tenants.[19]

The public housing sector was required to make similar reforms to those 'visited on other spheres of the social economy in the 1990s in the name of microeconomic reform, deregulation and competitive advantage'.[20] This brought a change from investment in public housing, to a greater reliance on the private sector. Government policies favoured direct assistance payments so that people could rent in the private market, and restricted public assistance. The policy shift was 'a significant redefining ... of the social contract in relation to housing assistance for the needy'.[21] Stephen Baker represented South Australia at a meeting of housing ministers in 1997, which encouraged the Commonwealth, through the CSHA, to provide most public housing assistance to those in greatest need.[22] Housing advocates such as Shelter pointed out that this Commonwealth policy had an equal effect on allocations as changes in state policy, and influenced the degree to which the public tenant population might include those who could afford to pay market rents (and so not be eligible for rental subsidies).[23]

These pressures accelerated the scaling back of public housing and its formal restriction to people most in need. By the early 2000s the profile of public tenants in Australia was very different from the working families of the post-war years. Most tenants received government pensions. Few could afford to use public housing as a stepping stone to private purchase, as many of their predecessors had done.[24]

South Australia's governments ran down housing stock, driven by the need to reduce debt and, by contributing to an increase in private renters, capture Commonwealth Rent Assistance dollars. Liberal and Labor governments, equally opposed to independent statutory authorities, were also determined on smaller government, placing greater reliance on the private sector, reducing housing services to the Australian average, and focusing state assistance ever more tightly on people with high needs.[25]

The total rental stock owned by the Trust dropped to below 60,000 in 1997 for the first time in a decade and, although the decline was small (to 59,339), it reflected not only increasing sales, but also a sharp contraction in construction. Land banking and large-scale joint venture projects halted altogether in 1996. Smaller joint ventures continued, especially redevelopment (see Chapter Three). The Trust's Real Estate Services section was still managing 143 joint venture projects in 1997 and buying and selling homes, completing settlement of 1,044 properties in that year.

Economic confidence revived in South Australia under the Rann government and the stimulus of new mining projects, but the culture of small government and a preference for private sector development persisted. In the welfare sector the 'retreat from the state' kept on, while the roles of commercial and non-government organisations continued to expand.[26] The Trust had survived the fallout from the State Bank collapse in its original form when other important agencies had not, but the best efforts of board members and managers could not ultimately avert a similar fate.[27]

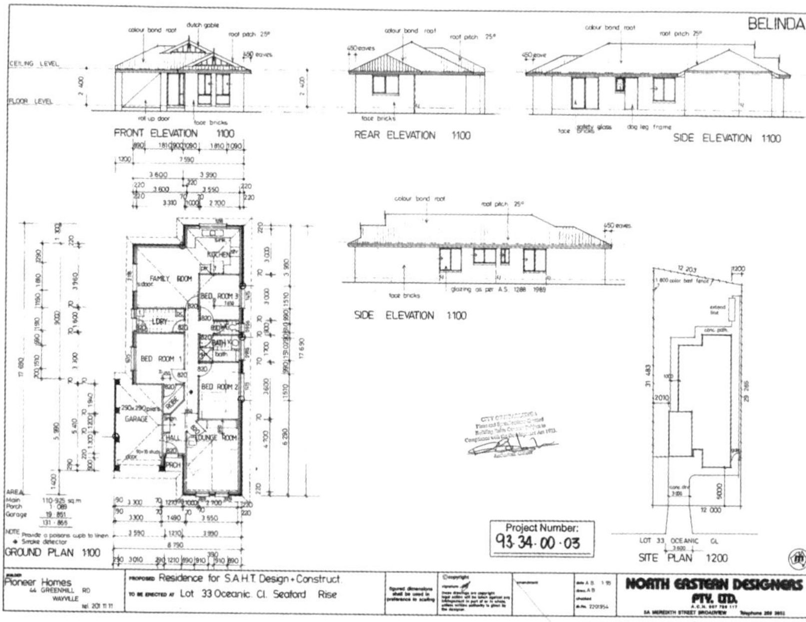

Newbuild homes: plan detail for 'Design and construct' house, Oceanic Close, Seaford Rise, by North Eastern Designers, 1995.

Institutional repositioning

Dean Brown was Liberal Premier until 1996, followed by John Olsen (1996–2001), then Rob Kerin. John Oswald was followed as the Liberal government's Housing Minister by Scott Ashenden (1996–97); and Stephen Baker (1997), succeeded by Dean Brown (no longer Premier) was Minister for Human Services (1997–2002).[28] The Board usually sent their minister the minutes of meetings only. In Tina Lloyd's recollection,

> Minister Baker took a direct interest in the housing portfolio. He read board papers every month and met with the chairs and general managers of SAHT, HomeStart and Community Housing before their monthly meetings, frequently raising areas of concern. As could be expected he took particular note of the financial modeling being undertaken in relation to the proposed redevelopment of The Parks and other financial matters.

Under these ministers, as the Auditor-General reported in 1996, there was 'significant restructuring and reorganisation' of the Trust, against a background of

Commonwealth proposals to alter funding arrangements. Contributing legislative changes were the *Housing and Urban Development (Administrative Arrangements) Act 1995* and the new South Australian Housing Trust Act.[29]

John Strang remembered that 'When the Liberal government tried to rewrite the SA Housing Trust Act, they left a lot of things out which we picked up'. He was a member of the Trust Tenants Advisory Council set up in 1989 which made recommendations about the bill. Nineteen provisions were reinstated from the original Act. For example, the government wanted proceeds from house sales to go into general revenue, 'not into the SAHT coffers', but the tenant representatives recommended that the money should be used for refurbishment, rebuild and maintenance. Funding of the Advisory Council ceased and it was dissolved in 1996, to be succeeded by Regional Advisory Boards.[30]

The new SA Housing Trust Act came into operation on 1 January 1996.[31] In the same year, Trust tenancies came under the limited jurisdiction of the Residential Tenancies Act. The Housing Trust Act provided for 'the continuation of the South Australian Housing Trust' as a body corporate, but subject to the control of the minister. The Trust's functions were redefined. They were to: assist people to secure affordable and appropriate housing; provide houses to meet public and community requirements; manage public housing assets to ensure acceptable rates of return and protect their value; and undertake programs to improve community housing. The Trust could exercise other functions and continue to buy and sell land – with ministerial consent. The minister also controlled staffing. This removed two principal management functions from the Board: control of decisions on major expenditure, and staff appointments.[32]

The Act also allowed the minister to transfer assets and rights to another corporation.[33] This was done at once with the transfers to the Urban Projects Authority, and later to the Aboriginal Housing Authority. The Aboriginal Housing Authority and HomeStart Finance were new statutory corporations with functions that had at times previously been the Trust's.

The Liberal government, massively reorganising South Australia's public service, created a super department amalgamating health, welfare and housing. The Department of Human Services (DHS) was established under the Housing Trust Act in October 1997. Combined agencies included the South Australian Health Commission, the Department of Family and Community Services (renamed Family and Youth Services), and the Department of Housing and Urban Development (itself a recent integration of agencies that included the Trust).

DHS was responsible for public health, hospitals, family and community services, disability services, ageing and housing. The colossal department employed 33,000 people and had a budget of more than $3 billion.[34] Dean Brown was Minister, and Christine Charles, a senior public servant heading Cabinet Office, was appointed Chief Executive.[35] The reorganisation placed the Trust in a human services portfolio for the first time. Christine Charles told the Board that this was 'a logical grouping of related activities with the aim of caring for South Australians', as part of a broader reform integrating similar service types to 'improve access ... for users ... reduce the costs of infrastructure and generally improve efficiency of government'. Existing services would continue.[36] The new department acted as a service provider to the state's housing authorities.[37]

Brown was an experienced minister, but the size of the new health portfolio allowed him little time for public housing.[38] As for Christine Charles, in the view of Don Lee who was appointed to the Board in 1997, the chief executive knew little about housing, or the way the Trust was run, and she made a dramatic gesture of transferring all Housing Trust employees to the public service.[39] Staff came under the *Public Sector Management Act 1995* from April 1998. From then the Board could no longer approve staff allocations, which became Charles' responsibility as chief executive of DHS.[40] Helen Fulcher noted the change as a definite 'signalling of moving from a statutory authority and our own way of working into a departmental mode with less flexibility about some of the decisions that were made'.[41] Shirley Trebilcock recalled

> a loss of identity when the Housing Trust was consumed within the Department (Human Services). From dealing directly with customers on various house sales schemes, I found that our tenants trusted us and were confident that we would be straight with them. Many were confused about the changes taking place at that time.[42]

There was no specific housing division within DHS. Fulcher described this as a challenging time. When representing the Trust in a section called 'Metropolitan', she found that 'health was very dominant and housing's voice was therefore a relatively faint one'. She worked hard 'to get some synergies ... in the area of community renewal, where we had clear links particularly with community health'.

Charles was chief executive of DHS from 1997–2002 and was followed by Jim Birch, who remained head of Health when DHS was again divided into separate health and welfare departments. Lee described Birch as 'a big improvement', and also commended James (Jim) Davidson, the department's director of strategic planning. Lee's observations were underlined by a 2003 review that noted criticism of 'the culture of DHS in recent times', and praised Birch for opening debate about it. While noting 'the culture of blame', and how leaders could influence systems for better or worse, the review emphasised underlying forces such as politicisation of the public service. Over the past decade there had been significant changes in relationships between ministers and staff. Employed on short-term contracts as direct appointments, CEOs and senior staff were beholden to their minister. The principal objective of public sector CEOs to provide frank advice changed to meeting 'the short-term political needs of individual Ministers'.[43]

The Aboriginal Housing Authority (AHA) was proclaimed as a statutory corporation in October 1998 under the Housing and Urban Development (Administrative Arrangements) Act. Like the parent Trust, the AHA was part of the Human Services portfolio. Chris Larkin was General Manager. Transfer of stock, staff and services from the Trust to the new organisation was completed in 2000.

The creation of DHS repositioned public housing from an urban and economic to a health and welfare context.[44] These changes were cemented by the government's 'Housing Reform Agenda' of 1998, which came into effect in July 2000. The informal and incremental welfare role of public housing was formalised from that date, with the allocation of Trust homes restricted strictly to applicants assessed as being of 'high need'.

In the midst of relentless institutional change, continuity was provided by the Trust's people: board members, staff and customers. For example, Tina Lloyd, a Trust employee since 1977, was seconded to the position of Ministerial Liaison Officer in 1994 and worked with Ministers Oswald, Ashenden, Baker, Brown and Key. She returned to the Trust in 2004 as Executive Officer to the General Manager, Malcolm Downie. As a statutory authority, the Trust retained a Board, despite erosion of its autonomy. Whatever their agendas on joining the Trust, members usually came to appreciate the advantages of working at arm's length from government. Susie Herzberg recalled that she and the other Board members took their corporate governance responsibilities seriously and were concerned about funding arrangements and unofficial directions from ministers that required the Board to govern in ways that were at times in conflict with the Housing Trust Act.

Ministers were less willing to allow the Trust to fulfil its statutory responsibilities, and some of them acted to curb its independence. Essential work, such as CSHA lobbying, was removed to departmental officers. The Board often acted simply as a sounding board for government decisions. Political considerations limited Board action to address the potentially fatal issue of funding. A powerful lobby prevented rent increases in favoured inner city tenancies. The Trust had also to compete for political attention, and for limited public funding, with new agencies such as the AHA.

Five new members joined the Board in 1996, including Jay Hogan and Susie Herzberg, but Professor Rod Oxenberry remained Chairman until 1999 when he was replaced by Hogan. Hogan had a private development background, having been Chief Operations Officer with AV Jennings in South Australia. His many contacts in housing were put to good use during his two three-year terms as chairman. Herzberg, also a Board member for ten years, chaired the audit committee. Both left the Trust at the end of 2005, Hogan praising the staff for 'their outstanding performance in a changing environment'.[45] Continuity was also maintained at Board level by the appointment of a former housing minister, Stephen Baker, from 2001–04, and Jan Connolly, who was appointed in 2004 by Minister Key.

The split into Property Management under Peter Jackson, and Housing Services under Jan Connolly, did not work well. Shirley Trebilcock described the Trust as becoming 'a divided culture'. Other people more bluntly recalled 'the boys' in one division not talking to 'the girls', and competing for funds. Helen Fulcher remembered a 'time of tension between the social and the commercial objectives … played out in quite a highlighted form'. She said,

> I remember that we were locking heads often with one of the more colourful characters in Assets, and when it came to something like modifying houses for people with physical disabilities the Assets side, who were driven by a commercial agenda, wanted to charge us internally a much more significant rent than we would usually pay in order to cover the costs of both the renovation and the modifications, but also they were anticipating that when they sold that property its capital value would be less.

In 1996 Greg Black returned from Western Australia to become Chief General Manager, above Connolly and Jackson. Trebilcock said that 'It was very important when Greg Black was appointed ... to bring the Housing Trust back together again'.[46] He encouraged managers 'to increase face to face contact (and in particular their listening skills)'.[47] Fulcher, who had previously worked with Black at HomesWest, said that, 'He was very successful in the way he invested very generous amounts of time in staff forums ... listening to staff. I always remember very early on meeting Greg in HomesWest and being impressed by the fact that he wore a T-shirt that had "Hassle me" on it'. Fulcher saw how well staff responded to 'having absolute clarity of direction, and that was the great strength of Greg's'. Much quoted by Trust employees from that time was Black's mantra 'The Three S's: Sustainable communities, Successful tenancies, and Service integration'. These brought new activities. 'Minister Brown introduced housing visits and made the media announcement with tenants on a Sunday morning at Stowe Court flats on Fullarton Road.'[48] A total of 21,913 tenants were visited in 1998 when the program began.[49]

Black described progress on developing a 20 year vision for the Trust, and grappled with 'complex and interrelated issues' such as predicting funding; customer needs; the effect of government reforms; changing demand for Trust homes by location and type; and quantity versus quality.[50] What he did not predict was that those pressures would bring an end to the Housing Trust as he knew it within five years of his departure in 2002.

A tradition of appointing general managers with prior experience at the Trust was maintained with those who followed Black: Malcolm Downie, appointed in 2003, and Philip Fagan-Schmidt (2006), as well as the first General Manager of Housing Services in Housing SA, Helen Fulcher (2007).

Top: Department of Human Services Chief Executive Christine Charles and Kym Freer (the Trust's Mitchell Park Project Manager) hold the plaque awarded in the Australian – New Zealand asset management competition, 1997–98. The Trust was runner up for an entry on 'The Vines' (at Mitchell Park) prepared by Freer, John Hewson and Bevis Kennett (second from left).

Bottom: inaugural Aboriginal Housing Authority, 1998. Chairman Charles Jackson to the left of Dean Brown, Minster for Human Services (centre, striped tie), with Christine Charles (front, second from left).

Above: Trust Chairman Professor Rod Oxenberry (left) with Elizabeth's Mayor Marilyn Baker (right) at the opening of Rosewood's 500th house, c1996. The Cities of Elizabeth and Munno Para merged in 1997 as the new City of Playford.

Below: Jan Connolly signing a head lease agreement with Upjay representatives, March 1996.

General Manager Greg Black cutting the ribbon at Whyalla Eco Renovation Information Centre (WERIC), with Jim Pollock then Mayor of Whyalla.

The ALP returned to government in 2002. Premier Michael (Mike) Rann had a long association with government. He had been press secretary and adviser to the three previous ALP premiers, and a minister in the Bannon government (1989–93). He gained a firmer hold as Premier in the elections of 2006 and 2010. Rann retained the human services departmental structure, but (as advocated by Black) he set up a Housing Management Council (later, Housing Executive Committee) made up of the minister's representative and board chairs and general managers of South Australia's four housing authorities which operated in DHS; the Trust, HomeStart Finance, Aboriginal Housing Authority and SACHA.

Rann appointed Stephanie (Steph) Key as Minister for Housing in March 2002. Key had a unique understanding for a new minister – she had been a Housing Trust member for 12 years (1984–96). Key described this knowledge as 'particularly useful when we had the first Commonwealth State Housing Agreements', and could refer South Australia's representative, Senator Amanda Vanstone, to known areas such as Peachey Belt. Dean Brown, the previous Liberal minister, gave her helpful advice on the housing portfolio and 'was always very supportive'; she noted that the Liberal government's sale of Trust houses had not been 'as wicked as it seems', because many were transferred to community and Aboriginal housing.

Key described herself as 'a traditionalist' who saw the value of having a broad-scale public housing authority rather than a narrow welfare authority, but that was not a view understood or shared around Cabinet table. There was no understanding of the CSHA 'and how difficult the feds were making it for public housing', nor of the benefits of having tenants paying full rent to support those on reduced rent. The change to welfare housing was 'something I'd also fought against'. She regretted the loss of commitment to public sector statutory authorities and to the value of having a large public sector.

While shadow minister, Key wrote the ALP's housing policy, proposing a strategic plan. As minister she set in motion a review of the housing system and production of a 'Housing Plan for South Australia'.[51] The Trust's contribution to the plan was less than might have been expected, as in line with Labor policy, the Party employed its own ministerial advisors. The first version of Key's plan was never approved by Cabinet. Although Key had prior knowledge of the Trust and

Mike Rann, when a mew member of Parliament, at his Briggs electorate office with Mrs MP Taylor, regional winner of the Trust's garden competition at Salisbury North, c1987.

a great deal of respect for it, she did not enjoy the strong position within Cabinet held by her Liberal Party predecessors. Jim Birch believed that Key's draft plan was rejected because Cabinet didn't want to lose control of public housing, and that the plan was 'sanitised' when revisited by Key's ministerial successor.

Key was succeeded in March 2004 by Jay Weatherill as Minister for Housing and for Families and Communities. Weatherill was from a Housing Trust generation – his parents had bought a rental purchase home in the 1960s, and he remembered the whole of Henley South as a Trust suburb. 'I think they built everything from the doctor's surgery to the local shops and parks and everything in between'. On election in 2002 he first became Minister for Planning, in which position he had contact with the housing system. He worked with Key on affordable housing and contributed to the Housing Plan: 'that was my first effort at trying to come up with some overarching housing policy for South Australia'.

The main effect Weatherill's background had on his role as Minister was having parents of modest means who had to work for a living.

> I suppose also recollecting that the Housing Trust back in the days when my parents got into their house was quite a different beast from what it is today has had an effect. I've had a clear understanding of what the Housing Trust has been to some people, and so I reflect upon what it is now, what it has been, when I've become Minister and look at its possibilities in that context.

Acts committed to the Minister represented several longstanding responsibilities. They were the: Housing Improvement Act; *Housing Agreement Act 1991*; South Australian Co-operative and Community Housing Act; Housing and Urban Development (Administrative Arrangements) Act; and the new South Australian Housing Trust Act.[52] The change of minister brought renewed work on the Housing Plan, which introduced a raft of new legislation. While this was underway, the Department of Human Services was broken up in July 2004 to form the Department of Health and the Department for Families and Communities (DFC), the latter keeping responsibility for the Trust. Kate Lennon was the first DFC Chief Executive appointed, followed by Sue Vardon.[53]

Vardon was well acquainted with the state's role, not only in welfare (having been chief executive 1985–92), but also in land development, as a member of the South Australian Urban Land Trust from 1987 to 1994. Once a community social worker employed in the western suburbs of Sydney, she said she 'knew intimately, having traipsed the streets, of the problems of new suburbs', and of the desirability of mixing public and private housing, as her predecessor Ian Cox had advised at Golden Grove. 'So I wasn't unfamiliar with housing when I came here.'[54]

She knew that South Australia's 'Health/Welfare amalgamation had been a disaster', but when Weatherill recruited her to head DFC she looked forward to 'coming back to this bigger department. I would never have come back to the department if it had just been the one I'd left'. What was different was that DFC

Housing Minister Steph Key (left) with Ms McKenzie, state winner of the Trust's 2002 garden competition.

also had responsibility for housing and disability services, and she liked the idea of looking to the connections between them.[55]

Early in 2005 Vardon discussed the minister's priorities with the Board, which needed to connect strategic plans with Department and state plans, and pursue 'opportunities for shared services'. (There was some overlap. DFC had a High Need Housing Unit, while the Trust had a Special Needs Housing Unit and a Crisis Accommodation Program.) Planning had also to fit with the Triennial Review, the Housing Plan and legislation. Even so, the Board saw 'financial viability and the long term direction of the Trust as its responsibility and this should be communicated to the Minister'.[56]

Finances

> The federal government has taken its money back, therefore there is less money for newbuild, refurbishment and general maintenance. Eighty-eight per cent of tenants receive subsidised rent. The pressure towards welfare housing is coming from the federal government. (John Strang)

Funding lay at the heart of the Trust's stock reduction and repositioning. Grants dwindled and the number of tenants rose, but rental income dropped due to changes in government policy and the need to house poorer tenants whose complex needs added to administrative costs. Changes to housing policy meant the Trust had to offer housing to those most in need, and the percentage of tenants paying reduced rents increased. In 1964 only 3.3% of 25,916 rental households paid reduced rents at a minuscule annual cost of (the 2010 equivalent of) $1,400. Forty years later there were 45,451 households, 84% them receiving rental subsidies (93% of new tenants) at a cost of $134.9 million. Only $39.9 million was returned by Commonwealth and state grants, the balance was revenue foregone by the Trust.[57] The cost was only slightly offset by raising rents to 25% of income for most tenants.[58]

Repositioning itself was expensive. In 1996, when industrial and commercial assets were transferred to the Urban Projects Authority and houses were provided to SACHA, the Trust suffered a net loss of $14.7 million.[59] In 2005 the Board noted that the Trust urgently required reimbursement of another $14 million lost due to the new Equity Start program replacing sales of homes to tenants, but it was told it would not be reimbursed.[60] A 1996 federal study found that the increased use of CSHA funds by the states to cover losses on rental operations, and extra expenditure on upgrading dwellings, was one of the major reasons for the decline in stock additions.[61] They also had to cope with an increasing degree of customer indebtedness, and the Trust noted with concern the effect of gambling when poker machines were legalised in South Australia.[62]

Triennial reviews in 1994, 1998 and 2001 concentrated on financial viability, defined in 1994 as 'sufficient capital assets and income streams to be able to meet the long term mission and objectives of the Trust'. The 2001 review marked 'a point of transition in which the majority of housing allocations are based on ... complex need'. In 2000 the Trust made 68.7% of new allocations on assessed needs that were well above simple poverty. The corresponding figure in 1995–96 had been 15.9%. The Trust had become 'an efficient and effective social housing provider'.[63] But the transition added to an already high debt load and threatened long-term sustainability.

The Trust embarked on the 'Future of Service Delivery Program' in 2001 to deal with an increasingly complex customer base, and to contain administration costs. In Downie's view, the Trust adapted well to a changing client base and reduced funding. The Future of Service Delivery brought important changes 'that resulted in less revolving doors for clients and more efficient operations'.[64] At the same time the Trust was grappling with inefficiencies caused by having to work within departmental budget lines, which also made planning large redevelopment projects difficult, as funds needed to be rolled over from one financial year to the next. Even more seriously, as the chairman wrote to the new minister in 2002, 'housing funding props up the health cash position'. Over the past four years $33 million of annual CSHA funding had been retained by DHS and not forwarded to housing. They also paid DHS more than $20 million in corporate service fees, and felt that 'the department is almost certainly making a profit from these arrangements'.[65]

The Commonwealth's assumption of allocation of CSHA funds resulted in a more even distribution than had occurred when the states themselves had determined allocation. This brought an end to South Australia's historically high share. Funding hit a peak in 1983–84, for the first and only time reaching the same level as NSW and surpassing Victoria. This was followed by an equally dramatic plunge.[66]

Under Keating's Labor government, Commonwealth funds for public housing generally went into decline, a trend perpetuated by John Howard's Liberal-National coalition government which held power from 1996 until November 2007.[67] The 1996 CSHA required 'targeting' of housing to people with highest needs, and required that housing assistance be coordinated with other support services – without providing funds for them. The government confirmed the change of direction for the CSHA under a new agreement finalised in 1999, which emphatically redirected funding to private renters.

The result of the CSHA changes was plain: over the 1990s the proportion of priority allocations increased nationally from 17% to 49%, while capital funding for public housing fell by 25%, forcing the authorities to sell 12,000 rental houses.[68] Radical reform that would have halted Commonwealth funding altogether was debated, but this was opposed by the states and territories.[69]

The Commonwealth imposed a new cost burden in 2000 when it introduced a goods and services tax (GST) that placed a tax of 10% on the price of most goods and services. The Trust had been exempt from income tax and sales tax but was now placed in the same position as every other business. The added cost was $14.54 million in 2000–01. As a public landlord, the Trust could not raise rents to cover that cost and was still out of pocket after receiving Commonwealth compensation which ceased in 2003. The GST also affected income by reducing house sales.[70]

Declining Commonwealth and state support meant less building activity, more public–private partnerships, and the further sale of Trust homes to clear debt, which stood in 1997 at $1.2 billion. When Housing Minster Baker issued a press release about funding changes in that year, he made no mention of construction as a major activity, and instead described the Trust's main functions as upgrading dwellings and paying off debt. Sales were seen as the only way to raise enough money to deal with the maintenance backlog. The Trust was locked into selling houses so that the remainder could be maintained or redeveloped to decent standards. Downsizing did help to update and diversify public rental homes. A total of 492 dwellings were built or bought for rental use in 1996, dropping to a minuscule 129 in the following year – the lowest number added to South Australia's public stock since the Trust's second year of operation in 1938. The government's share of new dwellings completed in South Australia dropped from a high of 20% in the 1980s to an average of 4% between 1994 and 2003. This also had the effect of bringing public housing into line with the Australian norm; the government share of new dwellings dropped from almost twice the national level to just below it.[71]

The ten-year debt retirement strategy was realised a year ahead of schedule in 1999 when the Trust paid the last $25 million of the $372 million commercial (common public sector) interest rate borrowings. But the Annual Report also noted an operating loss. The Trust would not survive if such losses were sustained, and so it continued to sell stock, combined with cost cutting through 'efficient management practices'.[72]

The most damaging change in fortunes followed the Commonwealth's decision to help private renters rather than public housing. The Hawke, Keating and then Howard governments partly replaced funds for new public housing with cash grants to first-home buyers and rent allowances to private tenants.[73] In the words of a South Australian minister,

> we were being penalised for the size of our public housing stock: we had double the national average in terms of the size of our public housing stock, and that was relieving the Commonwealth of what it would otherwise have to do, that is pay Commonwealth Rent Allowance to people that would be renting in the private sector.[74]

Over the ten years after 1996 the Commonwealth 'slashed funding to South Australia through the CSHA by around 36% ... forcing the State Government to reduce the number of houses it rents out in order to meet the funding shortfall'.[75] In Weatherill's words, 'the Housing Trust was actually chewing up houses just to remain viable [as] there was a shortfall between our revenue and essentially our expenses'.

Maintaining assets: Trust gardening staff.

This was partly also a matter of choice by his own government. The Board proposed an alternative strategy in 2004 of strategic sales of 1,200 high-value properties. Weatherill rejected the plan, although the Board also pointed out the costs of retaining these properties, and said that his Equity Start proposal would not resolve the Trust's problems.[76] A copy of the submission was leaked to the media and, as Malcolm Downie recalled, 'Kevin Foley as Treasurer came out in an article in *The Advertiser* and said the Government would never do that'. Former DHS chief executive, Jim Birch, confirmed that the Board did propose to sell high-value inner city properties as an effective means of retiring much of the debt, but said that this was politically unpalatable. However, Birch endorsed Weatherill's aim to make Treasury, that is, the state overall, responsible for the Trust's debt.[77] The Minister himself described this issue as a frustration that he couldn't resolve politically in the short term. There was no acknowledgment that the debt 'was really a debt for the State Government; because the Housing Trust was always a separate entity, that debt really remained on *its* books'.

> The analogy I like to give is that the debt that presumably was raised to build the pipes to go into the Murray River that services our state's water needs doesn't sit in the books of SA Water, whereas the Housing Trust has to labour with that debt, even though it's been converted to the benefit of the state, in so many different ways. So the Trust has had to labour on with what is essentially an increasing community service obligation as it subsidises more and more of its tenants, and that burden isn't shared with the rest of the budget, it's expected to be resolved internally, and the Housing Trust has essentially been cannibalising itself to maintain that degree of support.

In the view of Board member Don Lee, over the decade,

> [w]hile the funding problems and decline in housing stock were negatives, there was much in that time that reflected favourably on the Trust, its management and staff. This organisational performance was, to my mind, driven by two main factors. The first of these was the nature of the statutory authority, an entity with largely favourable public recognition, and a purpose with which its staff could identify. The second factor was the continuing adverse financial situation, particularly in the latter years, which required its management to be repeatedly challenged to look for improvements in efficiency. Out of these challenging times successes came.

Tenants and customers

> I have been involved with the regional board and managed customer tool bank for some years and have never had trouble with any staff ... The Trust have been good to me. (Ray Dunstall, history questionnaire, 12 January 2007)

The needs of public housing tenants have often taken second place to economic goals. Their dwellings, modest in design, kept down costs but spurred them to leave if their income improved. The introduction of market rents also penalised tenants financially if their income rose.[78] As Suzanne Millard commented, 'The only beef I have with Housing Trust is that every time we get a small rise in our pension they always hit us with higher rent!' 'Zoi.W' included in her list of 'Things I think are unfair and (may/can) prevent one from rising above the poverty level': having her rent raised at once, unlike Centrelink, which allowed a person to earn $100 a fortnight before reducing payments; and 'If/when one *does* obtain work, the rent is calculated on one's *gross* income *before tax*'.

Elizabeth Ostermann recalled the brusque treatment she received after moving into her rental home in 1987. Having just started work as a teacher her income increased, but she failed to notify the Trust at once. 'Via a telephone conversation in the staff room I was threatened with eviction if I didn't pay the arrears immediately. The pay system at the school meant a delay in wages and although I pleaded ... for a little time, he was adamant'. Embarrassed and tearful, she made a formal complaint to the General Manager about the man's attitude towards tenants, and did gain time to pay the arrears. She added,

> [o]ver the past 18 years the customer service that I've experienced from the Trust has improved enormously. There is a good system with forms to complete that ensures you are ahead with the rent. The yearly visits from the area manager have been a terrific contact with the Trust to discuss any problems ... I think there is more understanding and tolerance of tenants' needs and their particular situation.

Patricia Sumerling calculated that over her 24-year tenancy she'd paid over $60,000 in rent, more than the initial cost of $56,000.

> Technically, I've paid it off, but I am just a rent payer to a landlord who is on my back the moment I am in financial difficulties. They may not kick me out, but they make life immensely difficult for me and pressurize me to jump through a lot of silly hoops to fit into their requirements to enable me to benefit from a lower rent.

Tenant representative Bryan Atkinson wrote,

> I believed that affordable housing i.e. public housing should be available to working class people. I was soon disenchanted by the standard of customer service given by S.A.H.T. and by the attitude of the contractors used by them. I am more than concerned that the level of service has worsened over the 42 years I have been a tenant.[79]

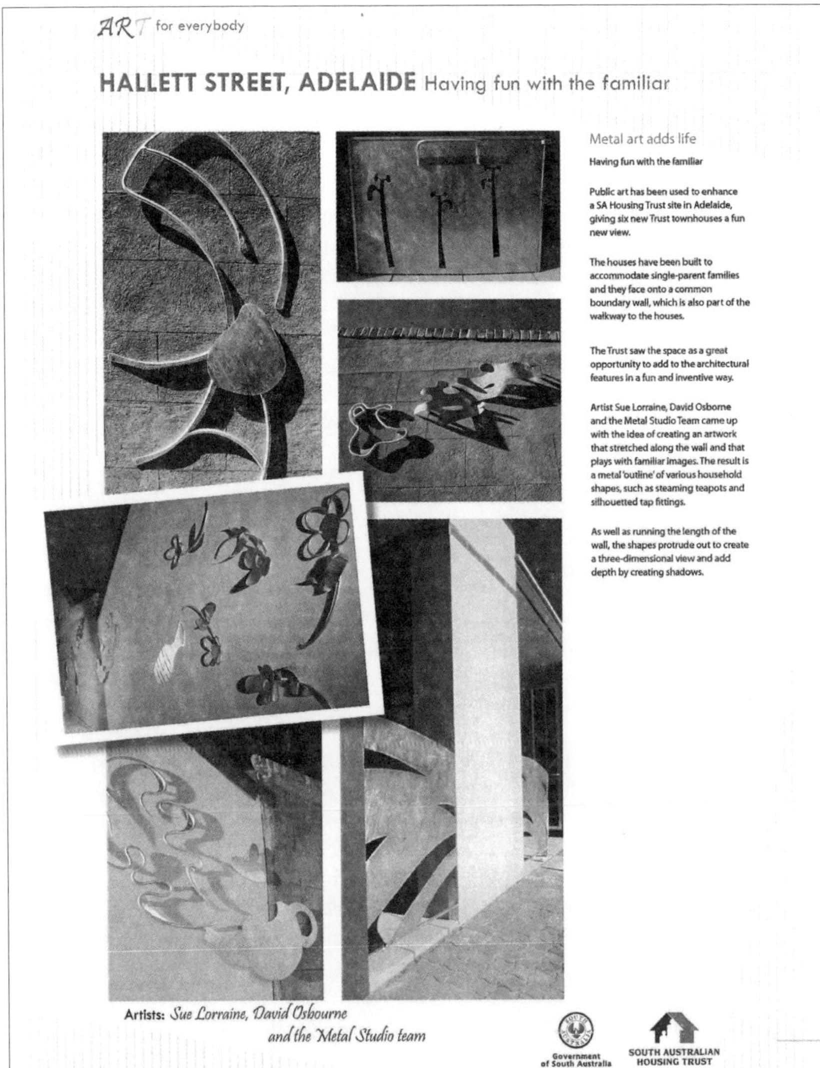

Hallett Street houses, designed by Phillips/Pilkington Architects, were completed in 2002 in Adelaide's south-eastern corner, and provided new benefits – such as art – as well as demands on tenants. The dense development complied with heritage guidelines with a low-scale built form, supplied adaptable housing at street level, as well as environmental features unusual in city dwellings, including north orientation, solar hot water, shade, rainwater tanks, and no car parks – tenants had to agree not to own a car.

The first Tenants' Association was formed by trade unionists Tony Elmers and Frances McGill in 1982–83. Elmers explained that 'we thought it was about time to have a tenants' association'. McGill remained chairperson: 'She was SA Businesswoman of the year, a real go-getter!' Elmers recalled the association having 'a habit of being right' in its criticisms and suggestions, and although the Trust often opposed them initially, they were later adopted. For example, the association proposed automatic deductions for rent payment, or, when the Trust was closing rental offices, allowing tenants to pay at post offices. (Rent collecting was contracted to Australia Post in 2002.) 'You know you've had a big impact on Trust policy ... but the association has never been acknowledged by them.' Three ministers, Hemmings, Crafter and Oswald, were supportive. Oswald, a Liberal minister, told Elmers 'that he wasn't just another economic rationalist'. The 'best person of the lot was the Federal Member for Adelaide, Kate Ellis'. But the association often publicly challenged ministers. 'We did a few militant things to say, "Hey, here we are". We put a picket line around Kym Mayes' office.' Their most outspoken member, Tony Olivier, was often in the news.

The Tenants' Association proposed that CSHA funds should support advocacy for tenants. When adopted, the association gained funds in 1992 and opened an office on Prospect Road, but, Elmers said, 'we didn't realise that going out to tender would knock us off. It was all political'. In 1997 the association lost its funding when a tender to provide advocacy was won by Anglicare, which also won succeeding tenders. 'We were all tenants and we formed a union. How could you put that out to tender?' The association continued despite the loss and, when people ring up, Elmers gives them the best advice he can – sometimes referring them to Anglicare.[80]

The Trust also introduced its own Tenant Participation Program. Helen Ottaway, who was appointed Tenant Liaison Officer in 1989, recalled Tenant Participation Officers being established in each region. 'Our role was to encourage tenants to form resident groups to take a pride in their local area, identify issues of concern and work collectively to address those concerns'. They included developing garden groups to maintain common gardens and raise funds for garden furniture, lobbying for better security, and establishing recycling groups.

In the 1990s, after the Trust's restructure, these positions were replaced by Tenant Management Coordinators.

> There were three of us: Helen Ottaway, Jon Moore and Roy Fanton. Our Manager was Tom Pears. Our role was then to train the Housing Managers so they could work more closely with the tenants in their area to establish these resident Tenant Participation groups. The emphasis was on community development. The spirit of the program was that of communication and cooperation – let's work together to improve the area in which we live.[81]

Information sharing was also improved. Until the 1980s the Trust had communicated with tenants only by letters or through the media. The first newsletter for tenants was the *Eyre Regional Newsletter*, soon followed by the *Southern and Riverland Newsletter* of which Ottaway was editor. She said,

> The *Southern Star* was printed on a photocopier in the office and then collated and stapled at home ... The popularity of the newsletter was high. It came out every few months and tenants looked forward to receiving their copy and finding out what was happening ... In the mid-90s, we became more sophisticated and coordinated, and *Focus 2000* was created. This was a glossy publication which was distributed to tenants state wide. Later it became *Trust Talk Tenant Link* and now *Customer Chat*. Throughout this whole time, tenants were also being encouraged to have their say about our policies and services. Regional Advisory boards were established. Each month representatives from each of the local resident groups would meet with the Regional Manager to discuss policies and services and provide a tenant's perspective on them. The feedback was very useful and indicated a shift in the organisation's attitude from that of being paternalistic (we know what our tenants want) to actually asking them what they want and whether our services met their needs.

Regional Advisory Boards (RABs) were elected locally and worked with regional managers on service changes. Adelaide RAB member Alison Murchie said that the managers were good at informing them about the broader picture, not just about local developments. This enabled members to answer more questions from tenants. She commented, 'It's a two-way street.' Marlene Littlewood (Marion RAB) said that issues were brought to her board, and that she was also often contacted individually. 'I get stopped in the shopping centre at Marion, or round the local shops. Complaining about the housing management, next-door neighbours, maintenance. They're the main issues.' Other RAB members agreed that dealing with maintenance problems was their major activity. Littlewood said that the decision to take maintenance away from housing managers was 'a big mistake', but Betty Alberton rarely received complaints about maintenance once it was better managed, an improvement that all agreed dated from Helen Fulcher's appointment as the Trust's first female Maintenance Director.[82]

One member from each RAB was nominated to the state-wide Operational Policy and Advisory Committee (OPAC). This group advised the minister on public housing policy and met quarterly. As General Manager, Malcolm Downie attended the start of every meeting. 'They had input into all policy changes impacting on the provision of services to tenants and applicants and ensured changes occurred without problems or surprises.'[83]

OPAC grappled with topics common to many community-based advisory boards. For example, in 2002 members asked if a community representative should become chair – and if so, what would happen to 'Executive support' for the committee – and heard that 'the group is currently lacking in representatives from the Mental Health sector, Indigenous and non-English speaking background sector and the aged sector'.[84]

RABs also sent representatives to a new Public Housing Customer Forum. By the 2000s the Tenant Participation Program was not as active as it had been – partly, Forum members suggested, because representatives were getting older and the young were disinclined to join community groups – but its legacy still affects the organisation. Ottaway said, 'Now, we are very aware of the need to consult our customers and tenants. When we are redeveloping areas, establishing a Boarding House or making changes to service delivery or policies, we consult. It's not an optional extra. It is integral to the way we do business'. And she added, staff no longer did the 'glove test' and tenants and customers referred to her as 'Helen' not 'Miss Ottaway'.

But the Trust also became 'more formal in its dealings with customers'. In Ottaway's early years events like carpet bowl tournaments between elderly cottage flat tenants were held with a staff member as captain. She also arranged workshops on gardening and home maintenance.

> One of the participants was celebrating his 80th birthday on the day of one of the sessions, I baked him a birthday cake which we all enjoyed for afternoon tea after we had sung to him. Many years later, he could still recall the occasion and how special he had felt. I don't think we do those things as often nowadays. We may not have the resources or time to arrange workshops and probably having a carpet bowl tournament would be questioned. Is it part of our core business? How much is it likely to cost?

Recent social events are more formal, arranged to celebrate Youth Week or Mental Health Week or a redevelopment. One housing manager who bought food for a sick tenant was told by his line manager that this was beyond his job role. Others who helped clean an elderly tenant's unit because it was taking too long to get support services were also reprimanded. 'I don't want to debate whether they should have assisted ... or whether there were Occupational Health and Safety policies ... My point is simply that these behaviours were more common and accepted 15–20 years ago.' Managers became 'far more conscious of public liability, safety and security, working alone, dealing with challenging behaviours and it may prevent staff from doing some of the things they would have done in the past'.[85] The Trust was at the same time assuming more complex responsibilities for customers, for example promoting local job training through urban renewal. By 2002 it was contributing to training and employment through nine renewal projects.

The National Customer Satisfaction Survey, introduced in 1996, documented increasing satisfaction with the Trust. One issue picked up through feedback from the national survey was the frustration felt by customers due to having to call and leave messages for staff who were out in the field or in interviews, and not having their calls returned until the next day. In response, the Trust established a Telephone Customer Service Centre in 2005 and channelled all incoming calls to trained staff who gave immediate and consistent advice to applicants and tenants.[86]

A longitudinal study in 2001 noted South Australia's good and improving results, and the Trust maintained its leading position in the survey. The location of their home attracted the highest level of satisfaction from residents: 'Statistically significant improvements in *very satisfied* scores were evident in NSW, Queensland, and South Australia'.[87]

Special needs

> I have a mental illness, and was in receipt of a pension ... I applied to be sure of secure long-term housing. I received Rent Assistance for some years before I became a tenant in mid-2000. I first applied for tenancy in 1994 ... Private landlords tend to be more fussy about housekeeping standards. SAHT Housing Managers seem a little more understanding of tenants' abilities and disabilities ... My disabilities have made implementation [of his obligations as a tenant] difficult, requiring assistance from a support worker ... There were problems at various times ... some bad conflicts with neighbours over the road. In some cases, I made formal complaints to the Housing Trust. I also needed to contact the police a few times. (Elijah)

As housing stock was reduced, applications again rose steeply, including from new arrivals in South Australia. Unlike in the Trust's early years, customers came from diverse cultural and linguistic backgrounds and comprised 12% of new allocations by 2006. Translation services were provided in 34 languages; most frequently Serbian, Vietnamese, Arabic and Croatian.[88]

State policies gradually reversed the last century's slow rate of immigration to gain additional settlers, rising from 3,657 in 2002–03 to 10,061 in 2006–07.[89] Most refugees were helped through the Private Rental Assistance Program.[90] As part of a 'multi-agency Immigration Promotion Task Force ... to facilitate the arrival of skilled immigrants', the Trust provided transitional housing for them. Expecting to get funds for furnishings, the Trust was directed by Cabinet to deliver the program from its own resources. In 1997 an initial 43 houses were provided to the On Arrival Accommodation Program, but because of the cost the Trust resolved to ask for assistance from agencies with a more explicit economic development function. The Board was told there was a risk that the Trust 'may be seen to be diverting resources away from those in housing need'.[91]

Special needs were defined more broadly than in the past. Services were focused on 'people with special needs, including mental health, homelessness, youth and the aged, domestic violence, disability, and those from culturally and linguistically diverse backgrounds'.[92] The emphasis on housing people with special needs was shaped by the growing longevity of South Australia's population, de-institutionalisation, long-term unemployment, and declining access to home ownership, private rental and public housing.[93] In effect, as in the past when

PARKS LIBRARY
BIENVENIDOS A LA BIBLIOTECA DE "THE PARKS"
WITAMY W BIBLIOTECE THE PARKS
THƯ VIỆN PARKS XIN CHÀO CÁC BẠN
欢迎来PARKS图书馆

Left and above: Cultural diversity: two views at The Parks Community Centre in early 2007.

large institutions housing the aged poor and destitute women and children were closed, other forms of state-funded housing were required.

A survey documenting the impact of industrial restructuring in Woodville North in 1985 found a population split into two groups: young people (aged below 24) and elderly people above 50 – both groups being vulnerable to unemployment.[94] Over the next 20 years both groups figured largely as public housing applicants and tenants. The ABC TV program *Lateline* reported in 2001 that the number of single-person households was increasing so quickly that one-third of Australia's population would be living alone within five years. Most were widows, but their proportion was declining, making way for younger divorced and unmarried people. Single people were by far the most numerous group to apply for public housing – more than 60% of new applicants in South Australia – but by contrast with the single population generally, the majority was under 25, unemployed and unable to rent privately. General Manager Greg Black told the ABC that 'Many young people are part of families that have been in poverty for generations and so their levels of skills, aspirations, communication are all very low. So we find in many instances they have very poor track records in terms of being able to share with other people'.[95] Single person households had lower incomes than couples or larger family groups, and Commonwealth Rent Assistance did not benefit singles as much as families, and so a greater proportion of them applied for public housing. In 1981 fewer than 20% of Trust tenants were single; by 2004 this proportion had risen to 63%.[96]

Discrimination was a contributing factor. A landlord's comment: 'If you are a single mother on a pension, then you can't afford my rent' was quoted in the report *Sexcluded? Women, Homes and Sex Discrimination 2004*. In this survey, 68 women reported being treated unfairly over accommodation. All but one sought low-cost rental, and 51 lived on a pension. There was discrimination 'right across the rental market: from landlords, agents, Housing Trust employees', and as a result, more than half of the women were refused a lease and were left homeless. These 68 women also had 100 dependent children.[97]

General economic recovery did not translate into renewed prosperity, or even jobs, for many housing applicants, but there were changes over the decade. In the early 1990s, when unemployment was high, men lost jobs when retrenched from male-dominated manufacturing, while women picked up work in the hospitality and retail industries. A decade later the situation was reversed as a boom in mining, trades and construction engaged men in well-paid work. In 2006–07 women, who represented a third of Australia's full-time labour force, gained only one-fifth of the new jobs. By 2007, for the first time, unemployed women outnumbered unemployed men, and a greater proportion of women workers held lowly paid part-time jobs.[98] Although applications from the unemployed fell due to the halving of unemployment in Australia in the decade after 1996, the proportion of people receiving disability support pensions only fell from 8% to 6% of the workforce. A tiny 1% of people on disability benefits found work, and those who did moved in and out of employment.[99]

The state's response to these events formally confirmed the Trust as a welfare housing agency. Leith MacGillivray remembers receiving information near the end of her tenure 'which said in a roundabout way ... that from now on the Trust would have to cater for the very destitute and homeless and not for those who could rent elsewhere'. An income test was announced in 1998 and further changes were effectively imposed by alterations to federal housing policy. In 2000 a new Commonwealth State Housing Agreement directed that public housing was to be targeted at those most in need. In March 2000 the South Australian government's Housing Reform Agenda introduced a major change to eligibility, requiring high-need applicants to satisfy income and asset tests, and restructuring the waiting list into four categories. Every applicant had to satisfy three criteria: basic eligibility, income and assets, and a needs test. Requirements for meeting the needs test included a life-threatening living situation; homelessness; family violence; long-term ill health or disability; living in crisis accommodation or leaving institutional care; refugees who had arrived within the past two years; and people who encountered serious discrimination, preventing them from renting privately.

Applicants were categorised according to their assessed need. Category 1 had the most urgent need, with 'Housing issues of extreme difficulty and seriousness'. Category 2 were people without an urgent need, but whose other housing choices were 'not suitable long term options'. Category 3 applicants met the income test, but not the needs criteria set in Categories 1 and 2; and those placed in Category 4 passed the basic eligibility test but had no housing need, although they could register for 'low demand areas'.[100] A hint of the old purpose of the Trust was evident when people applied for housing in regions of low demand, where the tests did not apply.

'Guidelines for writing support letters for early housing assistance', issued to professionals such as medical specialists, explained that in March 2000, 'due to limited housing resources', the Trust had changed allocations from 'wait turn' to a process of assessment to ensure those most in need were assisted first. The guidelines asked for information about the special circumstances relating to a customer's housing crisis 'and why Trust housing will assist', to be provided in a 'Housing needs report form', or a support letter. 'For a customer to be approved for Category 1 or 2 ... a thorough assessment of their circumstances is undertaken. The severity of their situation will determine the category for which they will be approved.'

The effect of the new allocation policies was soon apparent. Trust research had suggested that those most likely to be ineligible would be singles and couples with children, and that there would be a high vacancy rate.[101] This was confirmed. There was a high, and costly, turnover of Category 1 and 2 tenants, who often had to be re-housed by the Trust. Kilner asked, 'Was fast-track public housing the answer to their needs?'[102] Peter Chigwidden, a tenant from 1990, suggested that the Trust had 'gone backwards ... in the sense that lower paid working people are left without affordable housing while Category 1 people usually last 6–12 months (in our complex) before they leave or get evicted'.[103]

The income and assets tests confirmed informal practice and made little change, but the segmented waiting list abruptly increased the number of tenants with special needs. Applications fell by one-third, and the proportion of high-needs tenants leapt. In 1995–96 the proportion was 16%; by 2000–01 it was 69%. New staff skills and extra resources were required to serve an increasing proportion of tenants with multiple social and physical needs.

RAB member John Strang lives in a two-storey block of 98 units at Paradise South where turnover is so rapid that he can no longer get to know people, making it much harder for him to act on their behalf.[104] Within the Trust, Mignon Schneider noted the 'revolving door' problem and staff efforts to deal with it.

Allocation based on need brought other challenges. The most fraught and contentious was the increase in difficult and disruptive tenancies. As a survey of the impact of these changes at a national level noted,

> Given the reduction in stock numbers since the early 1990s, State Housing Authorities are now managing tenant groups with high and complex needs

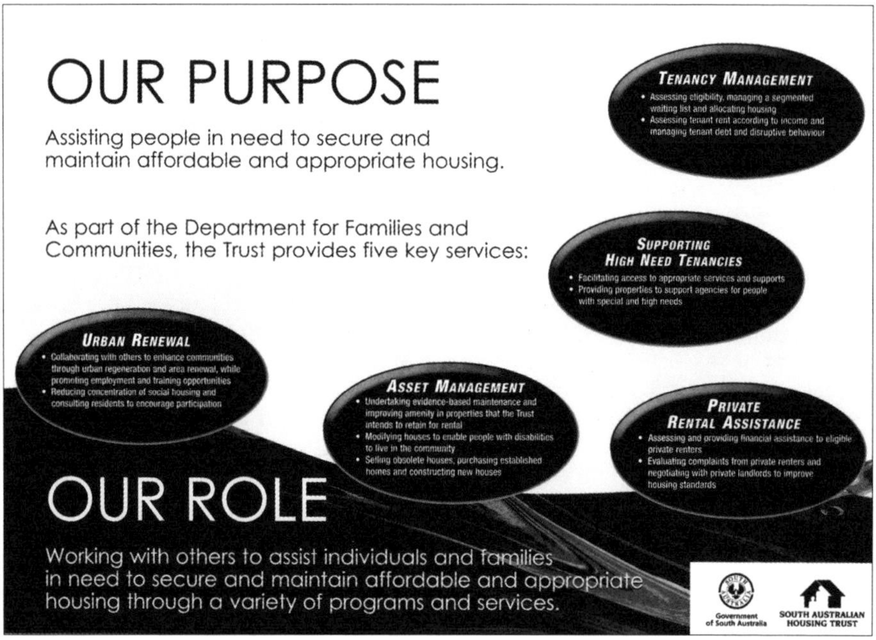

Housing Trust poster c2002.

> concentrated in increasingly smaller enclaves of often older and less desirable housing, a combination of circumstances that could have been designed to increase complaints of anti-social behaviour.[105]

Housing Trust regional staff and customers had to deal with many 'neighbours from hell', as several history questionnaire writers called them.

The Trust internally reviewed their management, but the problem built into a public campaign, vigorously pursued by Independent MP Nick Xenophon, and spurred on by talkback radio. As a result, a parliamentary inquiry was held into the way that the Trust managed disruptive tenancies; it reported in 2003.[106] Acting General Manager Helen Fulcher, who appeared before the Statutory Review Committee, described this as an interesting period of trying to get politicians to understand that targeting public housing to those most in need, involved people who would not have access to other housing, and were rejected by private rental agents. 'Therefore our philosophy was that we needed to work with them to be able to sustain their tenancies.' Some critics believed that the Trust should evict more swiftly, 'whereas we would see eviction as a state of last resort in that particular context'.

Most of the Review Committee's recommendations were implemented by the Trust, and involved more active and earlier intervention in disruptive tenancies. Even so, levels of disruption continued to rise as more and more high-needs people were housed, including those de-institutionalised from Glenside and other psychiatric hospitals. 'But', Fulcher added, 'we've not gone as far as some of the discussion in that review. It was, for instance, quite salutary for me to have politicians suggest that we should acquire from applicants their criminal record and on that basis decide whether or not we would house them.'[107]

The issue gained the Trust – and its customers – an enduringly bad press. As a later Housing Minister recalled,

> We established some tenant awards scheme, because we were being overwhelmed by all this talkback radio around disruptive tenancies, and we were conscious the Trust was spending a large amount of its time and effort on a very small proportion of its customer base. Disruptive tenancies take up a lot of political room, but they really are a tiny proportion of the total number of tenancies [although] they make people's lives a misery when it gets out of control. [On the other hand] going to the tenants' awards presentations, just seeing the extent to which small communities of tenants support one another, people who themselves may have difficulties, yet they still find the capacity to reach out and help other people – might do somebody's gardening; might support them through illness – and overcoming their own difficulties. What struck me about that was that many of the people who were being presented with their certificates looked to me like they'd never been publicly-recognised for anything before and some of them were quite moved by the ceremony. And that was a wonderful experience.[108]

Despite the transfer of 1,790 houses to the Aboriginal Housing Authority, demand far outpaced its capacity and many Aboriginal people continued to rent from the Trust.[109] Black reported in 2002 that 'the Indigenous population will be mostly affected by the Westwood redevelopment project in the next 5–7 years'. 'There is also a proposal to expand the current program of providing housing for people travelling from the country for health services such as the Queen Elizabeth Hospital's Renal Program.'[110] Aboriginal tenants should be kept informed about the Parks redevelopment using 'less paper and more face to face interaction. Basically it needs to be made more culturally appropriate'. The Trust discussed this with community groups and Aboriginal workers, and engaged local Aboriginal elders.

In 2002 the Trust reviewed youth access to all programs. Karen Hughes, who directed the review, found that few young South Australians knew about the services. 'Should information on this be put into schools, agencies and Centrelink etc? Should the information be changed to make it brighter and easier to read?' Young people did use the Direct Lease and Private Rental programs, but with difficulty, due to inexperience and a high demand for private rental. The Trust's own advisory group confirmed that young people were less satisfied than older customers.

Hughes pointed out that 26.3% of the waiting list were young, and 25.4% of new housing allocations and 36% of all private rental assessments were for young people.

Residents with special needs were not limited to public tenancy, and included many who were renting privately or living in 'supported residential accommodation'.[111] They were often the same people, moving in and out of private, public and community homes. The Trust's Special Needs Housing section was responsible for managing leases of supported accommodation to non-government agencies, community housing and other organisations that sheltered people with disabilities, those who were escaping domestic violence, or who were homeless. Shirley Trebilcock oversaw a review and restructuring of the branch in 2001–02 which regionalised some of its functions.[112]

Many public housing applicants included people struggling to buy a house. A report issued in 2008 found that affordability had worsened in all states between 1996 and 2006, with house prices increasing 400% but income by only 120%. Only one in 20 Australians aged under 30 were home owners.[113] Treasury acknowledged that affordability was 'the worst on record'. Between 1996 and 2006 the proportion of 55–64 year olds spending more than 30% of their income on housing rose from 5.8% to 9.6%, the percentage 'just a few years out from retirement' still paying off a mortgage expanded from 13% to 27%, and renters rose from 14% to 17%.[114]

Trust applicants could apply for private rental assistance while awaiting public housing. From 2000, when the Trust introduced changes to the waiting list, until 2003, a total of 2,858 applicants categorised as priority 1 or 2 received bond assistance to rent privately. The private market was not a viable long-term option for people assessed as having high needs and so most stayed on the Trust's waiting list.[115] The task of collecting information was helped when the electronic transfer of customers' Centrelink income details to the Trust began in 2000 through the Income Confirmation Service.

While public renters dealt with difficult neighbours and social stigma, private renters faced other problems. Their rents were higher than those of public housing and they had less security of tenure. Data collected in Adelaide in 1991 showed that the five year mobility rate for private renters was 83.8%, compared with 47.6% for purchasers and 50% for public tenants. Private renters moved more often than other residents.[116]

But, as state and Commonwealth funding declined, the Trust's support for private rental households also came under threat. In 2000 the Trust assisted 10,775 households with rent relief, but the program was closed to all new applicants other than country tertiary students living in Adelaide. Within two years the number of renters assisted fell by 70%, even though there was greater need for help. By 2002 South Australia's share of national rental assistance was half that in the previous decade, but the state's newly elected Labor government made no move to reinstate its own rent relief program.[117] By 2003 an estimated 14,000 households in Adelaide were paying more than 50% of their income in rent, even with Commonwealth Rent Assistance.

ART for everybody

MIKAWOMMA Community art in reserves

Mikawomma Reserve

Community art in reserves

Residents are helping to celebrate the history and culture of their suburb through a variety of community arts projects in the Westwood redevelopment.

An important aspect of the Westwood project is the creation of open space. As these spaces are developed, the community becomes involved in enlivening those spaces through art.

One such space is Mikawomma Reserve, at the corner of Liberty and Ridley groves, Woodville Gardens, where art has been an integral part of designing the space.

The key theme has been the Kaurna people's culture and technology, as they are the traditional custodians of the Adelaide Plains.

To design the reserve, the Westwood Neighbourhood Development Officer and artists Bridgette Minuzzo and Adrian Potter worked with local Aboriginal groups, councillors, residents and school students.

Then Aboriginal artist Mark Blackman worked closely with the Council's Aboriginal Advisory Panel, Aboriginal residents and students to create the artwork concepts. Ridley Grove Primary School students were heavily involved, providing ideas, research, concept drawings and participating in workshops. They also helped to plant a section of the reserve.

The result is Mark's sculpture, titled World of Knowledge—Tip of the Iceberg, which represents the Kaurna people as teachers.

Other artworks scattered throughout the reserve include stepping stones and Kaurna numbers and animals carved into boulders. To help visitors find the animals, their images are depicted on the reserve's bridge, with their names given in Kaurna language, English and Latin.

Community workshops were also held where residents created mosaic tiles that portray things found on the forest floor. The tiles were then used to create gum-leaf shaped seats. The bridge's railing was styled on traditional netting made from bulrush fibres and resembling Kaurna fishing and hunting nets.

Artist: *Mark Blackman & Youth of Ridley Grove Primary School*

Government of South Australia

SOUTH AUSTRALIAN HOUSING TRUST

Kaurna history in artwork created by Aboriginal residents, students and the artist Mark Blackman at Mikawomma Reserve, Woodville Gardens, part of the Westwood redevelopment.

By the first year of the twenty-first century, homeless people were once again camping in tents in Adelaide's Park Lands.[118] This did prompt a response, with extra help offered to people with an obstinately enduring need. Links were strengthened between housing, health and welfare services, facilitated by their reorganisation as part of DHS, and later DFC, and the Rann government set up the Social Inclusion Board and the Social Inclusion Unit committed to act on homelessness.[119] The new Social Inclusion Unit funded a project managed by the Trust, which from 2003 employed liaison officers to help homeless people rent private accommodation, and private tenants facing eviction. Funds were committed to halve homelessness by the end of 2006 and the number of rough sleepers was cut by 42% within two years.[120] An outreach program, 'Street to Home', assigned a caseworker to each homeless camper in the Park Lands. Mick and Kenny, interviewed in the west Park Lands where they had camped for the past seven winters, mentioned contact with the program, which had helped 2,222 people into homes by the end of 2007.[121]

Despite such efforts, the Trust's Board drew attention to the mismatch between housing stock and Category 1 and 2 customers, and told the minister that 40,000 houses should be kept to meet demand – a figure challenged by Treasury's estimate of 20,000.[122] Nor could the Trust overcome the inherent deficiencies of welfare housing, both for customers classified as permanently 'needy and dependent', and for the provider facing 'a major financial crisis'.[123]

Professionalism and compassion

> Although there may be differences of opinions at time between staff, we share a bond and that is the desire to maintain the tradition of the SA Housing Trust and ... a desire to assist members of our community ... Why have I stayed working in the SA Housing Trust for so long? Because the organisation, its history, culture and values are intertwined with that of South Australia and as such also our profile as South Australians (Helen Ottaway, questionnaire, 24 February 2007).

The Trust gained first place in the National Social Housing Survey of customer satisfaction for six years in succession, with 76% of tenants in 2005 saying that they were satisfied to very satisfied with the services.[124] The Trust was highly responsive to housing people with complex needs, treating them humanely while also improving rental homes. In the 2005–06 Annual Report, his last as General Manager, Malcolm Downie praised the 'professionalism and compassion' of 'our staff, contractors and key stakeholders' in delivering housing services.

Shirley Trebilcock described the Trust as 'bigger than any one person – it is/was an organisation with a heart. From my experience, there is a great caring by employees for each other, for tenants and for the organisation'. Housing Manager Carmel Hallion has worked for over 20 years in several regions 'and can honestly say, I have enjoyed my career and found it very satisfying being in a position to

In 2003-04 the Trust provided $94 100 to support ninety seven projects which aim to build the capacity of local communities. Examples of projects supported by the Trust are outlined in Table 7 below.

Table 7 – Examples of Projects Supported by the Trust

Region	**Participating Group**	**Project**
Adelaide	Kilburn Blair Athol Community Action Group	Chicago Fair – an annual event in the community
Elizabeth	Peachey Belt Residents Association	Peachey Belt Christmas Pageant – initiated by members of the community
Marion	Southern Youth Support Services	Upgrade of Community Venue – to conduct living skills workshops for young people
Modbury	Northern Women's Health Centre	Aboriginal Mural – created by Kaurna women
Murray Bridge	Adelaide Hills Community Health Service	Community Foodies Program – to provide nutritional information through peer education
Noarlunga	Neporendi Aboriginal Forum Inc	Elders Garden Maintenance Program – where volunteers mow the lawns and maintain the gardens of Indigenous Elders in the southern metropolitan area
Port Adelaide	Mt Carmel College	Work Experience and Housing Improvement Project - eight students with disabilities participated in cleaning, replanting and maintaining the garden of local Trust tenants with special needs
Port Augusta	Centacare Port Augusta	Community Curtain Project – provides opportunities for community members to learn how to create curtains
Port Lincoln	Local Community	Community Event – to mark the successful completion of the Lincoln Gardens urban renewal project
Port Pirie	Risdon Grove Community Reference Group	Risdon Grove Garden Tool Library - for use by local residents
Salisbury	United Care Wesley	Living Skills Program – to help young people develop skills and strategies to live independently
South East	Mount Burr Youth Committee	Bike Track for Mount Burr – to be created with the involvement of local youth
The Parks	Athol Park Community Group	Volunteer Training – for group members to enhance their ability to respond to local issues
Whyalla	Young Parents Peer Group	Talking Realities – provides training for young parents on all aspects and responsibilities of teenage parenting

Building community capacity.

help people in need and see the positive impact that gaining secure housing has made in their lives'.[125]

The Trust's Social Club, formed in 1946, kept up a program of dinners and happy hours. Between 1964 and 1998 staff also raised $50,000 for the Spastic Centres of SA through payroll deductions.[126] All hands were called on to help in emergencies. In 1997 the maintenance centre took nearly 3,300 calls on the last weekend of October, after wild storms struck across the state. All available operators and regional staff worked 25 phone lines non-stop, and Comskil and maintenance contractors attended to the damage.[127]

There is a line of thought that the most important public servants are not the policy makers but street-level bureaucrats, such as staff in the Trust's local and regional offices who interact directly with clients. Whatever the formal power structure, in practice these officers have discretion over how they operate, and their implementation of policies depends on their relationships with the people they serve. 'This boundary-spanning role allows the street-level bureaucrat simultaneous access to information about clients and about the organisation.'[128]

Interaction at regional office level in country towns customarily allowed for less formal, more human relations than in the city. Tracey Roissetter, who started work at the Mount Gambier office in 1989, described doing a 'lolly run around the concentrated trust areas' every Christmas.

> We would use the Contractor's ute with a trailer. All staff would be on the back of the ute with one very handsome young man dressed as Santa. We would get donations from various business houses of lollies, chips and drinks which we would give out from the back of the ute and trailer to the kids who would come running when we rang the bell. It was a lot of fun and made us all seem so much more human to the residents of our homes.[129]

When Mignon Schneider joined the Trust in the 1990s she found a welcoming, friendly and embracing environment with a family atmosphere. When she moved to the Port Adelaide office as housing manager, her team gave her a bunch of flowers with a card saying 'Welcome to the A-team'. All the staff knew each other and each other's families. Most had attended the same Catholic schools or church. Those who were attracted to work for the Trust tended to have a strong sense of social justice, and there had been 'a lot of Catholic recruitment'. She described the culture within the Trust as very strong, 'and those who don't fit, leave'.

Schneider also worked at the Adelaide office as an advisor. This was a 'culture shock' for a middle-aged, middle-class woman. She had an academic understanding of the people, but the reality hit hard. She was shocked by the scale of the problems. Many customers coming to this office for help were 'homeless people from the underclass'. This was the first time she had been exposed to the reality of life for them. There was a lot of shouting by those who couldn't be helped. After a while Schneider became desensitised to raised voices.

General Manager Malcolm Downie presents a 'Westwood award' to Lucina.

As Malcolm Downie observed:

> Trust staff had difficult jobs because they worked with clients who had so often hit the end of the line. The Trust's key partners were often non-government organisations who have very limited resources. Because the Trust had the capacity to assist people by accommodating them in both the public and private sectors, it was often Trust staff who bore the brunt of managing the clients through difficult times, especially when those other issues were impacting on their tenancy and or neighbours.

Leith MacGillivray offered a view from the other side of the counter. Her relationship with her liaison officers 'deteriorated quickly and dramatically' soon after she became a tenant in 1995.

> Tenants could reach them only by phone and only rarely. This meant going to the main office in Angas Street and waiting ... waiting ... waiting with countless other unhappy, and often belligerent, noisy tenants in a building staffed with Security Officers. Housing liaison officers had to keep behind closed doors with a security system and rarely came into the main room. We waited until our name was called by someone at desk.

Relations were improved for many tenants when regular visits by housing managers were introduced in 1998 after testing in Elizabeth and Port Augusta. Feedback from one tenant described 'a relaxed, casual atmosphere with no pressure and no feeling of landlord versus tenant'.[130] A further change in 2000 introduced the positions of service delivery manager and housing support coordinator to regional offices.

An ambitious plan

The most definitive change in the Trust's history was the result of frustration with the lack of federal support for affordable homes. Weatherill argued later that the Commonwealth government saw its only role as involving interest rates and capital grants or income support payments, when it should also acknowledge links with taxation and housing finance. 'In the absence of any real national leadership on this issue, we developed our own ... ambitious $145m Housing Plan for South Australia'.

In 2002, soon after the ALP won government, Housing Minister Steph Key began to prepare 'a 10 year strategic plan which engages industry, government and the community in the development of affordable housing options and strategies towards reducing homelessness'. The state renowned for affordability was facing 'increasing costs of home purchase and rental, ongoing discrimination against some groups in the rental market, and a widening gap between rich and poor'. Programs to supply appropriate housing would form 'a critical part of our broader strategies to reduce poverty, improve living standards, and create inclusive and sustainable communities'.[131]

Advocacy group Shelter (SA) Inc argued that the Housing Plan should be intended to maintain the stock of social housing; foster sustainable tenancies; improve indigenous homes; give incentives for investment in rental housing; increase support to private renters, the homeless, boarding house and caravan dwellers; and improve housing design for lifelong needs. Shelter and many other groups were consulted in a drawn-out planning process. Kilner suggested that the 'long gestation' indicated 'housing policy's struggle to remain a significant policy issue ... the complexity of the issues and the difficulty of attracting additional resources'.[132]

Stretton wrote in *Australia Fair* that 'housing hardship and homelessness are now increasing in our rich country. What should we do about it?' Wainwright's 1930s strategy for a Housing Trust would no longer work. 'It's the guts and intelligence and invention of that old South Australian achievement rather than its details that should inspire us now.'[133] The new Minister for Housing, Jay Weatherill, who was familiar with the Trust's history, intended the Housing Plan to do just that.

> One of the criticisms of the state housing effort up to that point is that it very much had become collapsed down into a welfare effort. We were seeking to say, 'We need to look at the whole of the State's housing needs and there'll be

> a continuum of government involvement and obviously at the most vulnerable end there'll be a lot of government involvement, and at the end where people are wealthy the housing effort will be more akin to a regulatory role rather than a direct provision. So there'll be a level of involvement in descending order, depending on people's incomes.

Stretton argued that 'the fundamental lesson' of the Trust's history 'is that you should stop thinking that the only function of public housing is to house the poor and unemployed in welfare housing ... and realise that in a society like ours ... the spread of incomes makes it impossible to have a decent distribution of housing to the bottom third or so'. While this may not necessarily require 'a great big apparatus of public housing ... you do want a public supplier into that market, into its middle and lower ranks, determinedly putting plenty of houses on the market'.[134]

Weatherill agreed, but argued that as the Trust was the largest single institution in the state's housing effort, 'what passed for housing policy really became Housing Trust policy, and what passed for Housing Trust policy really became policies around the viability of the Housing Trust'. As a result, 'everything was getting sucked into that vortex of the survival of the Housing Trust, and it crowded out room for much other innovative thinking'.

Key's reworked Housing Plan was launched by Weatherill in March 2005, and set out the Trust's future, and introduced EquityStart home ownership and the Affordable Housing Innovations Program.[135] The main aims were to boost the supply of affordable housing; strengthen the roles of the Trust and the Aboriginal Housing Authority as high-need providers; and promote energy, water and waste management efficiency. The plan confirmed a commitment to special needs housing. The subsequent state budget (2005–06) predicted that two-thirds of new Trust tenants would fall into the high-needs category.

The Housing Plan revived the older requirement for public support for low-income earners who were again struggling to rent or buy homes. This did not mean the Trust would resume that role. 'Affordable housing' was defined differently from 'social housing', which is what the Trust was now intended solely to provide. The Affordable Housing Trust, a division of the SAHT and an echo of its origins, was intended 'to address the needs of those who aspire to home ownership, those who need affordable rental while they are establishing their careers and families and those who want to live near their workplaces and extended families'.[136] The new trust would work with the private sector to provide homes for low-income residents, including the working people who were once the Housing Trust's responsibility. The new Affordable Housing Innovations Fund drew on CSHA funds that had been diverted to other portfolios, new state funding, and (once again), money from selling public housing.

The Housing Plan did not prevent a further rundown in stock, although 1,500 inner city houses were quarantined from sale. The plan did not address the Trust's debt problem and did not set targets for the eventual size of its stock.

In the main, the plan confirmed established trends and formalised the role of public housing as high needs housing.[137]

The Minister told the Board that as a 'lead agency' the Trust was crucial to the plan's success. It was critical for the Board to collaborate with other agencies, critical to the management of a different clientele – tenants.[138] The Board noted that the new EquityStart program would supplant the Trust's sales to tenants (which raised $14 million in 2003–04) with a significant impact on capital programs. Reimbursement was raised as an urgent matter, but members were told that none would be provided.

The drafters of the housing plan proceeded from a pragmatic view of the Trust's financial context, assuming no likely increase in state or federal funding. In Weatherill's words they asked,

> What assets do we have? What do we have in the housing system that enables us to think innovatively about these things? And the first thing we had was a history of innovation; we had good collaborative relationships between the various sectors – there's always been a very strong relationship with the private sector, largely because of the role the Trust has played over the years; we've got a good planning system and a culture of respect for planning; and I think a willingness to sign up for particular social goals; we had a relatively mature Community Housing sector ... and a lot of assets – despite the fact that the Housing Trust ... was actually chewing up houses just to remain viable ... we were nevertheless sitting on about six billion dollars' worth of assets ... So it was really looking at all those things and saying, 'Well, look, what can we do with what we have?'

It looked as if doing what they could with what they had would bring an end to the Housing Trust itself.

Top: Housing Minister Jay Weatherill (left) and Trust staff Josie Pastore and Paul Ogden with a tenant (right); Above: her house in Salisbury North Urban Renewal, c2004.

Notes

1 *HTN*, 8, Dec 1998, p. 1.
2 SAHT, Board Minutes 19 Dec 1995.
3 A. Parkin and L. Hardcastle, 'The impact of targeting housing assistance', Final report, DFC & Southern Research Centre, AHURI (Australian Housing and Urban Research Institute), Nov 2004, <www.socsci.flinders.edu.au/spis/staff/Impact.pdf> viewed Dec 2007.
4 SAHT, Performance Agreement Report to Minister, Sept quarter, 2000, p. 2. (SAHT, Board letters).
5 Hasan, p. 22.
6 DHS, SAHT Triennial Review 1997/98–1999/2000, DHS, Adelaide 2001, p. xi.
7 Kilner, *Housing policy*, pp. 264, 265 (quotation).
8 ibid., p. 266 (quotation).
9 SAHT, Board Minutes 24 March 1998.
10 Milligan & Randolph, 'Privatising public housing: cases from Australia', 2006, p 3.
11 The number of co-ops and associations peaked in 2000 and 2001 (at 93 and 49); numbers of properties grew from 1,469 in 1992 to 4,216 by 2004. Kilner, *Housing policy*, p. 342 (table 6.10).
12 Kilner, *Housing policy*, p. 291.
13 Hayward, 'The Reluctant Landlords?'
14 Kilner, *Housing policy*, p. 408.
15 *Adelaide Review* archives 2004–05: on Hugh Stretton, <www.adelaidereview.com.au/archives> viewed Oct 2007.
16 SAHT, Board minutes, 22 Dec 1998 (outgoing chairman's comments).
17 Hayward, 'The reluctant landlords?'
18 D. J. Walmsley and HC Weinand, 'Is Australia becoming more unequal?' *Australian Geographer*, 28, 1, 1997, p. 72.
19 ibid., p. 83.
20 B. Badcock, 'Replacing "problem" housing: a South Australian case study', *Just Policy*, 9, Mar 1997, p. 3.
21 ibid., 1997, p 4.
22 Parkin and Hardcastle, 'The impact of targeting housing assistance'.
23 C. Johnston, 'After the 2003–08 Commonwealth-State Housing Agreement: a background to some debates in national housing policy', paper, Shelter NSW Incorporated, Nov 2007, p. 4, <www.shelternsw.org.au/docs/rpt07postcsha-sb34.pdf> viewed Mar 2010.
24 C. Cameron, 'Redevelopment of Public Housing Estates', Shelter WA Occasional Paper, Oct 2000, <www.shelterwa.org.au/publications/resandproj/OP2000-1.pdf> viewed Feb 2007.
25 Based on the summary provided in Kilner, *Housing policy*, p. 331.
26 See also A. Vicary, 'Social welfare', in Prest, Round & Fort, eds, *Wakefield companion*, p. 497.
27 ETSA (Electricity Trust of SA), created when Premier Playford nationalised the Adelaide Electric Supply Company in 1946, was disaggregated and privatised under Premier John Olsen in 1998 – an act intended mainly to pay the State Bank debt.
28 The Housing Minister's title changed frequently during this decade, as follows: Minister for Housing, Urban Development and Local Government Relations (1992–96); Minister for Housing and Urban Development (1996-97); Minister for Human Services (1997–2002); and Minister for Housing (from 6 Mar 2002, still current in 2010), compared to Minister of Housing prior to 1984. Parliament of South Australia, 2007, Statistical Record, 'Ministerial Offices 1856–2007', p. 179.
29 SA, Report of the Auditor-General, June 1996, vol II, p. 609.
30 John Strang, Forum of the Regional Advisory Board (Public Housing Customer Forum), Adelaide, 19 Dec 2006. The Forum was made up of representatives from all the Advisory Boards.
31 The new Act, assented to on 12 Dec 1995, repealed the 1936 and 1958 Acts, and amended the 1940 Act and the Housing and Urban Development (Administrative Arrangements) Act (*SA Government Gazette*, 21 Dec 1995, p. 1,759).
32 South Australian Housing Trust Act, 1995 <www.legislation.sa.gov.au/>. The Board could approve the sale of land or property up to a maximum of $2 million, and purchases to a maximum of $1m; sales between $2 and $4 million required ministerial approval, and sales above

$4m or purchases over $1m required Cabinet approval (SAHT, Board Handbook, April 2006, p. 18).
33 SAHT Act <www.legislation.sa.gov.au/>.
34 SA Dept of Health and FAYS split to concentrate on their 'core' roles, Ministerial, 16 Dec 2003 (Archive, 2007), <www.health.sa.gov.au/> viewed May 2007.
35 S. Marsden, 'An overview of past and current practice. A brief history of State involvement in the care of children and young people in South Australia', 2006, DFC, pp. 86, 87. See also Kilner, *Housing policy*, p. 367.
36 SAHT, Board Minutes, 28 Oct 1997. The phrase 'a logical grouping of related activities with the aim of caring for South Australians' was repeated in the SAHT Annual Report, 1997–98, p. 7.
37 DHS, Annual Report, 2001–02, p. 8.
38 Interview, Steph Key, 13 Feb 2008 (information given to her by Brown).
39 Questions were later raised about Charles' own dual public service and statutory authority positions as CEO of both DHS and the Health Commission (from 1999). The state Auditor declared that under the *Health Commission Act 1976*, public servants could not be appointed as CEO; that there was 'a very real potential for conflict' for Charles; her Health Commission appointment was unlawful. Public Governance: Appointment of Chief Executive Officer of the South Australian health commission pursuant to Section 68 of the Constitution Act 1934 (SA): Section 19(A) of *South Australian Health Commission Act: Audit Comments 1999*, <www.audit.sa.gov.au/98-99/a3/section19a.htm> viewed Mar 2007.
40 SAHT, Board minutes 28 July 1998.
41 Helen Fulcher interview, 11 Jan 2007.
42 Shirley Trebilcock, Oct 2007 (Q).
43 SA, Generational Health Review: Submission No: 00184 – Child and Youth Health, Final Report of South Australian Generational Health Review presented April 2003, <www.health.sa.gov.au/generational-health-review/documents/Submissions/00184.pdf> viewed June 2007.
44 Kilner, *Housing policy*, p. 299.
45 SAHT, Board Minutes, 13 Dec 2005.
46 Trebilcock, (Q) 4 Oct 2007.
47 *HTN*, (new version), no 1, Sept 1997, p. 1 (including quotation); SAHT, Board minutes 22 Feb 2000.
48 Tina Lloyd, additional recollections, 2010.
49 SAHT, Operational Policy Advisory Committee minutes, 21 May 2002; Chronology (1998); *Fulchat* no 1, 26 July 2006, p. 2.
50 *HTN*, 7, Oct 1998, p. 1.
51 See also: S. Key, 'Why a State Housing Plan. Statement by the Minister for Housing', in *The South Australian State Housing Plan: Discussion Paper*, Housing Management Council, Adelaide, 2002.
52 SA Parliament Research Library, In-house database, 'Acts committed to ministers', 8 April 2008, p. 13.
53 Marsden, *A brief history of State involvement in the care of children*, p. 87.
54 Sue Vardon, interview, 24 Mar 2010 (R) (SLSA, OH 807/3). Vardon was CEO of the Department for Family and Community Services 1985–92, returning as Chief Executive Designate, Department for Families and Communities, in Dec 2004, and as Chief Executive in Jan 2005.
55 ibid.
56 SAHT, Board Minutes, 25 Jan 2005.
57 Kilner, *Housing policy*, p. 333; Report of the Auditor-General, June 2004, vol II, p. 656; AHURI, 'Social housing rental policy in Australia and overseas', Issue 75, June 2006: in June 2004, 88% of public tenants in Australia paid rebated rent, making the agencies unviable, unlike authorities in Europe, New Zealand and North America where central governments paid subsidies to the housing providers to cover the difference between the subsidised rent and ongoing housing cost.
58 No tenant paid more than the full market rent for their house regardless of their household income.
59 Report of the Auditor-General, June 1996, vol II, p. 608.
60 SAHT, Board Minutes 28 June & 26 July 2005.

61 Monro,'The Results of Federalism: an examination of housing and disability services', PhD Thesis, University of Sydney. Economics and Political Science, 2006, pp. 163–164.

62 SAHT, Board Minutes 22 Dec 1998. Poker machine gambling was legalised in SA in 1992 and the machines were introduced in 1994. See also S. Marsden, 'Len Ainsworth: Patriarch of the Pokies' (typescript, 2008).

63 DHS, SAHT, Triennial Review 1997–98, 1999–2000, 2001, pp. ix, x.

64 Malcolm Downie, (E) 27 Dec 2007.

65 Chairman Jay Hogan, letter to Minister Key, 28 Mar 2002 (SAHT, Board letters file).

66 Monro, pp. 310–311: Fig 9.3 (p. 311) shows each state's percentage share of Commonwealth funds under the CSHA from 1945 to 1995–6. From 1985/6, funding to Queensland reached and then rapidly outstripped that provided to SA. Western Australia's population overtook that of SA in 1984, and from 1989 WA also received higher levels of Commonwealth funding

67 The Productivity Commission in 2004 found that CSHA expenditure in real terms fell by 18.6% between 1993/4 and 2002/3. (GA Wood, *What is happening in Australian housing markets? Why policy makers should be concerned*, University of Melbourne, Carlton, 2004, p. 7.)

68 AHURI, 'Housing management practice and support', Issue 71, Jan 2006, p. 1.

69 Monro, 'The Results of Federalism', pp. 171–172. The new CSHA also reflected recommendations by COAG. COAG was established in 1992 to provide for regular meetings of Commonwealth and state heads of government with a focus on micro-economic reform, and areas of joint Commonwealth-state responsibility.

70 Kilner, *Housing policy*, p. 376; SAHT, Performance Agreement Report to Minister, September quarter, 2000, p. 2. (SAHT, Board letters). The extra cost imposed on the Trust by the GST was not compensated for by the state government despite the fact that the revenue from this new tax, collected by the Commonwealth, was given to the states in the form of a general purpose payment.

71 Kilner, *Housing policy*, p. 287.

72 SAHT, Annual Report, 1999–2000, pp. 9, 35 (quotations).

73 Stretton, *Australia Fair*, p. 120.

74 Weatherill interview, 11 Jan 2007.

75 Government of SA, 'News: Howard plan will end public housing in South Australia', quoting Minister Weatherill, 24 Aug 2007 <www.ministers.sa.gov.au/news.php?id=2056>. Weatherill's media release was in response to the Federal Minister's proposal to abandon the CSHA altogether. The state government announced in early 2007 that more than $700 million in loans was owed to the Commonwealth for the construction of homes over several decades, and that a quarter of the remaining public housing might have to be sold 'because of spiralling costs and falling revenue'. *ABC News* quoted Mark Henley from Uniting-Care Wesley, who said, that the Trust's unusual accounting practices had overstated costs and undervalued the capital value of the housing. He added, 'We've also had some cost shifting where housing authorities have really picked up more and more welfare costs rather than being just a housing focused organisation' (ABC News 10 Jan 2007).

76 SAHT, Board Minutes, 14 Dec 2004.

77 Jim Birch, personal communication, 9 May 2008.

78 Hayward, 'The Reluctant Landlords?'

79 Mr Bryan Atkinson, interview/recollections, 21 Nov 2006.

80 Tony Elmers, interviewed (by telephone) 17 Jan 2007.

81 Helen Ottaway, (Q) 24 Feb 2007.

82 Forum of Regional Advisory Board, Dec 2006.

83 Downie, 27 Dec 2007.

84 SAHT, Operational Policy Advisory Committee minutes, 23 Apr 2002, viewed April 2007.

85 Ottaway, 27 Feb 2007.

86 Downie, 27 Dec 2007.

87 Department of Families and Community Services (FaCS), <www.fahcsia.gov.au/sa/housing/pubs/housing/Pages/nat_rentassist_recipients_report.aspx> viewed Nov 2006.

88 SAHT, Annual Report 2005/06, p. 32.

89 Hugo, 'SA's population policy', *Independent Weekly*, 9–15 Feb 2008.

90 SAHT, Board Minutes 22 Feb 2005.

91 SAHT, Board Minutes 27 Jan 1998.
92 Minister's introduction to 'Housing Plan', 2002, quoted in Kilner, *Housing policy*, p. 301. The term 'special needs' was later supplanted by 'high needs'.
93 Kilner, *Housing policy*, p. 358.
94 Marsden, 'A history of Woodville, 1977–1987', p. 66.
95 ABC TV, *Lateline*, 'Flying solo', broadcast 27 Aug 2001, <www.abc.net.au/lateline/stories/s353401.htm> viewed Nov 2006.
96 Kilner, *Housing policy*, p. 333.
97 *Sexcluded? Women, Homes and Sex Discrimination 2004*: a snapshot study <www.sheltersa.asn.au/Info/Womens%20Housing%20Caucus/sexcluded.pdf>. The report recommended that a new ground of discrimination be introduced into SA's *Equal Opportunity Act 1984*, that it be unlawful to discriminate against any person on the grounds of their social status (homeless, unemployed or in receipt of social security). This should include discrimination against a person who offers a Housing Trust bond guarantee in the private rental market. The report also recommended launching a Women's Housing Caucus, and this was established on 17 October 2005, becoming a branch of Shelter SA. Two of the report authors Michele Slatter (also a Housing Trust Board member) and Janet Adkins were respectively the caucus convenor and secretary. (SA Women's Housing Caucus, Convenor's Report 2005–2006, <www.sheltersa.asn.au/Info/Covener's%20Report.pdf>) viewed Oct 2007.
98 *The Australian*, 19 Oct 2007.
99 D. Uren, 'Amending disability legislation no walkover for new government', *Weekend Australian*, 5–6 Jan 2007.
100 Aboriginal Housing Authority, <www.housingtrust.sa.gov.au/resources/AHA.pdf> viewed May 2007.
101 SAHT, Board minutes 27 Jan 1998.
102 Kilner, *Housing policy*, p. 341 (statistics and quotation).
103 Peter Chigwidden, 6 Nov 2006 (Q).
104 Forum of the Regional Advisory Board, 19 Dec 2006.
105 Caroline Hunter, Judy Nixon and Michele Slatter, 'Neighbours behaving badly: Anti-social behaviour, property rights and exclusion In England and Australia', *Macquarie Law Journal*, 5, 2005, p. 155.
106 Parliament of South Australia, Statutory Authorities Review Committee, 35th Report Inquiry into the South Australian Housing Trust, 2003.
107 Helen Fulcher, interview, 11 Jan 2007 (SLSA, OH 807/2).
108 Weatherill interview, 11 Jan 2007.
109 SAHT, Board Minutes, 27 Oct 1998.
110 SAHT, Operational policy advisory committee minutes, 21 May 2002, <www.housingtrust.sa.gov.au/resources/21-05-02minutes.pdf> viewed April 2007.
111 Except for one year (2004) the Trust did not administer SA's Supported Accommodation Assistance Program (joint state and Commonwealth funding to organisations providing emergency support to homeless people), although the actual housing was often supplied through the Trust's Supported Tenancies Scheme. Kilner, *Housing policy*, p. 357.
112 Shirley Trebilcock, interview, 26 Mar 2010 (SLSA, OH 807/4).
113 *The Advertiser*, 18 Mar 2008.
114 *The Australian*, 2 April 2008.
115 SA Parliament, Family First Party, 'Answered question: Housing Trust', 30 Mar 2004, <pandora.nla.gov.au/pan/23288/20040910/www.familyfirst.org.au/south_aus/pqHousingTrust.htm> viewed May 2007.
116 S. Baum and R. Hassan, 'Home owners, home renovation and residential mobility', *Journal of Sociology*, 1999; 35; 23, p. 29. 36.9% of private renters made three to five moves 1986–91, compared with 17.8% for public tenants (p. 29).
117 Kilner, *Housing policy*, pp. 328–329.
118 ABC, *PM* Archive, 24 May, 2001 <www.abc.net.au>.
119 Social Inclusion Unit, Everyone's responsibility: reducing homelessness in South Australia, 2003.
120 Kilner, *Housing policy*, pp. 356, 359.
121 *City Messenger*, 29 May 2008, p. 9.

122 SAHT, Board Minutes, 14 Dec 2004.
123 Kilner, *Housing policy*, pp. 398, 400–401.
124 *TTTL*, 16, Dec 2005, p 3.
125 Carmel Hallion, (E), 22 Jan 2007.
126 *HTN*, 5, June 1998, p. 6.
127 *HTN*, 3, Christmas 1997, p. 2. Comskil was contracted to run the Trust's maintenance centre in January 1997, which responded to calls and paid maintenance contractors. (*HTN*, 5, June 1998, p. 1).
128 Monro, p. 84 (discussing the arguments of Sabatier and Prottasp).
129 Tracey Roissetter, (E), 29 Jan 2007.
130 *HTN*, 6, Aug 1998, p. 2.
131 Quoted in Kilner, *Housing policy*, p. 301; see also <www.infrastructure.sa.gov.au/documents/community_serv.indd.pdf>.
132 Kilner, *Housing policy*, p. 302 (quotation).
133 Stretton, *Australia Fair*, p. 122.
134 ABC, *Counterpoint*, interview with Hugh Stretton, 29 May 2006.
135 *TTTL*, 16, Dec 2005, p. 2; 1st Newsletter for Housing Plan for SA, SA Government [Dec 2005]. Housing Industry Association, Media releases, 31 Aug 2006 & 18 Oct 2007, <http://hia.com.au/> viewed Oct 2007; *The Australian*, 19 Oct 2007. This was a national trend identified by the HIA in September 2007 as a seven-year decline in affordability, falling to its lowest level since the series began in 1984.
136 CISA, 'Housing SA', viewed July 2007.
137 Kilner, *Housing policy*, p. 303–304.
138 SAHT, Board Minutes, 24 April 2005.

CHAPTER THREE

Living environments, 1986–2011

The very success of the SAHT in housing a considerable proportion of industrial workers as inexpensively as possible (in large, cheap estates close to industrial areas) now constitutes a grave problem of concentrated unemployment, near a barren landscape of abandoned or partially-used factory sites. The shaping of Adelaide to fit the requirements of ... foreign-owned manufacturing industry had the same historical limitations as in any town built to serve single economic purposes. (Susan Marsden, 1994)[1]

New Haven Village, a higher-density urban consolidation project at Osborne. This comprised 65 affordable dwellings incorporating a range of innovative urban-design and engineering systems ... The result is an enhanced living environment for residents and the promotion of an environmentally-sustainable model for future housing developments locally and internationally. (SAHT Annual Report 1995–96)

mitchell park, 2000
in hours this housing trust home   reduced to a pile
of red bricks bulldozedclinking/ booming   into
skips carted off as fill to new subdivisions ...
these homes held the children i taught thirty years ago

    their fathers
from the assembly line at chryslers coming Home of a
Friday after a few beers from the marion or the tonsley

    their mothers
from the upholstery cutting room   stuffed
    returning to linoed kitchens

these blocks   scraped of history
all ripe for gentrification   as poverty
moves further north or south to fresh suburban fringes. (Rob Walker)[2]

Introduction

Living environments in South Australia were strongly shaped by the Housing Trust as an urban developer, builder and landlord. The 70th anniversary exhibition in 2006 highlighted the Trust's 'enormous impact in regard to the built form, the social blend of population and the industrial development of the state'.[3] The Trust 'continued to give Adelaide's development a distinctive cast', and 'shaped South Australian urbanisation in ways that made Adelaide a relatively better place to live for more of its residents than in comparable Australian cities'.[4]

This chapter links to the spatial chapters in *Business, charity and sentiment*[5] and explores how the Trust and Housing SA transformed 'metro, fringe and country' environments over the 25 years following 1986. It covers old and new urban development and the experiences of residents. To provide 'affordable and adaptable housing', staff, contractors and joint venture partners built 'flexible' homes that were low-cost and energy efficient, and embarked on urban renewal to diversify housing type and tenure. Tracts of rental housing became places of the past. 'Elizabeth encouraged large public housing estates, the City of Adelaide and West Lakes significantly reduced them, whilst Golden Grove, Seaford and Rosewood Village have abolished them'.[6]

Metropolitan Adelaide was an artefact of the Trust's post-war policy of creating a linear city extending north and south, with neighbourhoods built around regional centres. This policy exerted an enduring influence on subsequent planning.[7] Trust construction in joint venture developments at Golden Grove, Northfield and Seaford on Adelaide's northern and southern margins were additions to that template. The Trust's own role as a large fringe developer ceased and most of the land required for a reduced newbuild program was bought at discounted prices in these joint ventures. When they were completed, another approach to supplying low-cost housing was urban regeneration, although success depended on 'the Trust's ability to access affordable land for replacement housing to facilitate the relocation of tenants, particularly in the middle and inner ring of Adelaide'.[8]

This approach tied in with state planning changes. In 1987 the government proposed controls to curb suburban sprawl and promote consolidation – an approach that was finding favour in Australian urban policy generally. Growth boundaries were drawn around the metropolitan area, and within them medium density development was encouraged on residual vacant sites or through demolition and rebuilding. The Trust was already recycling old commercial and industrial sites as 'infill' – an early form of urban consolidation. Hosting Australia's first annual meeting of housing authority executives in 1987, the Trust showed them over Mitchell Park and Hindmarsh. Paul Edwards noted that 'the other States felt that the Trust was tackling some very difficult long-term projects in both the areas visited'.[9] These new forms of development involved both infill on purchased land (Hindmarsh), and the first stage in redeveloping an old estate (Mitchell Park). Such work earned many awards, including one from the Royal Australian Planning Institute in 1991, for Excellence in

Metropolitan Planning, for the Trust's pioneering role and high standard of design in urban consolidation.

Consolidation had many benefits. It helped to retain low-cost homes in inner suburbs and sustain their diverse streetscapes by the adaptive reuse of historical buildings, such as the colonial horse-tram barn at Maylands, and Goodwood Technical High School, both converted by the Trust. There were critics of consolidation. Patrick Troy argued that low income households were restricted to outer suburbia as controls on broad-acre fringe development pushed up inner-city values.[10] There was also public outcry over the destruction of heritage in the redeveloped inner suburbs. Stretton believed that some consolidation was unavoidable, given the environmental constraints society faced. Taking note of water scarcity, George Seddon went so far as to advocate concentrating metropolitan Adelaide inside its 1950 boundaries.[11] Stretton argued that consolidation could be done well

> by spreading city central activities better so that each can be the centre of a modest sized spread of city residents, then you can continue to give people the freedom that Australians love to have about their form of housing and the kind of mixtures in which they want to live.[12]

Internationally, urban renewal had developed a bad reputation because post-war schemes had obliterated many poor communities. Gentrification – the flip side of social mix – had also forced up prices, pushing poor residents further out. However, Housing Trust renewal typically involved a mix of demolition and renovation, transfer and re-housing, rather than total replacement.

A conjunction of four elements made South Australia's public estates ripe for redevelopment: a concentration of disadvantaged people; aged and mediocre building stock; increases in the value of the land occupied by those estates; and rising levels of state debt and declining funds for new public housing.

Paul Edwards' successor, Richard Parker, had a background in project management and, in 1991, went from directing the Urban Land Trust to the Housing Trust 'with an urban development agenda'.[13] The Land Commission was also put under his control. As General Manager, Parker placed greater emphasis on renewal and brought financial rigour to the program. He also appointed Peter Jackson, whose private sector experience included work for Baulderstone. Parker's urban policymaking was evident in his description of the Northfield project as one that would 'bring together the threads of the state's Planning Review and ... build on the Trust's excellent work on urban renewal. I have no doubt', he told staff, 'that the project itself will play a vital role in setting the direction of urban development in the next decade'.[14]

In 1992 South Australia's Planning Review Committee completed '2020 Vision: Planning strategy for metropolitan Adelaide', which endorsed the Trust's program of progressive redevelopment by reducing concentrations of public housing.[15] There were also elements of the Trust's work in the Development Act. This was

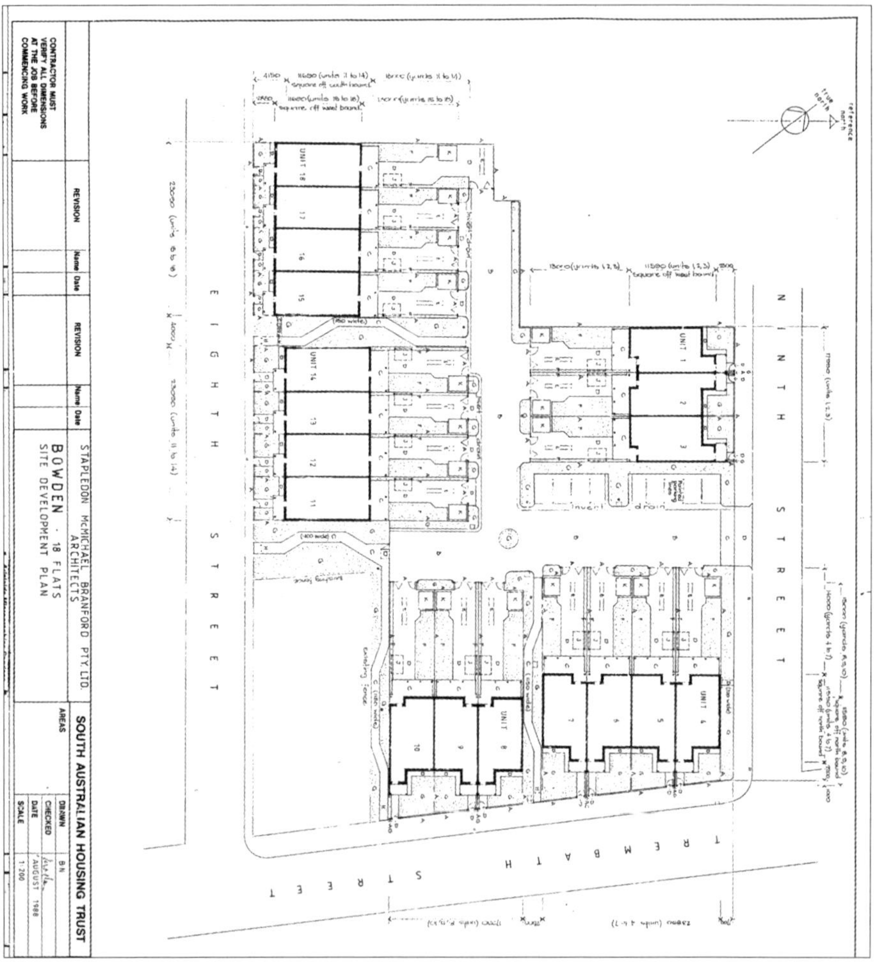

Above: urban consolidation. The Trust pioneered redevelopment in Mile End, Bowden/ Brompton and Port Adelaide. Site plan for 18 flats in 8th, 9th and Trembath Streets, Bowden, 1988, architects Stapledon McMichael Brandon;

Top right: Adelaide Cooperage group, infill at Mile End.

Bottom right: Minister John Oswald (second front right) signs the feasibility study for Hillcrest redevelopment with (from left): Gary Rusling (Barrett & Barrett Director), Richard Parker, Bob Townsend (Barrett & Barrett General Manager) and Harry Weira (Enfield Council City Manager),

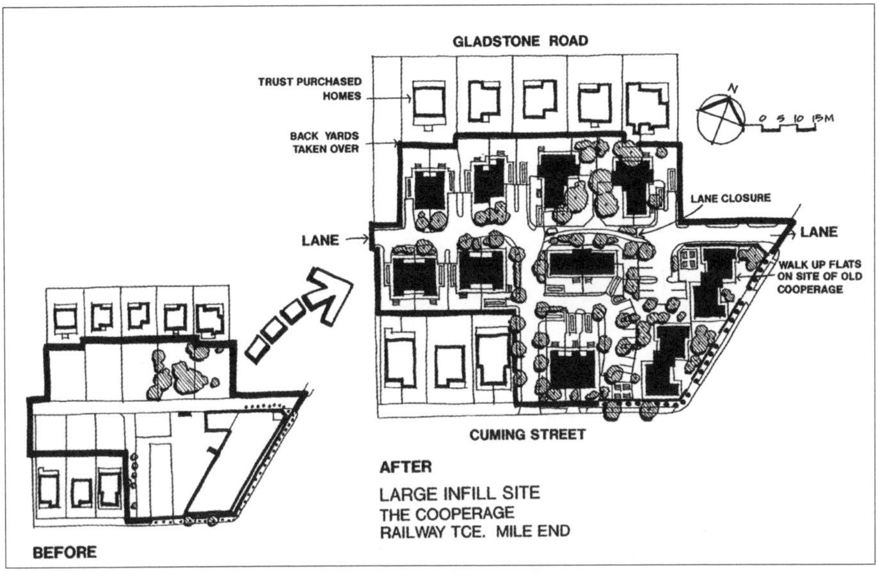
GLADSTONE ROAD
TRUST PURCHASED HOMES
BACK YARDS TAKEN OVER
LANE CLOSURE
LANE
LANE
WALK UP FLATS ON SITE OF OLD COOPERAGE
CUMING STREET
AFTER
LARGE INFILL SITE
THE COOPERAGE
RAILWAY TCE. MILE END
BEFORE

intended to promote consolidation, protect agricultural land in the south and redirect construction to the northern and north-western suburbs, diversify housing and urban design, and develop a multi-centred city.[16]

A number of new agencies contributed to the changing pattern of Trust development. Minister Crafter explained in 1993 that the SA Urban Land Trust (SAULT) was acquiring land identified by the Metropolitan Development Program and staging land releases. His new Department of Housing, Urban Development and Local Government Relations combined the resources of the Housing Trust, SAULT, and the Office of Planning and Urban Development, and aimed to spread public housing 'more widely throughout the metropolitan area. The redevelopment of bigger Housing Trust estates makes economic sense, while lifting housing standards and ... strengthening often depressed communities'. New principles would apply to redevelopment:

> no suburb will consist of more than 15 per cent of public housing; no single public housing development will contain more than 20 units; redevelopment may involve a substantial program of sale and renovation in order to provide a social mix and diversity of stock and tenures; there will be local consultation on redevelopment plans; and ... voluntary relocation of tenants.[17]

SAULT was abolished in 1995 and replaced by the more limited Urban Projects Authority (UPA). Urban scholar Max Neutze described such changes in Australian cities as 'the rise and fall of planning since its post-war eminence'. From the 1980s there was a 'complete decline as far as the federal government was concerned – but a strong maintenance of interest at the state government level but pretty serious defeats in some of these major development projects which were taken outside the planning system altogether'.[18]

The Urban Projects Authority had a far briefer life than had the equivalent Housing Trust divisions and was dissolved in 1997. Assets were transferred to State Development and staff to the Multi-Function Polis Development Corporation.[19] UPA was replaced by the Land Management Corporation, which retained a land banking function and could develop land in joint ventures, but lost the previous authority's social infrastructure role.[20]

The economic imperatives of urban policy were sustained under both Labor and Liberal governments. As Crafter explained in 1993, his department would 'unite land, housing and recreational needs' to help expand the economy, and establish 'the ideal climate to allow the urban development industry to flourish in this State'.[21] The Trust's regeneration projects also represented significant reinvestment in existing estates.

Redevelopment was already flourishing in Adelaide's city centre, but at a cost. During the 1970s and 1980s the Trust was a significant residential developer and had the support of the Adelaide City Council (often on council-owned land), as well as state and federal governments through the latter's Local Government and Community Housing Program (established in 1984). Between 1973 and 1999,

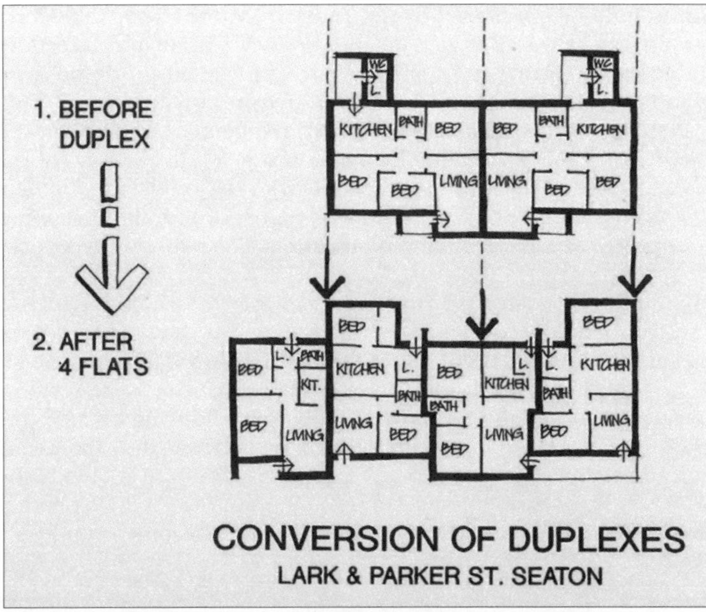

Conversion; double unit at Lark Avenue and Parker Street, Seaton showing the plan and the results after upgrading and alteration into four flats, 1986.

city dwellings built or purchased by the Trust grew from three to 592, although Leith MacGillivray heard, after moving into her new Carrington Street unit, 'that people had lobbied to prevent Housing Trust ... moving in'. Additions after 1990 were few and governments instead favoured private construction.[22] The City of Adelaide Plan Review of 1990–91 recorded a vehement debate between pro-development and pro-conservation factions, which 'left little room for [planning to meet] ... the needs of disadvantaged people who rely on the City for accommodation and support services'. Nor could low-cost accommodation compete with office development and residential gentrification. The plan reviewers continued:

> Recently the South Australian Housing Trust has indicated its intention to withdraw from the City residential development. The demand for up-market housing and the consequential rise in residential land values has meant that land owned by the Trust in the City can realise a price which will enable the purchase of more land for substantially more housing outside the City. The 1974 City of Adelaide Planning Study considered that the Trust and other agencies concerned with more affordable housing should provide a minimum of 10% of residential accommodation in the City. This percentage has never been achieved and its achievement will become even less likely

Adelaide city housing. Above: renovated boarding house, Carrington Street; Right: Albert Edwards Court, Alfred Street, looking towards 'Dunmoochin', a 1850s bluestone cottage typical of this historic street.

> under present circumstances, unless initiatives to implement a Residential Development Strategy are successful.[23]

Redevelopment was later revived in central Adelaide in 'affordable housing' ventures. Jane Lomax-Smith, a former Lord Mayor of Adelaide, was Minister for the City of Adelaide in 2006, when she was briefed on an estimated $8 million, 28 unit 'Eco-affordable' development on Council-owned land on Whitmore Square.[24]

In the meantime, building by the Trust was generally curtailed. For nearly 60 years the Trust had built as many as 2,000 homes per year, but in the decade after 1996 that dropped to an average of 200. Paul Ogden, Director Capital Projects, attributed the 'dramatic drop-off' to reduced government funding redirected to Commonwealth assistance for private renters. By 2005 the Trust was intent on replacing 500 obsolete homes per year, and even that work was self-funded.

> So there's no money going into the capital program so we have to raise that money through what we do in our development ... And we have currently seven urban renewal projects underway involving some 5000-odd public rental houses. And again, those urban renewal programs have to be self-funding ... last year we spent $115 million on capital works. We had to raise $115 million by the sale of assets.[25]

Ageing residents occupied ageing double units. As labour recruitment had been the main aim of the post-war immigration program, the age of most migrant settlers on arrival was between 20 and 40. By the 1980s that large group was aged between 50 and 70. As migrants in good health had been selected, many would reach an older age than other Australians. Their number was augmented by grandparents who arrived in the Family Reunion Scheme. The rate of growth in the number of overseas-born aged residents was more than four times that of Australian-born aged. By far the largest overall number of old people from non-English speaking countries lived in the Trust dominated Woodville (subsequently Charles Sturt) and Enfield (Port Adelaide Enfield) Council districts.[26]

The Trust's former selection policies favouring Australian- and British-born working families ensured that many estates were populated by a more homogeneous group than in other post-war suburbs. Those policies were reflected in a large stock of poor quality rental houses, mean suburban surroundings and, due to the uniform ageing of tenants, many elderly retired residents subsisting on small pensions. Elizabeth, and the middle suburbs built by the Trust from the 1940s to the 1960s, were losing population compared to the more diverse inner suburbs. As well, 'since the SAHT began to house an increasing proportion of "non-working poor", the legacy of single family dwellings and the scale and locations of estates have created serious problems'.[27]

Most new dwellings were completed in renewal areas where double units and cottage flats had been cleared or sold. This meant that most areas lost more Trust houses than they gained. In 2004, for example, 354 dwellings were completed, but there was a net loss of 800.[28] The outcome was a smaller number of better quality houses.

A high rate of construction during the 1980s meant that the subsequent loss of stock came from a large base, although this had also inflated debt and increased pressure to sell houses. Public rental stock reached a historical peak of 63,318 in 1989 and by 2006 had fallen by nearly 20,000.[29] The contraction made the character of public housing more metropolitan, as the reduction in country stock was proportionally much greater. The largest metro reductions were made in outer suburbs (as demand for social housing was higher in inner suburbs). These changes translated into a modest redistribution of public housing, although 40% remained in the outer zone in 2001.[30]

In the recollection of then Principal Engineer, Murray Hutchesson, in the mid-1990s, large-scale development was 'stopped dead' and the Trust concentrated on renewal. The development role halted with implementation of the new South Australian Housing Trust Act, which focused on public housing rather than land development, and enabled the Trust's surplus land and industrial and commercial property to be transferred to the Urban Projects Authority. This was effected in 1996. Most of the portfolio of industrial and commercial properties was sold. Joint venture equity ownership in the Seaford and Northfield projects was also transferred, although the Trust completed construction at Seaford.[31] After 1996 most of the Trust's vacant land was small parcels acquired for redevelopment, or allotments created by demolishing its older houses.

The state government's '2020 Vision' planning strategy identified Adelaide's northern region as the location for significant development. The community-based Elizabeth/Munno Para Social Justice Project was set up, with the main aim of reducing the proportion of public housing and improving access to ownership by upgrading and selling Trust dwellings. Both strategies were employed at Rosewood, the Trust's first northern renewal. In 1999, when Rosewood's final stage began, the Trust completed a Northern Metropolitan Study to address social disadvantage and 'inappropriate' public housing. The study region was colossal: Salisbury North, Peachey Belt (Smithfield Plains and Davoren Park), Elizabeth South, Grove and Vale, Gilles Plains/Windsor Gardens, Kilburn/Blair Athol and Taperoo/Osborne. The study set out principles for renewal planning: encourage community development; reduce public housing to a maximum of 25% of dwellings per suburb, with reductions of 2,000–3,000 houses by 2002; construct replacement housing and integrate this into other new developments; and promote local economies, job creation and training.[32]

Over the 25 years following 1986, the Trust's role as the state's largest landlord, its work on fringe developments, regenerating middle and inner estates, designing environmentally efficient houses, and updating post-war housing, helped to maintain its historical role in shaping living environments in South Australia's capital city and country towns.

Housing diversity encompassed new types of tenancies, sites and building materials, including mud-brick homes built for Hindmarsh Co-op Housing during the 1980s. Top: spreading mud over brick moulds at Earthwerks in Mount Pleasant; Above: house under construction; Top right: near completion in West Street, Brompton; Bottom right: two-storey mudbrick in 10th Street, Bowden.

Creating homes for individuals

> I asked for city or inner suburbs, particularly because I wanted to continue riding my bike to work, and ... with night lectures in the city ... I was delighted, at first sight, with my two-storied unit ... separate from the others, on Marion Street, just off Carrington St. It was very spacious; had a large area downstairs which could be divided into 'living' and 'eating' areas; upstairs there were two bedrooms, one with a walk-in wardrobe; and a large bathroom with bath and shower. It was newly built and I was the first occupant. I had room at the back for a small garden and a space to park my car. What more could I ask for? (L. MacGillivray)

Historically, in its choice of tenants and use of austerity house designs, the Trust preserved a 1940s social and architectural character in many suburbs and towns until well into the 1980s. Barbara Holt described old-style double units in Whyalla, as being 'a poor design for family life', with tiny lounge rooms and too-small bedrooms. As tenants in the late 1970s she, her husband and two children found the house 'very cramped indeed'. Later single units with larger bedrooms and living space were 'much improved on earlier designs'. Ronald Harding and his wife, who were allocated a unit at Whyalla Stuart in 1999, found it to be in a good location and of good design. 'Some rooms [a] bit small. In 2000 we were promised repairs and renovations, so far [in 2006] nil work'.

By the closing years of the twentieth century the Trust had bought or built one-fifth of all South Australian residences – over 120,000 homes – and still owned half that number. But they were no longer traditional Trust dwellings. Those still standing were upgraded, many others had been sold or replaced and emphasis had been placed on creating homes for individuals, catering for a more diverse tenant population. New forms of accommodation were also supplied, as illustrated in 1986 when the Trust and Western Community Hospital built the first independent cottage flats designed for aged people needing support. Two projects were completed with Greek communities as the first joint ventures that addressed the specific needs of ethnic groups, and a property was bought at South Plympton to become the 100th Youth Community Tenancy House. Another method to provide a continuum of care was followed in developing aged-care facilities in new residential projects, such as at Christie Downs. That project was also a response to the large number of family homes built locally by the Trust during the 1960s and 1970s, many now occupied by elderly people living on their own.

The range of youth residences also broadened, with joint ventures that included two with the Cities of Noarlunga and Elizabeth, both finished in 1989. The boarding house at Noarlunga used an old drive-in site.[33] In 1997 a pilot scheme leased surplus accommodation to student housing bodies which then sublet the properties. Other special purpose housing included emergency shelters such as the Aboriginal Women's Shelter (1988) and cluster accommodation for other women escaping domestic violence in the northern suburbs (1999).[34]

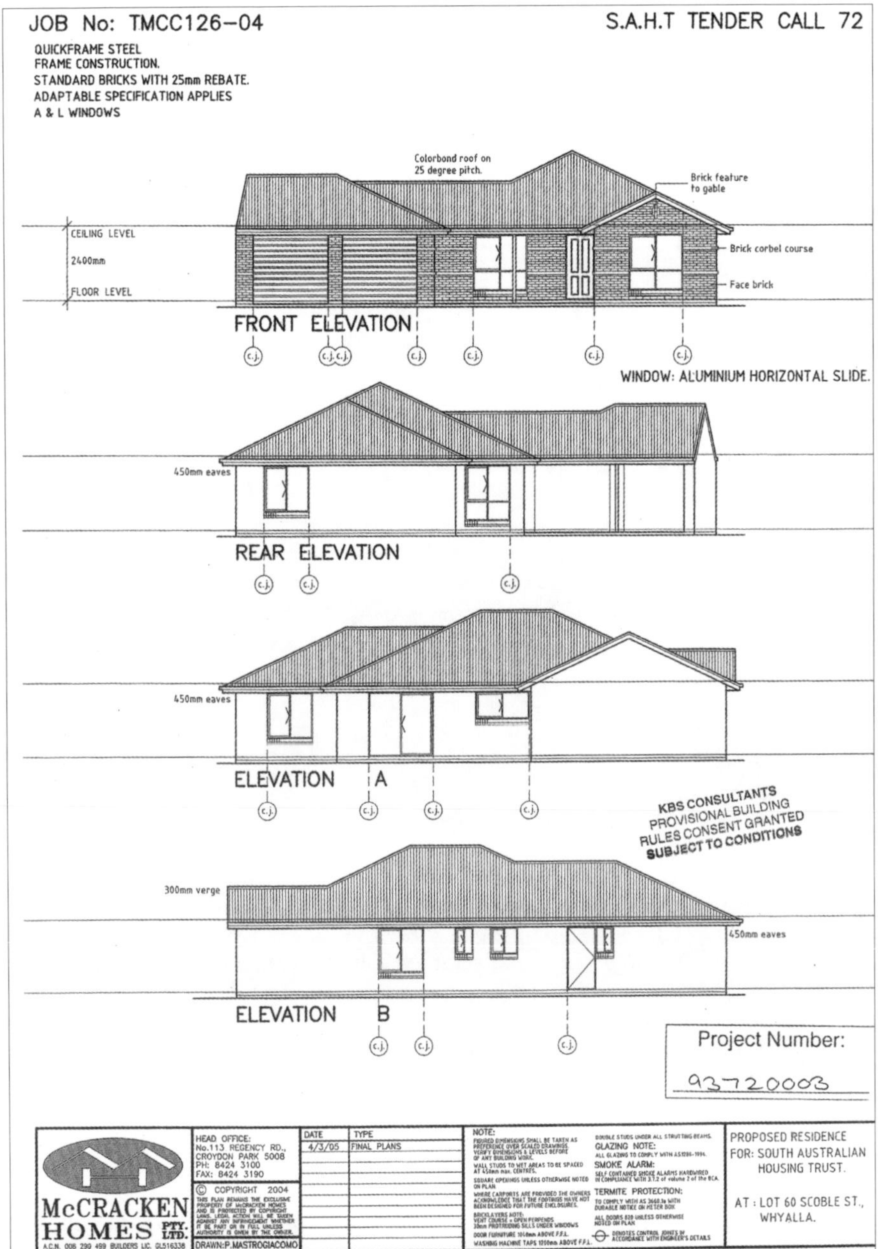

Single unit designed for Lot 60, Scoble Street, Whyalla, by McCracken Homes for the Trust, 2005.

Hundreds of cottage flats were built in country towns to help ageing South Australians live locally as they retired from farms. Port Vincent residents celebrate the opening of Glad Correll Cottage Homes in 1986.

Accommodating the aged and disabled

Fay Rohrlach, who is visually impaired, applied to become a tenant because she had been living in Blind Welfare Association units and wanted 'to be in the whole community at large'. Her previous home was too small and had only one fire escape, while her current Trust unit at Windsor Gardens has three.[35] The Trust started to build housing specifically for people with disabilities in 1967, and was the first public housing authority to do so. But 'disability' and the methods used to address it were narrowly interpreted in the 1960s. Modifications were made to existing houses, while later properties incorporated adaptable designs so that tenants did not have to move if their needs changed. 'Disability' was also interpreted initially as 'physical handicaps', with modifications made mainly for people in wheelchairs. The expansion of groups defined as disabled, and consequently the large increase in the number seeking social housing, followed de-institutionalisation.[36] Rising costs and low government subsidies also caused many private boarding houses to close, forcing many of their mentally ill and disabled residents to move.[37] However, the Trust redeveloped one of the most

LIST OF JUBILEE 150 PROJECTS WHICH MAY REQUIRE OFFICIAL

OPENING IN 1986.

TOWN		COMPLETION DATE	PARTNER
Bute	3 CF	September 1985	District Council of Bute.
Jamestown I	6 CF	September 1985	Corp. of Town of Jamestown.
Renmark	10 CF	September 1985	D.C. of Renmark.
Snowtown	4 CF	September 1985	D.C. of Snowtown.
Ceduna II	4 CF	November 1985	Far West Senior Citizens Inc.
Clare II	6 CF	November 1985	Catholic Church.
Gladstone I	4 CF	November 1985	D.C. of Gladstone.
Pt. Broughton	8 CF	November 1985	Pt. Broughton Hospital.
Murray Bridge	10 CF	November 1985	Murray Lands Homes.
Yankalilla	6 CF	November 1985	D.C. of Yankalilla.
Balaklava	3 CF	December 1985	Lower Northern Homes for Aged.
Christies Downs I	24 CF	November 1985	Greek Orthodox Church.
Edithburgh	4 CF	December 1985	D.C. of Yorketown.
Goolwa II	8 CF	December 1985	D.C. of Pt. Elliot & Goolwa.
Hendon	24 CF	December 1985	Corp. of City of Woodville.
Lobethal	6 CF	December 1985	D.C. of Onkaparinga.
Mt. Barker	10 CF	December 1985	Mt. Barker & District Homes for the Aged.
Ridleyton	2 CF	December 1985	Hindmarsh Diamond Jubilee Cottage Homes.
Stansbury	4 CF	December 1985	D.C. of Yorketown.
Warooka	4 CF	December 1985	D.C. of Warooka.
Laura II	6 CF	February 1986	D.C. of Laura.
Kadina II	8 CF	March 1986	Northern Yorke Peninsula Homes for Aged Inc.
Kapunda II	6 CF	March 1986	D.C. of Kapunda.
Robe	7 CF	March 1986	D.C. of Robe.
Moonta II	8 CF	March 1986	D.C. of Nthn. Yorke Peninsula.
Jamestown II	6 CF	April 1986	Corp. of Town of Jamestown.
Pt. Wakefield	6 CF	April 1986	D.C. of Wakefield Plains.
Loxton III	8 CF	May 1986	D.C. of Loxton.
Williamstown II	4 CF	May 1986	D.C. of Barossa.
Meningie	4 CF	June 1986	Yallarah Homes.
Naracoorte	6 CF	July 1986	Naracoorte Homes for Aged.
Marion	29 CF	August 1986	Resthaven Homes for Aged.
Tanunda	7 CF	August 1986	Lutheran Church.
Tumby Bay	4 CF	August 1986	Tumby Bay Homes Inc.
Waikerie	9 Cf	August 1986	Waikerie Aged Cottage Homes.
Saddleworth	4 CF	September 1986	D.C. of Saddleworth & Auburn.
Strathalbyn	7 CF	September 1986	D.C. of Strathalbyn
Crystal Brook II	6 CF	October 1986	D.C. of Crystal Brook.
Moonta (Heritage Site)	6 CF	October 1986	D.C. of Nthn. Yorke Peninsula.
Ridgehaven	30 CF	October 1986	Masonic Memorial Village.
Whyalla	12 CF	October 1986	Corp. of City of Whyalla.
Yorketown II	6 CF 3 AH	October 1986	D.C. of Yorketown.
Salisbury	21 CF	November 1986	Corp. of City of Salisbury.
Aldinga	6 CF	December 1986	D.C. of Willunga.
Ardrossan II	12 CF	December 1986	Ardrossan & District Retiremen Homes.
Lameroo II	3 CF	December 1986	Lameroo Homes for Aged.
Pt. Vincent II	4 CF	December 1986	D.C. of Minlaton.
Ridleyton	18 CF	December 1986	Aust. Greek Society for Care of the Elderly.
Stepney	13 CF 6 AH	December 1986	Corp. of St. Peters Council.

425 UNITS 49 PROJECTS.

important facilities, the St Vincent de Paul Night Shelter in Whitmore Square, which opened in 2003.

Trust applicants included those whose illness was age-related. David Schmidt's Alzheimer's disease brought him with his wife Barbara to Adelaide in 1988. They had applied to the Trust, which said they had to sell their Murray Mallee farm. Within five weeks they had sold and were renting a unit at Holden Hill. Barbara Schmidt needed to live near her daughter, who could drive them to the doctor. 'It's a beautiful unit and I love it and I will be here until I have to go into a home'.[38] Her story also illustrates the need to take ageing tenants into account when designing accommodation. Joan Beagley put her name down for a Trust house after her husband died. She had two children and worked part-time at a shoe store. She was given rent assistance, but waited ten years until 1997 and had retired, when she received 'great news to go into a brand new home at Fulham. It was marvellous, and I love my little home and have my garden out the back to give me plenty to do'. The houses were head-leased by the Trust from the owners, an approach that 'came into being when these were built'.

By 2005, when one-third of tenants were over 65, the Trust was embedding accessibility into designs. Existing housing for the aged included 20,000 double units and 6,000 cottage flats, walk-up flats and single dwellings, but turnover

Resident at Lockleys Retirement Village, 1986.

was high as few people liked living in cottage flats. They were small (40 square metres) and basic, and shared wet areas. Between 2001 and 2005 the Trust redeveloped the obsolete bedsits, relocating over 600 aged tenants into nearby homes, and built 1,000 replacements designed as flexible housing suitable for people of all ages and levels of mobility. Malcolm Downie, General Manager from 2003–06, recalled that David Bernard (Director Real Estate Services) had also developed a strategy for several groups of old walk-up flat and medium density complexes that were also unsuitable for a changing client group and in need of repair. This involved funding their redevelopment through partial sales to neighbouring aged-care providers. 'This met a critical asset replacement need but also ensured older tenants would now have access to support services and the option of moving into higher levels of care as they became more frail.'[39]

New features

The Trust came to build adaptable features into 90% of all new houses, counteracting the shrinking size, due to cost cutting, of design and construct housing with spaces too narrow for wheelchairs or pushers. This approach would also save money in the long term, as it was cheaper than retrofitting.[40] Other features included wider perimeter paths, stepless entry and shower alcoves, grab rails, door levers rather than knobs, and spaces under basins to allow room for people using wheelchairs or frames, adjustable kitchen shelves, and mixer taps with temperature controls: 'it's not rocket science ... it's just being thoughtful about your design'.[41] Adding new fittings to old houses was sometimes done at the resident's expense. When she became minister, Stephanie Key was disturbed to learn that older tenants were paying up to $5 per week extra for security doors and she decided that these should be free, and also provided to tenants who were subject to domestic violence.[42]

As other institutions closed, the Trust became the major public provider of housing to people with disabilities. The first joint venture that catered to the needs of the intellectually disabled was started in 1987. In 1989 the Australian Council for Rehabilitation of People with Disabilities awarded the Trust a Certificate of Merit 'in recognition of outstanding service to people with disabilities in the design and provision of accessible housing'. The most newsworthy project (in 1990) was an allergy-free house on Kangaroo Island built on their own land for a family suffering from 20th Century Allergy Syndrome.[43] In 1999 the Easy Access Display Homes project was launched to raise awareness of new disabled access building ideas. In 2005 the minister opened a home designed for residents with multiple disabilities that was built by Normus Homes.[44]

The Trust also introduced new technologies in engineering, building materials, energy and wastewater management, and land reclamation of contaminated areas.[45] Low density housing was replaced with medium density. These might be more accurately described as medium density suburbs, as the Trust built mixtures of attached and detached dwellings similar to those of private builders, who were constructing larger houses on smaller blocks than in the past.[46]

Constructing the Kings' allergy-free timber house on Kangaroo Island. Opposite: Mrs King in the laundry of her new home.

Tenants spoke of both the benefits and drawbacks of living in dense suburban housing. Patricia Sumerling went from renting a large old villa to a brand new townhouse in the Maylands Tram Barn redevelopment.

> At first I simply wept with disappointment as they were like little dolls' houses after my blousey roomy house in St Peters ... I let my children choose the house they wanted to live in. They chose the one at the end of the cul-de-sac, It had two lovely gardens on its boundary and was away from the main street ... I am grateful for small mercies. I was in no financial position to reject a house that was offered to me in the locality I was living in ... and where I had asked to be. I consider myself exceptionally lucky.
> However, I absolutely hate living in a two storey house. Further, I have a garden far too small for growing vegetables which I used to do in St Peters. I also think the development of the 16 odd two storey townhouses is far too dense. This is made worse as there is no policy about keeping dogs. Consequently, the last 5 years have been very stressful as we suffer a constant noise pollution.[47]

In 1987 the Board discussed the 17th 'design and construct' call for a typical mix of attached housing and pensioner flats in the central metro, and for detached

family homes in the growing town of Murray Bridge. Twenty-seven builders made 102 submissions for 1,005 dwellings, costing $68.68 million. The Board approved proposals for 320 units for nearly $20 million. Emmett's was the largest single project approved. It was for 63 attached houses on an infill site in Brompton and cost just over $6 million. Other successful tenderers included Koussidis (at Murray Bridge), Caj Amadio, Prominent Homes and Devon.[48]

Under the national building code adopted in 1990, the Trust started to install smoke alarms.[49] Courtyard housing was developed for the metropolitan fringe. In central Adelaide, Trust architect Peter Swalling designed communal housing to shelter 13 women 'in a supportive and secure environment'. The three storey building with five bedrooms and a refectory was slotted into a narrow city site. 'Using Housing Production's CAD (Computer Aided Design) system, it was possible to explore a variety of design alternatives in 3-D with the client ... CAD also proved to be a useful tool when negotiating planning approval with Adelaide City Council'.[50] While Sister Anne Gregory was setting up this place as Catherine House, her colleague Sister Janet Mead established the Adelaide Day Centre for Homeless Persons, again with Housing Trust help. In 1993, when the Trust wanted to build on the centre's Moore Street site, Sister Janet said, 'we found this place [in Queen Street] which was Menzel's Plastics, and it was just a great big grey besser block building, only four walls, and so we designed what it was going to be and they built it for us'. She added,

> All these small contracts people [from the Trust] were with us in our work. They brought people from all over Australia to have a look at the Day Centre to see what they were doing, hoping to inspire other people to do the same. They were wonderful people.[51]

Asset management

The double units that had been built in their thousands up until the 1960s, and retained in suburban rental estates long afterwards, presented the Trust with a challenge of a different kind. This was workers' housing, geared to the needs of industry, rather than welfare housing.[52] Placed poorly and designed ineffectively for people with high social needs, double units and timber single units also required costly maintenance and upgrading.

Asset management of the Trust's stock had mixed effects on the design of new dwellings. 'Welfarisation' could have meant that only single bedroom dwellings were designed, catering for single tenants. More small dwellings were built to cater for the large number of one and two person households seeking help. This also meant that the Trust resisted adding expensive improvements such as carpets and air conditioning, although these were common even in private rental homes. But such modest houses did not maintain their value and were harder to sell, so many new Trust homes kept to the standard two or three bedrooms. By 2005 the practice was to build mainly one and two bedroom houses (60%), with 30% three bedroom and the remainder four and five bedrooms for large

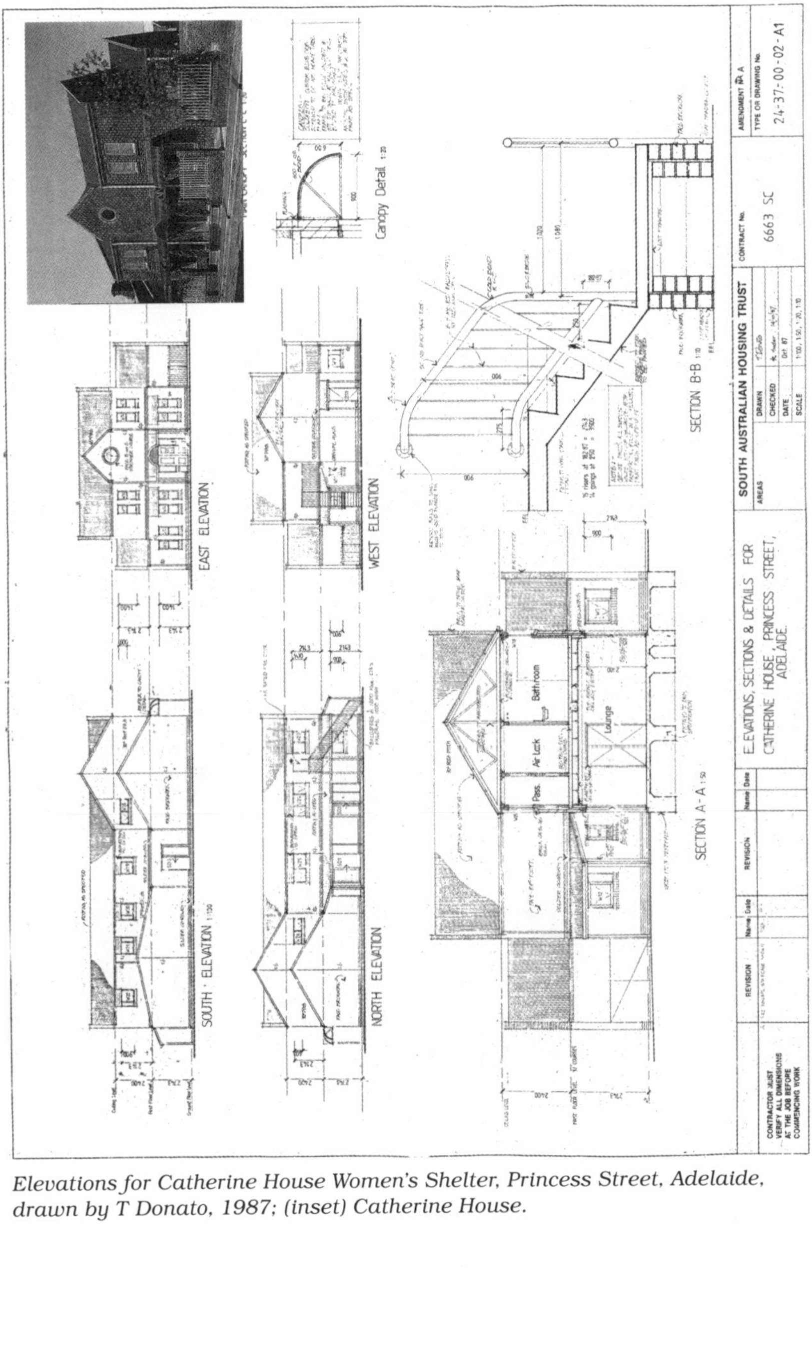

Elevations for Catherine House Women's Shelter, Princess Street, Adelaide, drawn by T Donato, 1987; (inset) Catherine House.

families. Redevelopment and sale of older stock reduced the proportion of flats and attached dwellings and increased the proportion of detached houses.[53]

Tenants began to help manage assets: they gained a greater say in their living environment, but also had greater responsibility. Glenice Bennett, a tenant on and off since 1953, recalled participation beginning in 1983 when she was living at Barwell Flats at Glenside. 'Tenant participation really revved up when resident officers were withdrawn from flats like Barwell. That made maintenance issues more and more difficult'. At her second advisory group meeting, the regional manager suggested that tenants organise maintenance and allocation. 'The whole group said, "No way. All of us have got lives and can't spend it on maintenance of SAHT houses"'. She also wrote in 'Life in a walk up flat' (at Barwell), 'Cleaning the stairs and foyer can be a nightmare or it can be a dream. Who cleans and when and what is clean? Trying to enforce a roster can put you at the edge of a nervous breakdown – in sheer desperation you do the lot yourself. Conciliation rather than confrontation has a better chance of producing positive results'.[54]

Contracts between the Trust and contractors were replaced by three-way contracts that included the tenant group. Tenant representatives had authority to supervise garden work and could quickly sort out problems with contractors. They also began to manage maintenance contracts, starting at Brownlow Flats in Henley Beach in 1990.[55]

In 1996 Jan Connolly presented the results of 'Check It', a pilot survey to help build an asset condition database. Inspecting 60,000 houses would have been costly and slow, and so the Trust decided to tap into tenants' knowledge and train them to collect the information. Connolly pointed out that confrontation between tenant groups and housing authorities often related to the quality of accommodation, and that the Trust had 'made a deliberate attempt to work with our tenants ... in the management of housing'. 'Check It' gave tenants another opportunity to 'have a say about what happens to their homes'. Expectations were exceeded. There was a remarkable response rate of 92%, although many people described the study as overdue. Their accuracy was also excellent (78%), and sufficient to rate the condition of each surveyed dwelling.

The survey confirmed regional variations in maintenance liability. For example, most of the houses in a northern suburb required repainting, but only 13% of Trust houses in one country town. The pilot 'proved that tenants are a highly effective and reliable means of collecting data on the condition of public housing stock', and created a database of great value for strategic planning, helping to 'ensure that we are providing an acceptable, up to date standard of housing for our customers'. The success of 'Check It' persuaded the Board to apply the approach to all housing stock.

Asbestos

The cost of maintaining ageing houses was not only financial. Tenants and contractors faced health hazards which the Trust also had to address. Before the 1980s many homes used materials containing asbestos. As a Housing Trust fact sheet explains, 'Asbestos is a natural material that separates into strong, very fine, flexible fibres, which has strong resistance to heat and chemicals'. Asbestos cement sheeting (fibro) was a cheap and versatile material used in low-cost housing throughout Australia, including Housing Trust homes. Marlene Littlewood, who grew up in a damp asbestos house at Brayville (Parkholme) remembered the doctor writing a letter to the Trust stating that the condition of the house was affecting the children's health, and her family was moved to a new home. Fibro was used for eaves and exterior wall claddings, splashbacks in laundries and wall linings in bathrooms. Asbestos wool was used for insulation. Fibro was described by the Trust as safe if undamaged and left undisturbed. 'However, sawing, sanding, grinding and drilling materials containing asbestos can expose people to asbestos fibres, which can cause health problems if inhaled ... Do not cut, rip or sand materials containing asbestos.'[56]

Exposure to asbestos fibres resulted in Australia having one of the world's highest rates of mesothelioma, a fatal cancer of the lining of the lungs and abdomen caused by inhaling airborne fibres. Between 1987 and 2010 asbestos dust exposure will have caused an estimated 16,000 mesothelioma deaths and 40,000 lung cancer deaths.[57] The Asbestos Victims Association (SA) wrote of a 'never ending ... trauma and anguish that people must go through simply because they were exposed to asbestos at some stage'.[58] Early victims were asbestos miners and milling workers in Western Australia. They were followed in a second wave by builders and tradesmen, susceptible to a disease that lies dormant for years. A third wave were children when their parents or workmen were constructing or renovating family homes. Their deaths contributed to a 25% increase in asbestos related disease between 1997 and 2005. The biggest increase was in South Australia, which overtook Western Australia and had the highest rate of malignant mesothelioma in Australia by the late 1990s. As *The Australian* reported, 'The South Australian cases have been attributed in part to the large number of old housing trust homes built of fibro cement in Adelaide's suburbs, which were then renovated by families in the 1960s, 70s and 80s'.[59]

Independent MP Nick Xenophon told Parliament of a damning report in 2003 into the removal of asbestos from Trust properties. 'Correct disposal methods have not always been adopted ... not enough notice has been given to tenants when asbestos is to be removed, and inappropriate barriers have been erected'.[60] General Manager Malcolm Downie received the 'significant and confidential report ... into all aspects of asbestos management' prepared by McLaughlin and Hodge in 2003–04, and implemented risk management procedures. Since that time Housing SA has managed asbestos in South Australian Housing Trust owned, social housing properties through a Memorandum of Administrative Arrangement (MoAA), with the Department for Transport, Energy and Infrastructure (DTEI) (formerly DAIS) for all sampling, testing and removal of asbestos products, and the coordination of contractors. In 2005 the Department of Administrative and Information Services began to remove asbestos from all government owned non-residential buildings.[61]

Downie believed that with this transfer to a separate authority 'very little criticism ... can sensibly be levelled at the HT and not also be applicable to every privately owned and rented dwelling constructed in the pre-1985 period'.[62] The 'Triennial Review 2005' described asbestos as a major maintenance issue, but not one peculiar to the Trust and that 'the Trust is handling this difficult and significant issue appropriately'.[63]

During 2004–05, for the first time in many years, the Trust acquired more properties than it sold and completed 400 new houses.[64] A new Affordable Housing Innovations Program funded other construction, including $798,000 in 2006 for seven units for the Trust and Anglican Housing Association at Seacombe Gardens, and $765,000 for construction of six units for the Trust and Lutheran Community Housing Support.[65] Church-based community housing associations supplied the majority of land for joint building ventures. Between the mid-1990s and 2007, churches provided land for almost 200 community houses.[66]

The Trust still owned 11,438 double units in 2006, one quarter of its total stock.[67] The necessity of selling properties to fund upgrades or newbuild not only reduced stock, but also prompted reforms that would permanently change the Trust. In June 2006, just before Housing SA was established, the Trust

Historical row cottages in Charles Street, Unley upgraded by the Trust, 1993.

managed 45,454 rental dwellings.[68] For long-term tenants like Fay Rohrlach, the change was 'sad for the many who've known the Housing Trust for a long time, but [acceptable] if it's going to improve the quality of housing in coming years'.

Environmentally sustainable

> There is no question re SAHT [needing to pay] attention to sustainable development eg need for rainwater tanks, solar hot water systems, insulation, facilities to make shading easier, even photo-voltaic cells. Tenants could be asked to contribute towards some of these ... Flats like mine (besser brick) get cold and hot (and retain cold and heat) ... houses/flats need to be adjusted so no need for air-conditioning or rarely. (Mary Cusack, SAHT tenant, history questionnaire, 2007)

The Trust was often an innovative builder and used new construction methods to contain costs. In 1992 test sites were established to test aerated concrete walls, composite panel walling, solar and heat pump centralised hot water services, and polyethylene and aluminium plumbing. The Trust was also an early innovator in what came to be called environmentally sustainable activities.[69] In 1997 a paper proposing further projects to the Board observed:

> Apart from the more overt sustainable development and energy efficiency demonstration projects with which the Trust has been associated, the less visible planning, design and construction initiatives which promote domestic energy efficiency have provided Trust tenants, Trust home purchasers and the State with the potential for very real savings in energy consumption, consequent costs and greenhouse emissions.[70]

Maintenance Manager Shirley Trebilcock affirmed the Trust's environmental leadership. 'We have conducted many pilot studies and research projects ... The only slightly negative slant on this is that because of the limited funding, some of these fantastic initiatives have only been run as "pilots" and not mainstreamed'. Environmentally sustainable insulation, low-flow shower heads and dual-flush toilets became part of normal programs, and all newbuilds had a mandatory five-star energy rating.[71]

Ceiling insulation was installed in cottage flats as early as 1961, solar hot water heaters were trialled in 1965 and common service trenches were introduced in 1969. A more systematic approach began in 1978 with construction moving from strip footings with timber floors to concrete raft slabs (with more thermal mass) and insulation in external walls and ceilings. From the early 1980s, low-flow shower roses were included in all new houses and, from the late 1980s, so were dual-flush toilet cisterns.[72] The stock of older dwellings was more difficult to improve. Paul Burger found his flat at Brooklyn Park 'old but suitable' when he moved there in the 1990s.

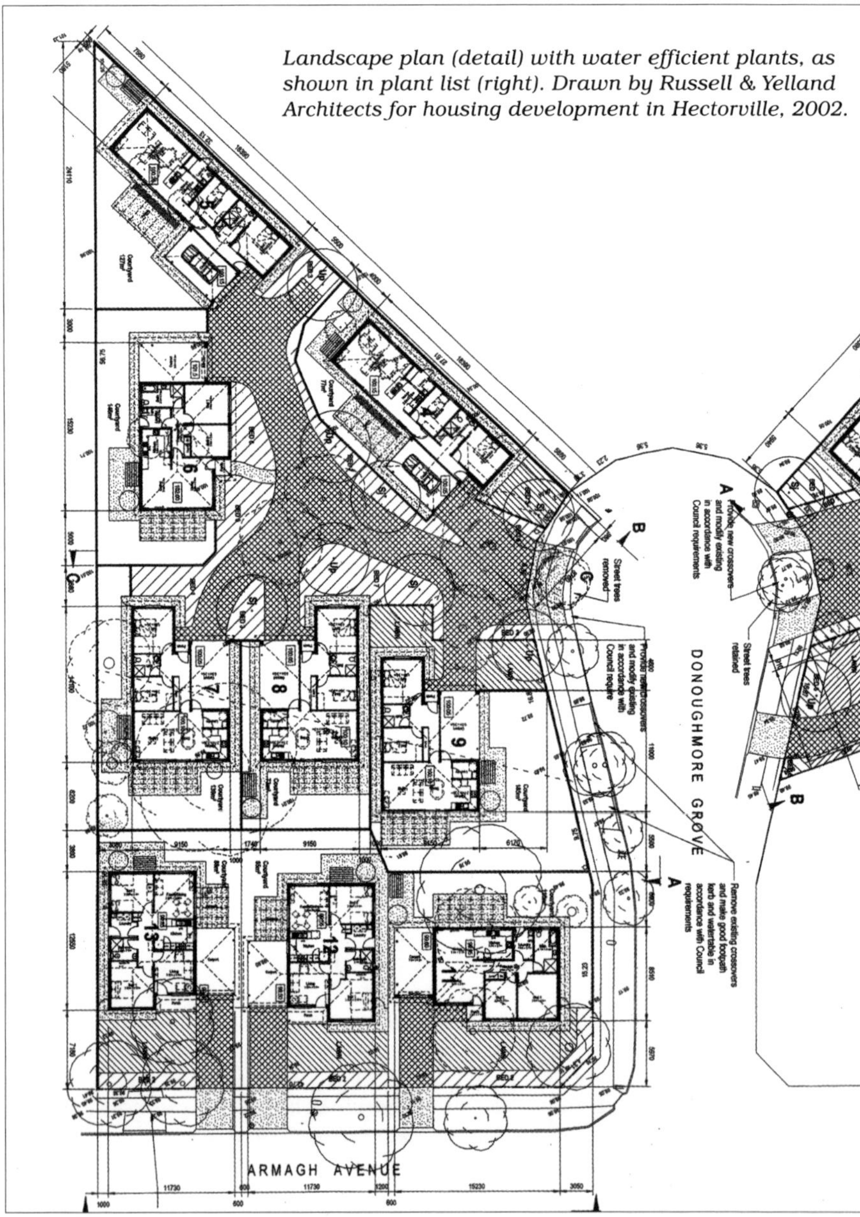

Landscape plan (detail) with water efficient plants, as shown in plant list (right). Drawn by Russell & Yelland Architects for housing development in Hectorville, 2002.

PLANTING SCHEDULE

BED 1	Agapanthus orientalis (mix blue + white) Dianella tasmainica Erigeron karvinskianus Helichrysum bracteatum
BED 2	Agapanthus orientalis (mix blue + white) Clematis montana 'Rubra' Dianella tasmainica Hebe buxifolia Helichrysum bracteatum Pennisetum alopecuroides Pittosporum tenuifolium 'silver sheen' Pittosporum tenuifolium 'sunburst' Sollya heterophylla Trachelopspermum jasminoides
BED 3	Agapanthus orientalis (mix blue + white) Clematis montana 'Rubra' Pittosporum tenuifolium 'silver sheen' Pittosporum tenuifolium 'sunburst' Trachelopspermum jasminoides Erigeron karvinskianum Hebe buxifolia
BED 4	Agapanthus orientalis (mix blue + white) Clematis montana 'Rubra' Dianella tasmainica Erigeron karvinskianus Hebe buxifolia Helichrysum bracteatum Pennisetum alopecuroides Pittosporum tenuifolium 'silver sheen' Trachelopspermum jasminoides
BED 5	Agapanthus orientalis (mix blue + white) Clematis montana 'Rubra' Dianella tasmainica Erigeron karvinskianus Hardenbergia violacea Hebe buxifolia Helichrysum bracteatum Trachelospermum jasminoides
BED 6	Agapanthus orientalis (mix blue + white) Dianella tasmainica Erigeron karvinskianus Helichrysum bracteatum Pennisetum alopecuroides
BED 7	Agapanthus orientalis (mix blue + white) Clematis montana 'Rubra' Dianella tasmainica Erigeron karvinskianus Hardenbergia violacea Hebe buxifolia Helichrysum bracteatum Magnolia soulangena Myoporum parvifolium Pennisetum aopecuroides Trachelopspermum jasminoides
BED 8	Callistemon harkness Callistemon kings park special Callistemon salignus Callistemon hanna ray Erigeron karvinskianus Coprosma x kirkii Myoporum parvifolium Sollya heterophylla
TREES	Up - Ulmus Parvifolium (1.8m, 25mm calliper) Sj - Sophore japonica (1.5m, 20mm calliper)

> Now, ten years on, my impression is that it is environmentally inadequate. The airconditioner doesn't work and … roofing and insulation do nothing to cool or warm the apartment; I went without off-peak electricity until about five years ago; despite huge surface areas on roofs, we have no solar panels … and we have an undue number of power blackouts during summer.

Water usage was another problem. Water conservation is vital in an arid state, a need made greater by global warming. Apart from technical improvements, the Trust acted on an often recommended approach to pass on the cost of water. Tenants in separately metered properties were levied excess water charges for the first time in 1991–92. A brochure advising on energy and water conservation was issued in 1993. Developing a computer system to follow up excess water debt was a big task with 63,000 tenants. Another difficulty was having many dwellings with shared rather than separate water meters. Julie MacDonald, a Housing Trust Tenant's Association member who campaigned for water meters for tenants, was later entered on the South Australian Women's Honour Roll.[73]

Minister Crafter reported that since having to pay for the excess, the amount of water consumed by tenants had almost halved. 'Water is a very expensive commodity … and discipline in its use can in fact bring about very substantial savings'.[74] The work of developmental agencies, including the Trust in collaboration with SA Water, made South Australia a leader in recycled water use. By 2006, 18.1% of metropolitan sewage was recycled, mainly by sewage treatment plants at Bolivar, Glenelg and Christies Beach.[75]

Urban planner Susie Herzberg was a Board member from 1996 to 2006; a crucial decade for promoting sustainable development. She was familiar with government environmental policies and seized 'the opportunity to champion these at Board level'. Projects had to fit the Trust environment and contain costs.

> Part of the challenge was to look at long term costs of building ... maintenance and management. Such life cycle costing meant that the short term higher costs would result in long term savings not only in reduction in water use and in greenhouse gas emissions but also in cheaper living costs for tenants and more sustainable houses in the long term.[76]

Herzberg was alert to the risks of imposing idealised, middle class, environmental solutions on poor, frail or inexperienced householders. Even rainwater tanks posed problems, and the Trust asked the government for extra maintenance funding before installing them en masse, because tasks such as gutter cleaning and downpipe repair were too difficult or too expensive for many tenants. Staff gave much thought to using technology that was low maintenance (for owner and resident) and had low environmental impact.

Herzberg valued Trust employees who were 'passionate about and technically expert in ESD innovations', and said that as a Board, 'we had to create opportunities for such people's ideas to flourish'. She regularly met with staff to discuss these ideas and to reinforce 'the need for support to low income households as a crucial component of any initiative'.[77] She said that Dennis Mitchell was instrumental in many of the partnerships in ESD. Another was Murray Hutchesson, who was awarded a Public Service Medal in 2006 for 'outstanding leadership in environmentally sustainable housing development'.[78] This had produced 'leading edge guidelines that address the impact of urban development on the natural environment, especially in the areas of urban design, energy efficiency, stormwater and waste management'. One initiative (in 2004) was a pilot solar project with Flinders Power in Port Augusta that installed solar hot water systems in 100 houses. 'Evaluation of the project determined that the use of solar hot water systems contributed to significant reductions in energy costs for residents and lowered the production of greenhouse gases'.[79] The Trust was also involved in the Commonwealth government's Solar Cities initiative.[80]

The Trust introduced its 'Energy Policy' in 1981, followed in the early 1990s by a system of four-star ratings in accordance with the National Housing Energy Rating System, as used at Mitchell Park, that also included a voluntary energy rating checklist and information for purchasers. From 2003 the use of recycled materials was specified in contracts, and ESD guidelines were implemented. It was only then, in 2003, that the state's housing code was amended to mandate energy efficiency (insulation) and rainwater tanks with all new houses. The Trust took early steps to require five-star energy management in higher cost projects, extending to all new and maintenance programs in 2005 before this was mandated for the state generally. By 2007 all public housing in South Australia was being built with five-star ratings.[81]

An ambitious series of demonstration homes illustrated technological advances between 1978, when a solar house opened at Seaton, and 2004 when the Solar Air Home went on display at Windsor Gardens. The Trust itself learned from these experiments and applied those lessons in later construction. The solar house was followed by the earth bermed (1982) and reverse brick veneer homes (1987), both at Port Augusta, designed by architect John Keipert; and the Breathe Easy Home in Hillcrest (1986), which demonstrated low allergy design, construction and services. The Southern Right Home Mk2 at Seaford (1993) combined energy efficient design and the Adaptable Housing Standard to reduce indoor allergens. This was probably the first housing built with adaptable features. The Easy Living Home was opened, also at Seaford, the following year.

Private developer, AV Jennings, collaborated in 1993 on the Seaford house and the Intelligent Home at Regent Gardens that demonstrated greywater reuse through reed-bed technology, energy efficient design, geothermal water heating and air conditioning, digital technology and low embodied energy walls – although it was found that the reed bed took up too much space in single backyards. At Whyalla another set of partners – Trust, Council and Energy SA – supported the Whyalla Eco-Renovation Information Centre to advise local residents. This was set up in 2002 in a double unit pair in Hincks Ave, Whyalla Norrie.[82]

Urban development offered opportunities for broader environmental improvements. Demonstration projects included central hot water services in Mary Street, Unley; a hot water solar tray project in Princes Street, Port Adelaide; stormwater detention at Montague Farm; the Walhalla development at Parkholme; and the Wandana project at Gilles Plains.

The largest sustainable project was New Haven Village, which dates from 1992 and was built at North Haven on Lefevre Peninsula, opposite the site proposed for the Multi-Function Polis (later built at Mawson Lakes). Trust employee, Josie Pastore, recalled New Haven as 'the most awesome' project, and was astonished by the massive stormwater tanks sunk beneath the oval. The Trust, in partnership with the Multi-Function Polis (and using some MFP funds), BHP and the City of Port Adelaide Enfield demonstrated on-site sewerage treatment and stormwater retention, reuse of greywater, energy efficient house design, and geothermal water heating and air conditioning. The Solar Sense demonstration home was added in 1998. The water management scheme later became standard in the main MFP development at Mawson Lakes.[83] Josie Pastore and other staff who were involved in New Haven were told that the higher than standard building costs must not be reflected in the selling price of houses. Even so, builders were frustrated by slow sales, pointing to buyer resistance due to the smaller than usual plot sizes and two-storey dwellings.

Urban wastewater disposal was also built into the Trust's largest renewal project

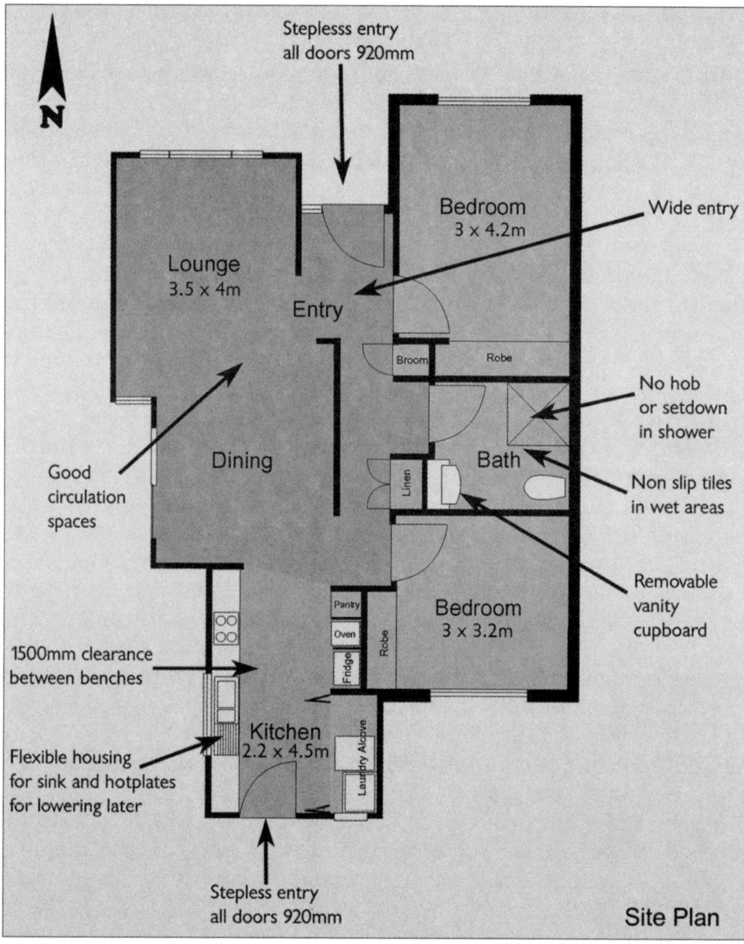

Above and top right: 'Innovative in design, affordable to construct and live in', this demonstration project at 5 Princes Street, Port Adelaide, designed by architect John Barrington, garnered several environmental sustainability awards in 2004. Five energy-efficient houses replaced five concrete block flats, and reflected the character of nearby old pressed metal cottages by using iron cladding and similarly angled roofs. These also maximised exposure to sunlight for solar hot water and photovoltaic cells. Accessible housing features provided 'for people of all ages and levels of mobility'.

Right: earth-bermed house under construction.

PV cells for electricity generation
Rainwater Tank
Sun Shades
North orientation to living area

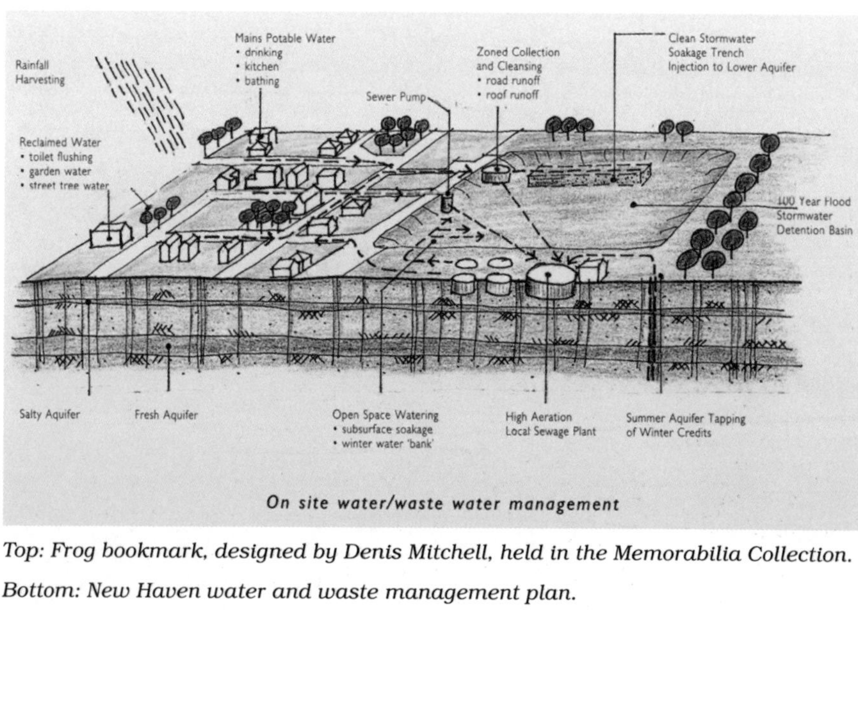

Top: Frog bookmark, designed by Denis Mitchell, held in the Memorabilia Collection.

Bottom: New Haven water and waste management plan.

at The Parks (Westwood), with provision for urban wetlands and large detention basins in new recreation areas, and installation of underground storage tanks connected to a shallow aquifer to reduce stormwater flows into the downstream drainage systems in Seaton and Woodville Gardens.[84]

Not surprisingly, given the Trust's pioneering of sustainable development, some urban renewals also demonstrated an understanding of the value of recycling heritage building materials. The minister announced in 2009 that the Woodville West renewal would reuse grey water, collect rainwater and use solar electricity, and recycle bricks and roof tiles from the existing double units. The old red bricks would be used for paving, fencing and landscaping in a new main street, and the terracotta roof tiles for roofing new dwellings. 'These materials are rich in character and history and will help to provide the new Woodville West with a character of its own, whilst recycling and minimising the energy required to create all new building materials.'[85]

The Trust collaborated with other agencies on energy audits, retrofits and in research. This included a demand management study with ETSA (1997), monitoring ceramic-based paint application at Port Augusta (2004), and working with the University of South Australia to develop a low-cost, roof-integrated, solar heating system (2002).

One tried and true environmental program was the garden competition held every two years, and which attracted up to 1,000 entries from tenants. Greg Black described the competition as 'an excellent way of getting together with family, friends and neighbours to improve the urban environment'. Ellen Greenslade, who loved her large garden at Parafield Gardens wrote, 'Excellent feeling to get prizes in the garden comps and a good neighbourhood award'. There were 450 cash prizes awarded with a maximum of $250 in each region. Regional winners entered state awards for a prize of $1,000. Categories included Best Overall Garden, Best Front Garden and Best Back Garden; Best Children's Garden, Best Vegetable Garden and Best Community Garden were added in 2000.[86] As for its own gardens, in 2004 the Trust used water efficient plants to cut water consumption, reduced the area of common lawns and upgraded irrigation systems. Two large underground tanks were installed at Stow Court, Fullarton, to capture stormwater.

My home is my castle

> My house is great. [I] actually saw it being built so it really felt like mine as I have lived in it since it was new ... 18 years ago. It was called 'special housing'. The type and location close to the city were answered. (D. Smith)[87]

There are thousands of histories of the people who rent homes from the Trust. Fay Rohrlach, who described her home as her castle, is 'very grateful for what I've got'. But her experiences also illustrate the part played by tenants in improving their own environment. Rohrlach, an activist in the Blind Workers Union,

FIRST MILLICENT

Opposite: state winner of the 1986 garden competition, and (above) her double unit home and garden at 3 Edward Street, Millicent.

joined the Trust's Modbury Regional Advisory Board when she moved into her unit in 1995. She brought attention to the difficulties people with poor or declining vision had, reading the cards of visiting housing managers for example, and of the need for promptness in repairs, such as fixing broken locks. 'It's very important that these needs are known.'

South Australia's Ombudsman reported that most complaints against the Trust were over maintenance, and that one-third were resolved in favour of the complainant. Having thousands of tenants, the Trust routinely received around 15% of all complaints against government agencies, the second highest percentage after Correctional Services (usually 40%).[88] One tenant, Joanne Holmes, wrote in the history questionnaire, 'Having to involve the Ombudsman to get the front fence patched up so my kids didn't fall in the lake and drown is outrageous. It was a 2 year fight and the fence is still inadequate'.

In 2003–04, the Ombudsman received 288 complaints against the Trust. One case, 'Alleged failure to adequately follow up complaint about noise generated by neighbours during the Christmas period', reflected the balancing act required in mediating individual and community needs. The complainant stated that every December other tenants in her block decorated their units with lights, spent longer outside at night and had more visitors. She said that the Conditions of

Tenancy required residents not to 'permit any interference with the reasonable peace, comfort or privacy of other tenants', but the Trust told her that Christmas lights were not a breach. The housing manager asked her neighbours, 'to dismantle the Christmas lights by 9.45pm and then to be as quiet as possible'. The Ombudsman acknowledged:

> As South Australia's public housing authority, the Trust attempts to create sustainable communities by promoting tenants' community participation and thus decreasing social isolation. It was appropriate for the Trust to conduct their own investigation ... [to use] the suggested interventions in the Trust's Difficult and Disruptive Tenants Policy ... [and to propose] a negotiated resolution and an endeavour to satisfy all parties to the complaint ... I acknowledged that the complainant did not agree that enough was done by the Trust to satisfy her concerns and ultimately chose to move to another residence to avoid the problem.[89]

Living environments encompass personal relationships as well as physical settings. In 1997 Greg Black arranged a forum on disruptive tenancies for government and community agencies, hoping to develop 'better approaches, policies and directions'.[90] But the problem persisted. Satisfaction with their Trust homes was counterbalanced for many residents by the stress of noisy or aggressive neighbours. Bryan Atkinson wrote that his unit 'satisfies all of my requirements except for the behaviour of disruptive neighbours who are not being asked to remedy their behaviour and who are almost impossible to evict, coupled with drug dealing tenants whose activities are not being dealt with by Housing S.A'. He likened his neighbourhood to The Bronx or the Glasgow Gorbals. His wife, Joy Riley, confirmed that their unit was 'lovely, [but the] location for old people terrible. Mixing old and young does not work'. Betty Alberton found that the Trust would not get involved in neighbourhood conflict. 'Things have changed but it was slow and only through political pressure and tenant participation did this come about'.[91]

A geography of social disadvantage?

> I was born and grew up there, in Elizabeth. Born to publicly-sponsored British migrants ... and taken home to our public housing, in which we lived until my mother's father died and left her a few hundred pounds, which could buy you a three-bedroom house in Elizabeth Downs because the public housing authority was allowed to build houses and sell them to people who had no chance of affording anything private builders could manage to provide. We didn't know it then, but Elizabeth had been placed upon a path into the future that would come to haunt it, as its jobs disappeared and its public housing was turned first into welfare housing and then – in the picturesque language of new prejudices – into 'housing of last resort' for the people no one wanted. I left just before Elizabeth's good times turned into hard times.[92]

Peel's story of *Elizabeth, Good Times, Hard Times*, describes the rise and fall of a workers' city, 'savaged by restructuring and recession'; and the transformation of 'a 1950s "new town" ... into a "welfare suburb"', perceived to be Adelaide's 'northern badlands', populated by jobless men, single mothers, criminals and delinquents.[93]

Elizabeth was the best known example of the Trust's past approach – the construction of large estates – and its social and spatial consequences. The early attempt at a social mix failed when disadvantaged groups were concentrated there. Stretton pointed out that the Trust did build for a mix of classes, and when completed, Elizabeth was 'a fully employed [workers'] town but there were doctors and lawyers there too. Then, bang! Comes about 1980. Ten per cent unemployment. Elizabeth rapidly becomes a terrible, different place'.[94]

Betty Alberton was a Peachey Belt pioneer in the first group of families that settled at Elizabeth West (now Davoren Park) in 1962. Of the eight families that moved into her street at the time, only three remain. There were no older residents and the men all had work, many at General Motors Holden. Since then she has seen employment wax and wane, with streets populated largely by the unemployed.[95] Manufacturing job losses were high, and jobs did not return with the general recovery, due to the restructuring of the Australian economy that accelerated factory closures. Elizabeth continued to suffer from high unemployment that was worsened by the stigma of low status.[96] Betty Alberton said that Elizabeth has a reputation as a place where bad things happened, and is a place easy to stigmatise.

The Trust's development of Elizabeth had long-term consequences, not only because it had the largest concentration of poor rental households in ageing homes, but also because other infrastructure needed fixing. By the 1980s, as Fred Foord recalled, the maintenance section was acting on a major 'unforeseen effect of putting electricity underground. The electrical fields so introduced produced electrolytic corrosion between dissimilar metals, notably between galvanised mains water pipes and copper services to each house'.[97]

Paul Edwards deliberately stood back from involvement in Elizabeth, believing that it was not in its interest to be seen as the Trust town. Many staff 'saw the Housing Trust and Elizabeth as the same thing ... It was best for the Trust to withdraw and it has been beneficial to the community'. Rather than get the Trust to fix things, 'They should feel that the solution is within their own hands'. He dropped dinner meetings with the Council and ended the Trust's administration of the Town Centre, placing this (and Noarlunga Centre) on 99 year leases.[98] The withdrawal came at a time when Trust construction was focused elsewhere, and when it was resumed in Elizabeth, it was redevelopment in partnership with local councils and private firms.

The Trust's 'marked disinclination to build rental estates in traditionally high-status suburbs in the east and south' had reinforced the low socio-economic status of Adelaide's northern and western suburbs.[99] These were the suburbs most affected by national policies to integrate Australia's economy into global markets. In Adelaide, urban restructuring formed 'cones of wealth' and dispersed a 'new urban poverty' to particular suburbs.[100] The financial and social deprivation caused by restructuring in the 1980s was experienced most acutely in outer metropolitan Adelaide where most disadvantaged people lived. Their economic position was further adversely affected by their location – with employment opportunities and public services mostly located in the inner city – and by poor public transport. As Baum and Hassan concluded in 1993, 'the benefits of the redistributive policies of the Labor government are being eroded by the spatial distribution of vulnerable groups in the outer metropolitan areas. There is, therefore, a manifest need to focus on the economic and social consequences of the existing urban form'.[101]

The Commonwealth government became concerned about locational disadvantage in the early 1990s, partly due to the effect of its own economic reforms that included reducing payments to the states and limits on the borrowings those governments could make to compensate. Deputy Prime Minister Brian Howe established the Social Justice Taskforce and the National Housing Strategy to consider spatial inequity, defining locational disadvantage as arising in areas where physical and social infrastructure was deficient, and there was inadequate access to jobs, education and recreation. In 1990 the social justice strategy was directed to urban fringe areas.[102] The Better Cities program supported state efforts to reduce the disadvantages of places such as Elizabeth.

The sale of public housing was intended to introduce diversity to Trust dominated suburbs, but in some areas, most evidently Elizabeth, stock was bought by private landlords who housed similar tenants in the same low-cost houses at market rents. The state's financial rather than social goals had been met, 'with concentrations of low incomes remaining in the same areas'.[103] Tenant representatives at a Regional Advisory Board forum described Elizabeth as going through a distinct change when Trust houses were sold. Betty Alberton observed that many houses in Davoren Park remained empty, while others were 'bought by the package by interstate landlords' who did not look after them. The Trust sold them as they were, and many were already run down. Marlene Littlewood could identify Trust properties by the split downpipes, unlike purchased double units (where these had been replaced by separate downpipes). But because they had been Trust places, most people thought the houses were still occupied by Trust tenants.

A tenant representative, John Strang, said that unsupervised rental attracted antisocial tenants and that unsupervised private tenants 'damage the amenity of the area for everybody. They were part of a different sub-culture – there were lots of hoons'. The Regional Advisory Board drew the regional manager's attention to the impact of the sale of Trust properties for private rental on Elizabeth. As a result the Trust stopped that sales policy.[104] Elizabeth retained both the largest number of Trust rental homes in South Australia (5,253) and the most double units (2,378).[105]

Despite many criticisms, Elizabeth's design was widely appreciated by residents. A typical ABC talkback session on the social problems also garnered praise, one caller describing Elizabeth as a beautiful place to live.[106] The generous tree planting also had long-term adherents. In 1989, when the Trust became a life member of the Trees for Life campaign, local 'Tree Lady' Pauline Frost led a group of tenants to form 'Tenants for Trees'. Trust staff helped by growing 1,000 seedling trees on the balcony of their regional office.[107]

Contrary to public perceptions of Elizabeth, an analysis of social indicators (statistics that assess social conditions) showed that West Adelaide (old metropolitan Adelaide) fared worst in the state in 1976, 1981 and again in 1991. North Adelaide (encompassing Salisbury-Elizabeth) recorded a higher level of wellbeing. Conditions in South Australia improved from 1976 to 1986 then deteriorated, but the same pattern did not occur in all areas. Whyalla and Port Pirie worsened, together with other industrial regions that suffered in the restructuring of manufacturing industry.[108] West Adelaide included the post-war public housing area known as The Parks. A researcher, Simon Neldner, described 'the series of estates (started before Elizabeth and with none of the planned outcomes)' as an area long neglected in terms of community facilities. Local activists brought some improvement, helped by 'receptive ALP governments at State and Federal levels willing to tip the ledger in favour ... of those places left behind'.

> This didn't last, and combined with a rolling recession in places and households reliant on protected industries and unskilled/semi-skilled process work, the fiscal restraint/rationalist philosophy of the 80s and 90s rapidly unravelled the small gains made on the ground. Unemployment – 2% in 1971; 11% in 1981; 30+% in 1991. This was especially so in the recurrent funding of services that made a *difference*. The demise of places like the Parks Community Centre – in terms of its original philosophy – is a classic example of this shift. Then the school gets closed, the redevelopment begins, and you have a completely different social mix – some residents remain, others are moved on ...
>
> In summary, the extent of poverty or deprivation ... has been masked by the 'boom' of the last decade or so, although the crisis in affordability has put the hard squeeze on the rental sector (the poorest having the least options), whilst at the same time public housing has been sold-off in the 000's. A dangerous mix.[109]

Neldner concluded that 'In The Parks, social exclusion and neighbourhood decline have complex geographies, where the intersection of housing and labour markets have both concentrated and deepened the disadvantage of its residents'.[110]

Despite 20 years of refurbishment and renewal by the Trust, Adelaide was described in 2004 as a city 'divided by socio-economic fault-lines and entrenched inequality'.[111] The property boom had made home ownership more elusive, and the stock of affordable rental housing had declined dramatically. A major contributor had been the loss of around 10,000 Trust rental homes.[112] Bernadette Kuhar made similar observations after becoming a tenant in 1994. Her early

Good news story: new tenants celebrate the opening of the Trust's 100,000th rental house at Parafield Gardens, 1986.

impressions of the Trust housing 'nominally marginalized people or low working class', altered as funding decreased with the change of government to Liberal, and never caught up again despite Labor's return. The Trust could now house only 'the most destitute', as evident at Plympton Park. Kuhar asked to move to an area not identified as 'Housing Trust', as she was unwilling to live with 'the very real social disadvantage that comes with living in "Housing Trust"'. After four years she was housed in a southern suburb, a 'non Trust' area. She had insisted on keeping this location preference, despite being 'repeatedly directed into the "traditional" low socio-economic areas eg Broadview, Clearview, Clovelly Park, Mitchell Park, Seacombe Gardens'.

The city's fault lines were illustrated in the census-based *Adelaide 2006: a Social Atlas*. Adelaide, with a population of 1.08 million, experienced a slow growth rate of 3.3% over the period 2001 to 2006, the second lowest in Australia. Slow growth lessened pressure for large tracts of new housing, but the state also had the highest number of single person households, indicating both an ageing population and the rapid formation of young households. Both groups were likely seekers of Trust help and preferred inner-city locations, the main focus of Housing Trust work over that time. Single parents with dependent children made up 11.6% of Adelaide families and lived mainly in the outer northern and southern

Trust dominated suburbs. Twenty years of redevelopment aimed at reducing local concentrations of public tenants had left unemployed people in 2006 still living mainly in the outer northern, north-western and outer southern suburbs.[113]

Country South Australia

> I facilitated the 'Mural Project'. South Australia had been divided into regions and the idea of the Mural Project was that tenants ... would stitch or embroider a square representing their region. Then all the squares would be joined to make a large Mural. It was a very creative exercise ... the South East Square had the Blue Lake and other symbols ... There was a lot of communication and goodwill between tenants throughout the state in creating this art piece. (Helen Ottaway, questionnaire, 24 February 2007)

Despite great changes in the fortunes of towns outside Adelaide, the Trust continued to build and provide other services in the country. Emergency Housing Office services were extended to non-metropolitan areas in 1986, and were fully integrated in the new regional offices in 1991. A plan was approved in 1987 for 86 houses at Ceduna South. Some dwellings were relocated from redevelopments in Adelaide; in 1993 Wallaroo District Council and Northern Yorke Peninsula Council gave their support for relocating Trust houses; and No 47 Lord Howe Avenue, Hillcrest, was trucked to Wallaroo.[114]

> Hillcrest was all lightweight construction, easy to remove. We had regular auctions and got up to $30,000 for them. They put them on a truck and took them away, mainly to rural areas such as Yorke Peninsula – most metro councils wouldn't allow them. (Michael Findlay, 2009)

Phil Miller bought one of the same set of houses from the Trust at auction in 1999 when it was looking to redevelop Hillcrest, Gilles Plains and Windsor Gardens. This group of houses was erected during the post-war labour shortage by a Swedish company contracted to supply kit houses. Miller said that these were made of Baltic Pine with bolt-together trusses for the roofing and modular sections for the walls, which all joined together to a basic plan. There were only two designs, 'one a rectangle and the other an "L" shape but they were also built as mirror images thus 4 different aspects'. Miller's house stood on jarrah stumps dipped in tar and set 'about 1 foot in the ground. My house was constructed in 1952 and in 1999 the stumps were still in perfect condition'. The method of construction was to place the stumps, then the bearers, then floor joists and then the floor. The walls were constructed on the floor then the roof trusses were erected. Sections were numbered so that a supervisor and unskilled labourers could put a house together.

Tenants were given first option to buy the homes and the Trust sold the others at auction, requiring them to be shifted so that the land could be subdivided

House on the move from Hillcrest (in January 1999) to Point Turton where cladding was added.The new holiday house was finally completed in 2004. (Photos Phil Miller)

into smaller blocks to increase density. Miller had to move his house within 30 days from auction date.

> The firm doing most of the moves was at the auction and said to me that they had done about 300 moves of these homes before mine. Cost at auction was $4200 and it cost a further $8500 or thereabouts to have the house transported to Pt Turton and resettled on concrete block pillars. The house had to be cut in two to move. (The front bedroom was cut off and rejoined on site.) The external walls were vertical Baltic pine in a shiplap pattern with sash windows all round. Because of the roof being trusses the internal walls were not load bearing and modification to the internal structure could be done with ease.
>
> Since getting the house to Pt Turton I have reclad the outside (over the existing timber) with Hardie plank (a fibre cement sheet), taken out the wall between the kitchen and the living area, rebuilt the bathroom from the ground up and replaced all the windows with aluminium except for the living area where I took the whole wall out and replaced it with glass and a pair of French doors.

The total cost of Miller's new holiday home on Yorke Peninsula – purchase, moving, installation, connection to services, refurbishment, a front deck and new windows – was around $23,000. He noted that ex-Housing Trust homes in the north-eastern suburbs are now about $300,000 to buy, about the same value as his place at Pt Turton.[115]

There were more problems with maintenance in the country than in the city. A Port Augusta tenant told researchers in 1986 that 'They've virtually rebuilt my home 4 times in the 30 years I've lived there'. There were still asbestos and timber houses in the town, and others built of 'second rate' bricks. Willsden tenants 'could watch what was going on in the streets, without looking out the windows!' Many agreed on the poor quality of construction, even of modern homes, because of the use of inexperienced contractors. The problem, they said, was worsened by bad maintenance and the Trust's failure to inspect the work done by subcontractors.[116]

The run down in country housing stock was proportionately greater than in Adelaide.[117] In the decade after 1991, stock was reduced by more than one-third (36%) in the country, compared to 17.1% in the city. The rapid reduction in rental stock in South Australia was less visible than it might have been because 45% of the reduction (to 2001) was in towns outside Adelaide.[118] The reason for the country run down was simple: there was much less demand. In 1991, 28% of the Trust's rental homes were in rural areas, falling to 23% (10,292 houses) by 2001. Further reduction was planned, as most rental stock was in regional towns whose population was falling, notably the Iron Triangle's Whyalla, Port Augusta and Port Pirie. Collectively, in 2001 those three towns held 4,513 dwellings, nearly half of the country stock. The Trust's management of this stock had

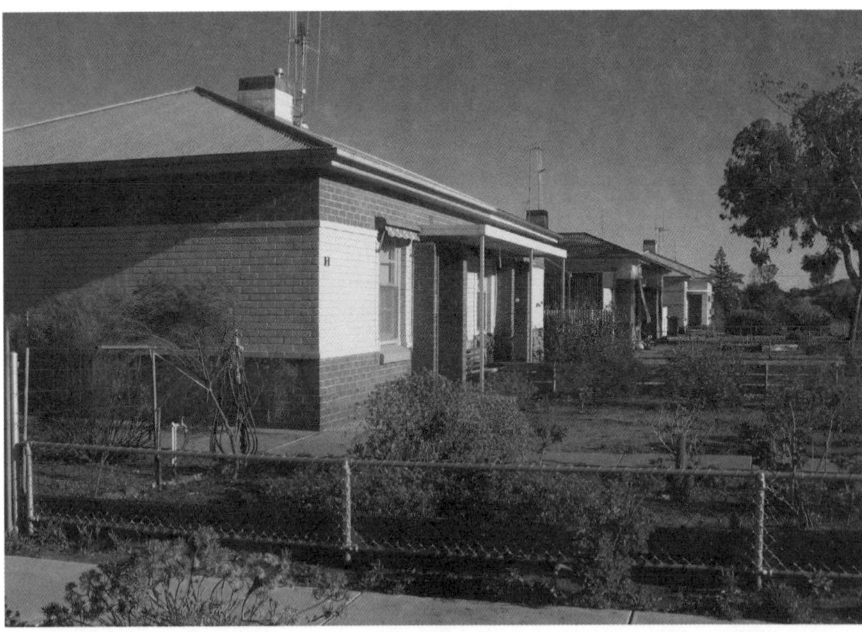

Top: double units in Weigall Street, Murray Bridge – constructed of local limestone and newly refurbished, 1987.

Above: 1940s double units in Syme Street, Whyalla, in 2005.

repercussions for whole towns because it owned so many of their houses: for example, around 40% of the total in Port Augusta.[119]

Whyalla

Looking back over Whyalla's history, Sue Scheiffers recalled the population climbing past 30,000 in the 1970s. 'The Housing Trust was struggling to build houses quickly enough. Schools were opened as quickly as they and the surrounding batch of houses could be completed and occupied.'[120] Speed and cost containment were of the essence. The old town centre, ignored by Trust planners, was left behind by new development around Whyalla Norrie. She continued, 'the change that was to have the hugest impact on Whyalla and virtually stopped development in its tracks ... was the closure of the shipyard in 1978'. Growth stalled 'and there was a rise in unemployment in a place where virtually everybody had a job in the steelworks, the shipyards or the town'.[121] In 2000 BHP sold the steelworks to OneSteel, which took on workers to supply sleepers for the transcontinental railway to Darwin (opened in 2004). Despite strenuous efforts to attract other employers, Whyalla's population fell by nearly one third from 33,000 in 1976, to 23,620 by 1996, levelling out at around 21,000 from 2001.[122]

The Trust owned 3,335 homes in Whyalla, a considerable 6.5% of its South Australian total, and the vacancy rate (as a percentage of all dwellings) was an extraordinary 35%.[123] Even in 1969, when Ronald Harding and his family first applied for Trust rental at Whyalla, they had to wait only two months. 'When [we] returned from Darwin [in] 1999 again applied and had to wait only 6 weeks'. Vacant homes were costly. In 2002 an arson attack on a vacant house in Choat Street, Whyalla Norrie, caused $10,000 damage.[124] The Board was told in 2005 that sales in Whyalla were 'mostly to small investors purchasing 3 or 4 houses', and that its task force was working closely with the council on houses to be sold.[125] The selection of houses for sale was based on a strategy to reduce housing in strata titled complexes.

Whyalla was eclipsed by Mount Gambier in 2001 as the state's second largest city.[126] The switch illustrated the decline of 'employment disadvantaged cities', wide variations in the adjustment of regional towns to global economic change, and their divergent housing problems. Whyalla, Port Pirie and Port Augusta were among the places worst affected by Australia abandoning protectionism and the consequent decline of manufacturing, sharing with other industrial towns above average unemployment and households suffering rental financial stress. Signs of revival in the Iron Triangle towns was evident after 2001, due (once again) to a mining boom, but by then the Riverland towns along the River Murray were reeling from the effects of a prolonged drought, and community representatives warned that the need for affordable rental and crisis housing was far outstripping supply.[127]

South East

Towns such as Mount Gambier and Port Lincoln benefited from the development of more diversified economies, including service industries and new forms of agriculture (aquaculture at Port Lincoln). They had below average unemployment, despite having more low income than high income residents.[128] Rapid growth also brought new housing demand. The regional manager told the Board in 1995 that the Trust's 'largest commitment' in the South East was at Mt Gambier (1,631 rental units), and that 'many customers ... are Victorian residents seeking work or housing'.[129] The General Manager reported housing shortages in 2002 in the South East and Port Lincoln due to economic booms.[130] A fatal bushfire on Eyre Peninsula on 11 January 2005 also destroyed 93 homes and Port Lincoln Caravan Park, worsening the town's already severe housing shortage.[131]

Redevelopment and sales strategies used to reduce metropolitan concentrations of Trust housing were harder to effect in country areas due to high vacancy rates, the age and type of the houses, low land values and a lack of interest shown by private developers. The South East 'enjoyed one of the highest profiles in the sale of existing rental stock throughout the State'.[132] Not so the Iron Triangle. In Whyalla, the sale of 600 half double units to private owners also limited opportunities for area renewal unless the Trust repurchased many of the properties.[133]

Regional urban renewal

Despite these problems, the Trust did not limit urban renewal to Adelaide. The Willsden redevelopment at Port Augusta was underway by 1993, and involved 99 dwellings at a cost of $1.3 million. Work began in 1997 on areas renamed Lincoln Gardens in Port Lincoln and Risdon Grove in Port Pirie. The redevelopment of Lincoln South was a joint project between the Trust and the Council with HomeStart finance and $2,000 cashback offers providing 'an excellent opportunity for Housing Trust tenants, first home buyers, retirees and investors'. House exteriors, gardens and Dickens Park were upgraded, but purchasers could refurbish the interior as they could afford it.[134]

Risdon Grove Urban Improvement Project aimed to 'regenerate the physical, social and economic environment' and finished in 2007. Double units were upgraded to sell and to keep as improved public housing. Port Pirie's strengthening residential market 'contributed to a healthy sales program providing a good return on the Government's investment in improving the area'. The council paid for footpaths and trees. 'The project area has been further enhanced with an artwork project by local schools and indigenous groups'.[135]

Regeneration also involved social development. Four sets of double units were provided to the BoysTown youth employment and training program in Port Pirie, and although Sandra Chapple's effort to set up a community centre had been frustrated (see Chapter 1), Port Pirie Community Centre did open in 2003 in a renovated double unit at 28 Symonds Street, Risdon Grove. Volunteers established a nutrition program, a food co-op and a toy library, and planted a community garden. 'While establishing the centre, community members thought about what

ART for everybody

PORT LINCOLN Lincoln Gardens Urban Improvement Project

Public and Community Art

Bush theme brings community to life

Visitors to Lincoln Gardens can have no doubt about where they are when they approach the suburb's entry wall on the corner of Shephard's Avenue.

The wall is a community art initiative that involved the whole community, from its concept and throughout its development.

Artist and cultural planning consultant Malcolm McKinnon consulted with the local community and took into account the area's cultural and historical features when developing the concept.

The entrance to Mortlock Street features a community-designed artwork with a nautical theme, in line with the area's location. The entrance-side of the wall is painted a vibrant yellow with metal sculptures of ocean-going birds and tall ships. The inside of the wall is painted with a colourful mural showing native animals and plants, against a seaside background.

Just around the corner the fence of the Lincoln Gardens Primary School features ten metal animal sculptures of land and marine creatures which were designed and painted by the students. The students worked with Malcolm to develop the artworks, which are full of fun and whimsy with an echo of indigenous art.

The project was sponsored by the South Australian Housing Trust, SA Country Arts and the City of Port Lincoln.

Artists: *Malcolm McKinnon & Youth of the Lincoln Gardens Primary School*

Government of South Australia

SOUTH AUSTRALIAN HOUSING TRUST

Community artwork at Port Lincoln redevelopment, Lincoln Gardens.

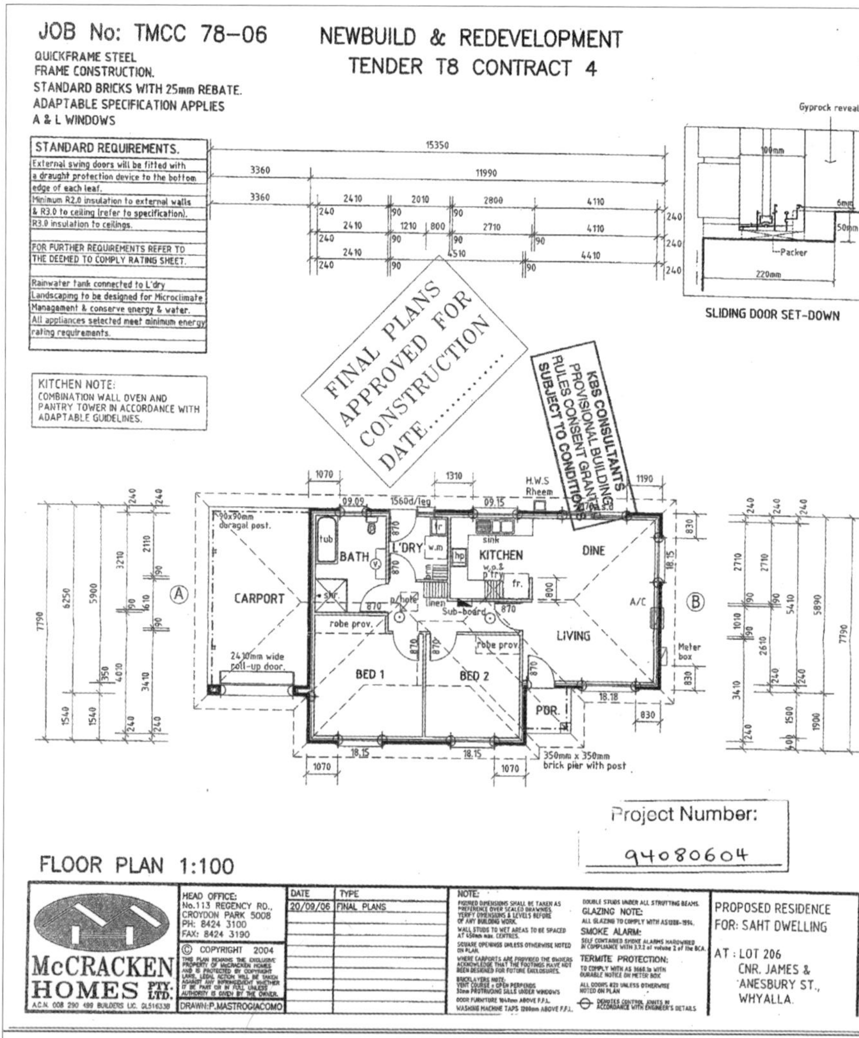

McCracken Homes plan for a house on the corner of James and Anesbury Streets, Whyalla, 2006.

sort of place it should be. They came up with the following statement: "A safe and caring place of welcome where people can gather, share and learn, to increase wellbeing within the community"'.[136] The Neighbourhood Development Officer gave further support to the Centre.

Myall Place, the demonstration project at Whyalla Norrie, was the first new Trust housing built in the town for 15 years. Myall Place Urban Improvement, a joint initiative with the City of Whyalla, was one of the Trust's most admired renewals. New houses were sold and the proceeds reinvested in building. In 2004 construction began on 10 energy efficient homes, a reserve, and street upgrades. In 2005 a retirement village was built on land sold to Village Life and double units attached to privately owned halves were modestly upgraded to improve their street presentation. In the same year Myall Place Project gained a Civic Trust award and the Urban Development Institute of Australia's Commendation Award for Regional Development.[137] Sales and renewal reduced the Trust's rental stock in Whyalla to 2,396 by 2006, but this remained the second-largest grouping with 1,926 double units in the state.[138]

Country work

The Trust's historical role of support for the industrial economy remained an important element of country work. Fostering regional development was highlighted by the Board in 1999, and the Whyalla task force prepared a situational analysis that included housing supply and demand, Trust programs, employment and economic development, population projections and industry attractions.[139] The Trust also sought economic partnerships, and considered supporting the magnesium plant in Port Pirie and the pig-iron plant in Whyalla.[140] The 2005–06 Annual Report described the 'Private Workforce Accommodation' planned for Whyalla. In 2005 the engineering company Thiess Pty Ltd was awarded the OneSteel Project Magnet contract to upgrade the steelworks. 'This project requires a large increase in skilled workers into Whyalla and has far reaching benefits for the economy'. The Trust was asked to supply worker housing and signed a lease agreement with Thiess in 2006. 'One hundred houses are likely to provide accommodation for up to 300 employees. Other workforce accommodation initiatives continue to be explored with OneSteel in Whyalla.'[141]

There was a very different form of economic stimulus to both Whyalla and Port Augusta when the Commonwealth government operated the Baxter Detention Centre which was located between the two towns. When the controversial centre for asylum seekers was closed in 2007, Housing SA negotiated with the Immigration Department to acquire a site in Ellis Close at Port Augusta where eight transportable units had housed women and children detainees from Baxter.[142]

Fringe development

The Trust's new fringe developments were anticipated by the prior purchase of rural land (land banking) for the mass construction that had once helped restrain house costs, but the new projects were very different from those of the

Vegemite the cat surveys the yard at Elizabeth Ostermann's new Trust home at 13 Alexander Drive, Mount Barker, 1988. (Photo Elizabeth Ostermann)

past. No longer the state's sole mass developer, the Trust worked in partnership with other agencies, councils and private consortia, and ceased to be a major developer in its own right. New rental homes were similar in design to houses for sale and were dispersed rather than concentrated in estates. Stretton, who retired as Deputy Chairman in 1989, said that he 'wanted of course to make public housing as mixed in and as indistinguishable from the others as you could'.[143]

The design and construct scheme and Jubilee 150 joint ventures were precursors to these more complex partnerships. Eight design and construct homes were built in 1985 in a Mount Barker Council subdivision in the middle of a flood plain. Two years later they were badly damaged by floods. Trust staff did 'everything they could to help the tenants, down to cleaning the houses and replacing children's pets', but as the minister told the press, the Trust would also seek compensation from the council.[144]

Elizabeth Ostermann, who moved in 1987 into a 'brand new' house in Alexander Drive at Mount Barker, told a story that would be familiar to earlier Trust pioneers in fringe areas.

> I'd already noticed the wide streets, old houses and huge farm land of the small country town but Alexander Drive was a newly created street for new housing and all the front yards were dusty and bare. There were very few trees left after the construction and it all looked very barren and in December was extremely hot …
>
> Over the years I did come to appreciate living in a rural boom town and the house in which I lived. I love the large rainwater tank with a tap into the laundry. I like the double sink in the kitchen and the colour scheme in the house was quite pretty. Eighteen years later the huge backyard has been transformed from weeds to an attractive, shady environment. I have converted dust into garden beds, made paths and arches, grown trees and shrubs, vegetables, flowers and fruit trees.

Golden Grove

The new approach to fringe development also reflected a more entrepreneurial role taken by state government in joint ventures with private enterprise.[145] Most allotment purchases for the Trust's reduced newbuild program were made at discounted prices from the major government joint ventures at Golden Grove, Seaford and Northfield.[146]

The precedent for large-scale development by special agreement (indenture) between government and private developers had been established in the 1970s at West Lakes and North Haven. Golden Grove, one of the largest new fringe developments, on 1,230 hectares north-east of Adelaide, was of a similar kind, but gave more generous terms to the private developer. The Trust was placed in a subordinate role, and rental homes were dispersed rather than clustered, as at West Lakes. The South Australian Land Commission bought rural land at Golden Grove in the early 1970s. A decade later the South Australian Urban Land Trust (SAULT) began to develop the area with Delfin Property Group Limited, the company responsible for West Lakes. It has since been taken over by the ANZ Banking Group. Delfin moved its site operations office from West Lakes to Golden Grove in 1985.[147]

The Housing Trust's General Manager, Paul Edwards, was on the SAULT Board during the venture negotiations, but voiced the Housing Trust's view that the public interest was not being adequately protected.[148] In an interview for *Business, charity and sentiment* in 1984, Edwards also criticised the negotiation process.

> The members of the Urban Land Trust Board although responsible for Golden Grove were not consulted on issues of principle before commitments were made in negotiations; they were not kept fully informed … and did not see

> key documents until it was too late for members to exercise any influence over the terms and conditions ...
>
> In this respect I believe the Urban Land Trust was a disgrace to public administration and the processes it followed were very very wrong. Nothing like that could possibly happen under the arrangements between Board and Management in the Housing Trust.[149]

Edwards disassociated himself by resigning from SAULT on 31 October 1984, the day after the joint venture was made public. The Golden Grove Indenture of 1984 did require the venturers to confer with the Trust on planning, development and pricing, but land prices rose higher than expected, disadvantaging both Housing Trust and low income buyers. Before submitting a subdivision plan, the developers had to determine public housing requirements; offer land at fair market value, and 'enable the SAHT to secure for its own purposes between twenty-five (25) and thirty (30) per cent of the total dwelling units'. All construction had to comply with Golden Grove's 'Paramount Objectives' and standard requirements.[150]

Ten thousand houses were planned to be built over 15 years for 30,000 residents in the new suburbs of Wynn Vale, Golden Grove and Greenwith. The Trust supplied 25–30% of them, scattered through the development area and of a variety of designs; an approach followed later at Seaford.[151] Shirley Trebilcock recalled that 'the developers had to declare to the buying public which allotments had been sold to the Housing Trust, so they could choose whether they wanted to live next door to Housing Trust rental properties'.[152]

As a pilot scheme, tenants participated for the first time in the location and design of their homes and occupied them from 1986. Adelaide's new O–Bahn guided busway operated from the same year using, in part, land bought originally by the Trust for such a purpose. In a typical transaction, the Board approved purchase of 33 lots from Delfin in 1987 at an average cost of $24,933.[153] Golden Grove's last allotment was sold in 2002, and the Trust's final contract was awarded in 2003 for seven homes at a cost of $690,519.[154]

Kenny's book, *State of denial*, describes Golden Grove as one of two major developments in the Bannon government's first term – the other was the Adelaide Station and Environs Redevelopment (ASER) project. Both projects involved private development of publicly owned land as well as other public support – in Kenny's view on over-generous terms. Golden Grove was praised for its design standards, but depended heavily on publicly funded infrastructure: the expensive O-Bahn. The terms of the partnership were 'most favourable – allowing a private company to make huge profits from public lands'.[155]

Badcock went further, describing the indenture terms as 'a grave miscalculation' by the government. SAULT was right to split the planning gain with Delfin but 'should never have handed over the land', as the Trust then had to pay prevailing prices for each home site it bought back. 'In effect the Housing Trust is helping to underwrite the profits of a partner agency, not to mention the private developer.'

On the other hand, the extent of the government's original land purchases at Golden Grove, Seaford and Northfield enabled joint venture partners to comprehensively plan whole suburbs and sell them in an orderly fashion, passing on 'real savings ... to home buyers and government departments requiring sites'. Government reserves of land in the northern and southern growth corridors also allowed the government to pursue its metropolitan staging plan.[156]

Seaford

> Seaford is the second major joint venture between Government and the private sector ... South Australia leads the nation in devising arrangements which result in much better all round communities. (Premier John Bannon, 1990)[157]

In 1987 a public–private joint development of Trust and SAULT land was proposed at Seaford, on the southernmost edge of suburbia. There was some backing and filling by the Board, which approved and then decided against selling Moana and Seaford land to SAULT.[158] As joint landholders, both agencies initiated the 728 hectare development, which was approved by Cabinet in 1989 as the Seaford Rise Joint Venture. Kinsmen/Jennings was chosen as the private partner. The Trust's Mark Henesy-Smith joined the management committee.[159] Premier Bannon and Noarlunga Mayor Ray Gilbert announced the ten-year project in June 1990. The agreement included financial arrangements that provided 'a satisfactory return at minimum financial risk to the Government land owners'.[160] However, only 5% to 15% of total dwellings were intended to be Housing Trust homes, much less than the 30% at Golden Grove.[161]

'Clever planning provided the urban framework which would facilitate growth, and a unique administrative structure provided the flexibility which allowed the Joint Venture to respond to changing conditions.'[162] Situated on a famously beautiful coastal site dotted with small villages, care was also taken to integrate the development with built-up areas west of Commercial Road, for a linear park linking the Onkaparinga Estuary with Pedlar Creek, and for 'strong thematic planting to create major landscaped boulevards defining and traversing the area and provide associated references to the coast'.[163]

The master plan designated 470 hectares as residential (close to 80% of useable land) for an eventual population of 20,500 'living in about 7,000 dwellings of which almost half will ultimately be other than conventional dwelling allotments'. Their variety would cater for families and single people and for a range of incomes. Public housing (15%) was similarly varied and, in the words of Noarlunga Council, was 'spread throughout the development in a "pepper and salt" fashion', and looked like other homes, 'thus destroying the belief held by many that public housing is visually unappealing'.[164] This was done by using uniform building materials and encouraging private builders to present their own plans to the Trust. A main street shopping area and schools were planned by the developers, as was a network of paths, roads and public transport routes.

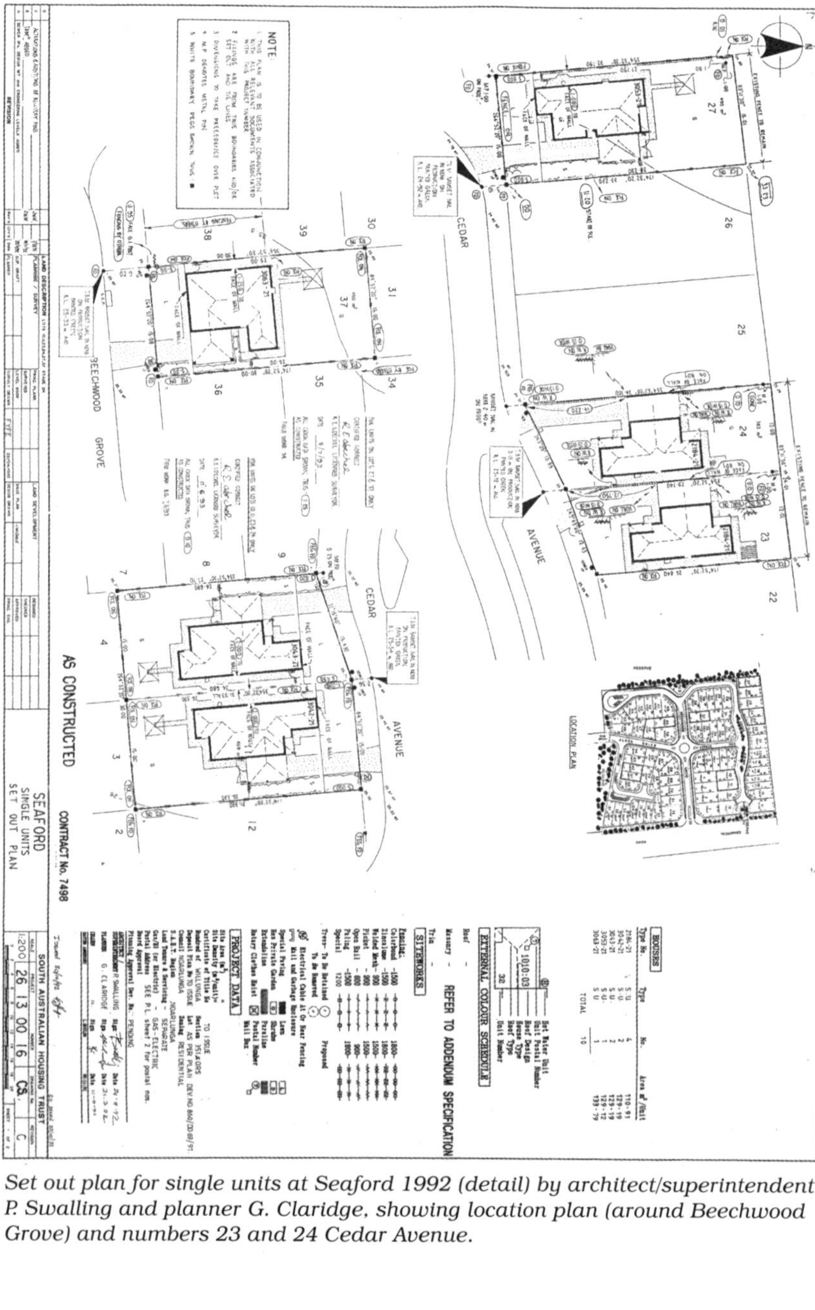

Set out plan for single units at Seaford 1992 (detail) by architect/superintendent P. Swalling and planner G. Claridge, showing location plan (around Beechwood Grove) and numbers 23 and 24 Cedar Avenue.

Jack Holder at Seaford. (Photo Susan Marsden)

By the end of 1990 a display village had opened and the first blocks were sold at Seaford Rise. By 1997 1,300 families had moved into their homes.[105]

Jack Holder, who had moved to Seaford in the 1970s and was a Noarlunga councillor, remembered having

> no say ... whatsoever in the Seaford design: it was simply 'put to council and passed. You really didn't know until it was going the problems that were attached to it ... A lot of the blocks are just so small, and there are little cul-de-sacs [sic] with no parking at all. If you have visitors there's nowhere to park.

Holder was appointed to the Seaford Trust Fund, formed to administer funds raised by the development (as done at Golden Grove) and anticipated to reach $10 million. 'A levy was put on every block sold to be spent in Seaford area, but they sold the blocks so slowly it didn't finish up $10 million ... It wasn't going as quickly as expected. But these things take time, and Holder observed 'building like mad there now, within no time at all there's a hundred houses there, and they're hundreds of thousands of dollars ... they're not cheap houses like they used to be'. In the late 1980s and early 1990s houses sold for $90,000 to $150,000: 'you'd pay that for a block of land now'. By 2008 he described the development as 'full up ... and they're moving so quickly to the north with new ... and huge homes, they're building along Seaford Road, two-storey homes all along the front ... Yes it's a success now because it's moving quickly, and obviously they're selling'.[166]

Blending public with private housing was not completely successful. Holder said that:

> at least every fourth house was supposed to be a Trust house, that was to not make ghettos of Trust people or Trust homes ...
> But you drive down the street now and you can see grass and rubbish in the front yard about half a metre high, and you can bet that that's a Trust home. I think that people can get the rent cheap, they don't care, and usually these people are on the dole, they've got nothing else to do but look after the place. Not everyone's the same, but unfortunately some are like it and they give everybody else a bad name.

The 'pepper and salt' approach was not universally approved of even at the time. Social mix assumed that people would socialise because they were neighbours, but Sarkissian cited studies showing that people from different classes were unlikely to socialise, advising that interaction was less important than 'protecting vulnerable residents from inappropriate behaviour by neighbours' and recommending instead clusters of 15–40 public rental dwellings.[167] The same message was delivered by Housing Trust tenants themselves, as a regional manager John Girardi later recalled. Golden Grove may have been lauded as 'the best suburb in the world', but the practice of marking on each new set of plans where the 25% share of allotments had been bought by the Trust meant that private purchasers bought blocks 'in most cases ... as far away as possible from those owned by the Housing Trust'. So, while the quality of the new public dwellings 'matched perfectly' those built privately, there was a general lack of community acceptance of Trust tenants.

> Requests began to be received from tenants, who had transferred from older double unit housing in areas such as Elizabeth into the best suburb in the world, to be transferred back to their modest housing within their original suburb, where experiences of community had been far more positive.[168]

But the Trust's fringe development was by then winding down. Expenditure on land purchase in 1989–90 was only $8 million, less than half that of two years previously. Further contribution was made to social facilities when the Trust built an aquatic centre at Noarlunga Centre in 1989 and contributed to the Southern Sports Complex that was opened in 1993.[169] The Trust's major role as town centre landlord was also coming to an end. Elizabeth City Centre was sold in 1995 as part of the government's asset realisation program, followed by Noarlunga Regional Centre, which was sold for over $28 million in 1997. In the same year the first stage of the publicly funded Southern Expressway was completed, shortening travel time between Adelaide and Noarlunga.

Northfield

> Regent Gardens is the first stage of Australia's largest urban consolidation program and has set a high standard ... [The project has received] many awards from professional organisations ... [In 1997 when residents were surveyed] the results showed a high level of satisfaction with the area. This result, more than any other award, is testament that Regent Gardens has been an outstanding success.[170]

Northfield, just 8.5 kilometres north of the city, broke new ground by encompassing both fringe land and redevelopment. The Trust had a 40% interest in a business undertaking with SAULT in land held for future development, and with SAULT, Residential Developments Australia Ltd and Co-operative Financial Services Ltd the Trust formed the Northfield Joint Venture consortium. Working with the City of Enfield, they aimed to promote a compact form to foster urban consolidation; develop a range of lot sizes and house styles; employ environmental management and energy conservation; develop a positive community image; use new development as a catalyst for renewing a disadvantaged area; and integrate adjacent communities.[171] As a business undertaking, the Board counted the project a success: it generated $54.93 million in sales and incurred $50.89 million in costs, including $19.72 million paid for the new land and $0.85 million contributed to the Hillcrest Community Trust Fund.[172]

Regent Gardens, a new section on 77 hectares, was started in 1992 at Fosters Road and Folland Avenue, and was directed by AV Jennings Project Management Services. Two objectives were quickly realised, with small lot sizes (mainly 300 square metres) and signs of an emerging community identity, such as a free newspaper, *Eye of the community*. More than 2,000 people attended carols by candlelight in 1996.[173]

By 1997 there were 1,350 dwellings, with one-fifth of them Trust homes – an outcome the Board considered 'disappointing', acknowledging 'the low (115) allotments acquisition level'. Parks, playgrounds and reserves were created, as well as a neighbourhood centre with a café deli. Landscaped and colour coordinated, Regent Gardens was pleasing to the eye and addressed environmental issues by retaining and treating stormwater on site.

Northfield Project included the Hillcrest Urban Improvement Area, where renewal of the adjacent public housing suburb began in 1993.[174] Northfield Project was unique in developing a new area, renewing and improving two others, and attempting to integrate all three.[175]

In 1990 Adelaide was recommended as the site for an international Multi-Function Polis (MFP) and Trust land at Osborne, adjacent to the MFP site, was used for a national housing and urban design competition to demonstrate MFP objectives. Planned in 1992, site works commenced in 1994 on New Haven, the MFP demonstration village in conjunction with MFP Australia, Port Adelaide City Council, Green Street[176] and private builders (see also New Haven, below).

Another development, Montague Farm, was started in 1992 in conjunction with the Housing Industry Association.

Metro: consolidation

The Trust's post-war building program hugely influenced metropolitan Adelaide, as did subsequent infill and the redevelopment of old estates. As state planning policy changed from extending suburbia to urban consolidation, the Trust became the most active infill developer of surplus industrial and government land. By 1986 it had already completed 36 medium density infill projects worth $51 million.[177] The Board purchased sites scattered across central metropolitan Adelaide. In 1987, for example, it considered purchasing State Transport Authority land at Goodwood, Largs North and Henley Beach, and approved an offer of $2.65 million for the site of the Enfield Receiving Home. This would accommodate 166 units, a mix of flats, and other medium density housing and single units. Negotiations were also opened with the owners of the Stock Paddocks at The Levels.[178] There were several purchases of closed state schools, including Goodwood High School in 1993 and, in 1995, $1.1 million was offered for the site of the Holden Hill primary and junior primary schools that occupied 3.78 hectares.[179] The subsequent Westridge Estate offered 80 allotments, 60% planned for sale in 1998.[180]

By the early 21st century, consolidation was moving to what were once outer suburbs. By then, owning only a few remaining Noarlunga sites, the Trust repurchased land at Christie Downs to construct denser living close to the Noarlunga Regional Centre and transport interchange. Purchase of the Christies Beach High School ovals allowed construction of a technical school and an aged-care facility on Beach Road, with other residential development behind them. Eighty per cent of the new houses would be sold to fund the development, while Commonwealth funding and Anglicare would supply the aged-care beds and independent living units.[181]

The Trust also contributed to early inner-city demonstration projects such as Green Street and Burley Griffin Estate in Brompton, where the sale of blocks around the heritage-listed, Walter Burley Griffin designed incinerator began in mid-1993. Also in 1993, Governor Dame Roma Mitchell opened Pennington Gardens in a new suburb built on the site of the Pennington Migrant Hostel. It was dedicated to the immigrants who had lived there. As many as 100,000 people had passed through the hostel between 1946 and its closure in 1985. Trees were planted to represent 11 countries of origin and included oaks, yews and cedars. Cast bronze diaries with statements by migrants were housed in a pergola that resembled the hostel's old Nissen huts.[182]

Soil contamination

Artworks, restored buildings and gardens were positive markers of land use history, but there were also damaging manifestations, when as in the words of an ABC broadcast, 'The past comes back to poison us'.[183]

> At first glance it seems like a great idea to recycle industrial sites, even rubbish dumps, and turn them into housing estates, but now we're seeing the downside of that policy ... the recent problems with contaminated land at Brompton, West Lakes and now Birkenhead have highlighted a health issue that seems is only going to get worse ...

Having only started to acquire old industrial sites in the 1980s, the Trust and tenants first encountered the problem of soil contamination. When Patricia Sumerling moved into her Maylands unit in 1983 she found that no attempt had been made to prepare the ground for future gardens.

> As the site is a former tram barn yard, less than two feet below the surface there is compact tar and contaminated soil, making it difficult to grow anything. None of the gardens were ever graded and developed with any top soil. To overcome this issue, I paved my back garden and made it into a courtyard.

In 1988 tenants at Albert Park also complained about not being able to grow vegetables. This site, a former tannery, was found to be saturated with arsenic. Murray Hutchesson said 'that rang some alarm bells', and the Trust found other purchased sites that could not be used for housing. The worst case soon hit the press. A century of brick making at Bowden and Brompton had left a legacy of clay quarries (pugholes) filled with industrial junk, lately acquired by state agencies to use for housing. New residents complained of illness, and investigation uncovered toxic chemicals dumped into the old pughole under the houses.

Tony Olivier, a member of the Housing Trust Tenants Association, who helped lead the campaign to clean up Florence Crescent, told the ABC in 2003 that soil contamination was widespread, and that 'Governments of all ilk have swept it under the carpets'. A Health Commission report in 1993 listed as many as 50 toxic sites in Bowden and Brompton, and parts of Port Adelaide, that had previously been used by industry. The Trust spent a huge amount of money to fix the problem at Brompton, relocating residents while replacing soil to a depth of 1.5 metres around 40 houses in 1993. The remediation led to the upgrading of the soils laboratory at Torrensville, rebuilt in 1993 as the Stolz Centre for Environmental Services, and the Trust became the state's largest investigator of sites for soil contamination. Staff also carried out commercial work for other agencies. Their very success engendered criticism as investigations held up building work. At least one building contract was cancelled. The Trust's downsizing in 1995–96 brought an early end, and the laboratory and the whole Torrensville depot, including the nursery, were closed. Minor remediation was later done

Transformation of Goodwood Technical High School into Trust housing.

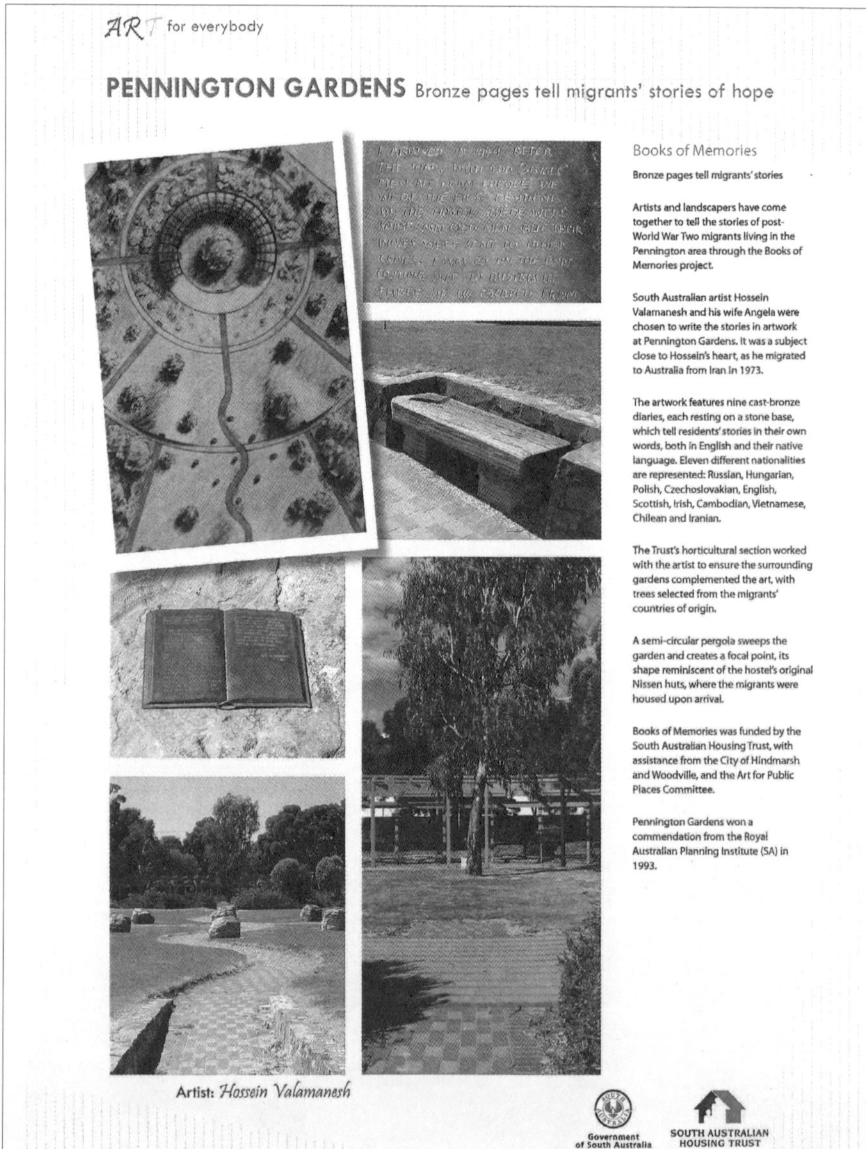

ART for everybody

PENNINGTON GARDENS Bronze pages tell migrants' stories of hope

Books of Memories

Bronze pages tell migrants' stories

Artists and landscapers have come together to tell the stories of post-World War Two migrants living in the Pennington area through the Books of Memories project.

South Australian artist Hossein Valamanesh and his wife Angela were chosen to write the stories in artwork at Pennington Gardens. It was a subject close to Hossein's heart, as he migrated to Australia from Iran in 1973.

The artwork features nine cast-bronze diaries, each resting on a stone base, which tell residents' stories in their own words, both in English and their native language. Eleven different nationalities are represented: Russian, Hungarian, Polish, Czechoslovakian, English, Scottish, Irish, Cambodian, Vietnamese, Chilean and Iranian.

The Trust's horticultural section worked with the artist to ensure the surrounding gardens complemented the art, with trees selected from the migrants' countries of origin.

A semi-circular pergola sweeps the garden and creates a focal point, its shape reminiscent of the hostel's original Nissen huts, where the migrants were housed upon arrival.

Books of Memories was funded by the South Australian Housing Trust, with assistance from the City of Hindmarsh and Woodville, and the Art for Public Places Committee.

Pennington Gardens won a commendation from the Royal Australian Planning Institute (SA) in 1993.

Artist: *Hossein Valamanesh*

Government of South Australia

SOUTH AUSTRALIAN HOUSING TRUST

Bronze diaries designed by Hossein and Angela Valamanesh tell migrant stories at Pennington Gardens. The garden design won a commendation from the Royal Australian Planning Institute in 1993.

Soil sampling at an inner city site planned for housing, c1991.

by construction staff. Problems continued to surface at early infill sites. As the ABC reported in 2003, when 16 units were built in 1982 on an old gasworks site in Mead Street, Birkenhead, the polluted soil was covered in plastic and a layer of clean soil. Toxic chemicals worked to the surface as the plastic broke down. Residents fell ill and were told their houses would be demolished. Judith Thomas, interviewed by the ABC, voiced 'going from tears and being upset ... talking with the other people about it, working through it, and then getting a little bit angry ... that we weren't better informed'. Olivier demanded a public register of all dangerous sites. The Environment Minister responded: how far back should they go to uncover contamination, and 'who takes on responsibility?' Downie said that the Trust was now using the best soil remediation techniques available, and thanked the Tenants Association for raising community concern over the past 15 years.

If there were problems with infill sites, there were many benefits, not just proximity to city services. Jenni-Lee Cotton loved her house at Prospect: 'It is amongst private homes and I will never willingly leave'. In 2007 the Royal Australian Institute of Architects gave a 25-year 'Award for buildings that have successfully stood the test of time' to Dr Kent's Paddock Housing Estate in Kent Town, designed by Newell Platten and developed in 1983 by the Housing Trust.[184] The Trust began to build such inner-city housing only in the 1970s, and so it was constructed to a better standard and in greater variety than the earlier mass-produced suburban stock.[185]

Jan Connolly spelled out the cost implications of those differences:

> in one outer metropolitan suburb where 28% of our dwellings were located, we found that we should spend 40% of our maintenance budget. On the other hand, in an inner metropolitan suburb, where 20% of our dwellings were located, our maintenance liability was only in the order of 4% of our budget.[186]

It was for this reason, as well as the fact that rising property values had begun to price it out of inner-city development, that the Trust turned next to the redevelopment of middle and outer suburbs where the ageing post-war public housing was concentrated.[187]

Metro: regeneration

> My role took me to a number of regional offices in which urban renewal projects were being undertaken. Each of these involved to varying degrees the existing community being dismantled as residents were relocated to alternative accommodation elsewhere and replaced over time with new residents and with their arrival, the creation of a new and different community. (John Girardi, 2010)[188]

Asset management also involved urban renewal or regeneration. The Trust used both terms, favouring 'regeneration' as emphasis shifted from improving houses to revitalising whole communities. The Trust embarked on serious renewal on its own estates in the mid-1980s. In metropolitan Adelaide they were Elizabeth Park, Hawksbury Park (Salisbury North), Hillcrest, Mapleton Grove (Kilburn), Mitchell Park, Playford North, Rosewood (Elizabeth North), Royal Park, Wandana (Gilles Plains), Westwood (The Parks), Windsor Green (Elizabeth) and Woodville West; and in country towns: Lincoln Gardens (Port Lincoln), Myall Place (Whyalla), Risdon Grove (Port Pirie) and Willsden (Port Augusta).

The first, and the only large southern project, was begun in 1986 at Mitchell Park. This differed from earlier regeneration such as The Parks, not only because of the larger scale and the reduction in Trust ownership, but also as it was a joint venture with the private sector. The partnership with Hindmarsh Adelaide Group was not announced until 1991, Minister Kym Mayes explaining that

> The arrangement with Hindmarsh has allowed the Trust to continue to satisfy demand for rental accommodation, but at considerably less cost than the alternative of undertaking the entire project by itself.[189]

The Trust then turned to renewal in northern metropolitan Adelaide at Elizabeth (Rosewood), Hillcrest, and both country and metropolitan projects. Some renewals nicely dovetailed with the Commonwealth's Building Better Cities Program that was introduced in 1990 to help redevelop large cities into denser and more diverse urban areas. A total of $68.7 million was allocated to South Australia. Projects included redevelopment of surplus land in Adelaide's industrial north-west and inner-west, and public housing in Elizabeth and Munno Para. The program was renewed in 1995 for two more years, and then expired under a new Liberal coalition government.[190] Critics had in any case pointed out that funding had never compensated for cuts made to the states for basic urban services. Places like Elizabeth that had won funding for a Better Cities project suffered badly from cuts to local and state government services.[191]

As corporate planner, Mignon Schneider developed a good understanding of the Trust's renewal program.

> Our rationale for doing urban regeneration was quite neat. Decreasing concentration of disadvantage by demolition of older style houses and bringing in residents who own homes (often working people who were not quite so socially/economically disadvantaged).

Where local government provided the infrastructure, 'there was a good result, but often the Trust was left with carrying the cost of streetscapes' and regeneration became costly. 'Dollars were not the only motive and renewing and refreshing a suburb has a great positive benefit on a community'. The programs also acted as a stimulus to the private sector, which was contracted to demolish, build, supply appliances and sell houses. 'We were also able to build socially responsible bits into contracts', such as stipulating that a large percentage of demolition materials were recycled.[192]

There was record regeneration during 2001, and the Better Neighbourhoods Program (BNP) was also started. As Schneider recalled, over time 'we changed our views from large scale to small scale redevelopment. BNP only redeveloped small areas ... there was an aim to make these programs self funding by selling land'.[193] In a typical project, a timber framed corner house was replaced by three new houses, and aged tenants across the road were moved into them. Their old houses were replaced in turn, and some of the freed up land was sold, helping to fund the program. And so BNP was rolled out through the metro area.[194] Royal Park, a smaller project than most (45 Trust properties and 52 new private houses), was planned in 2006, with replacement Trust housing sourced through BNP pocket redevelopments.[195]

In the first four years BNP relocated 700 tenants, demolished 600 obsolete houses and started 500 new homes.

> BNP provides new for old public housing which is more appropriate to tenants' needs, energy efficient, indistinguishable, adaptable and self funding from selling additional lots created ... BNP is creating a better, more sustainable social mix, reducing the SAHT's maintenance liability, enhancing streetscapes and slowing the loss of public housing.[196]

Tenants could stay in the neighbourhood, close to familiar services and friends. Renewal potentially benefited all clients because of the income derived from the process. BNP, by 2005–06, was a major revenue source for new Trust homes, contributing $22 million, compared to $15 million from house sales.[197]

Mitchell Park

In 1964 Marlene Littlewood, a second generation Trust tenant, moved with her husband and children to Mitchell Park, where she lives still: 'we were all young families. Fathers worked and mothers stayed at home'. When allotted their house, she said, 'I didn't know where Mitchell Park was'. Ten kilometres south of the city centre, Mitchell Park was well located, had good public transport and was close to employment at Chrysler's car plant and Marion Shopping Centre. The location was an ideal choice for a new kind of investment in urban renewal 25 years on. Three-quarters of Mitchell Park was owned by the Trust – a 1950s estate of 750 houses on large blocks, mainly double units in poor condition. The estate was a textbook illustration of asset management problems: declining property values, increasing maintenance costs, high vacancy rates, low demand and public stigma.

The Trust worked hard to change this perception. The main aim of the renewal was to improve the social and physical environment by reducing the concentration of public stock and improving the quality and choice of housing. The plans were to demolish over 450 properties and replace them with 625 new homes,

Mitchell Park redevelopment. Top: double unit pressed into service as project office; above: laying foundations.

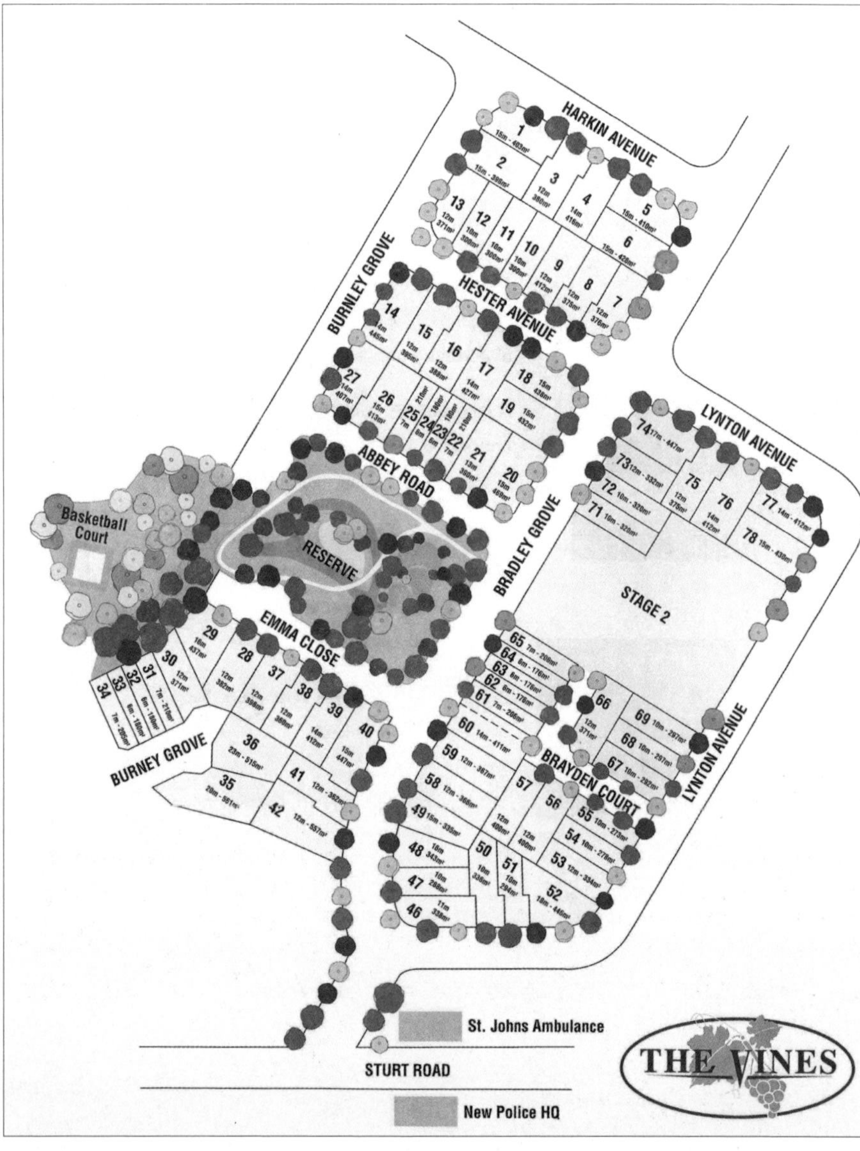

Mitchell Park redevelopment: The Vines project. Top right: under construction; and below: view across reserve in Emma Close.

retaining 30% for Trust tenants, with a further 150 renovated and either sold or retained. In the first stage, 400 double units were transferred into the project and 265 were demolished, creating 465 blocks varying in size from 194 to 430 square metres – much smaller than the old allotments. Two-thirds of them were sold to private buyers, as land and house packages ranging in price from $95,000 to $170,000. One hundred double units were upgraded. Trust ownership fell to 50%, the value of both public and private housing rose, and cash surpluses were gained from sales.[198]

John Girardi recalled that some of the new housing was 'ahead of its time in terms of density and form – particularly around the railway station. Although the terminology was not around at the time, it occurs to me now that this may have resembled a Transit Oriented Development'.

The renewal evolved from replacing public housing to regenerating the whole suburb. The City of Marion and the Trust upgraded streetscapes, buried power lines and created parks. In 1995, to draw attention to Mitchell Park's new identity, the Trust commissioned a mosaic, stained-glass gateway, designed in consultation with the community and placed at the Sturt Road entrance.

Finally complete, Mitchell Park renewal was celebrated on 29 August 2005, after 19 years and $30 million funding. The rundown suburb had been transformed to a mixed public–private community; 225 pairs of double units had been demolished, 50 pairs renovated, 210 new public housing properties were built, 425 allotments were sold, and a new community centre was built.[199]

Circumstances may change during the life of such large projects. When Mitchell Park's renewal began, one of the main attractions was the proximity to Mitsubishi's Tonsley Park plant. Trust housing had been built in the first place for car workers at Chrysler, which was taken over by Mitsubishi in 1980. In 2004 Mitsubishi reduced its workforce by 350 and closed the more southerly Lonsdale engine workshop that employed 650. Within three years employment at Tonsley Park fell from 2,800 to 980 and Mitsubishi announced the plant's closure in the same year.[200]

Elizabeth

While Mitchell Park was the Trust's first new-style redevelopment, Rosewood (Elizabeth North Redevelopment Project) was more prominent. Rosewood was a joint venture with Elizabeth City Council that started in 1993 in partnership with the Better Cities program and Delfin Property Group. The project encompassed 750 Trust and 600 private homes. The Trust was project manager and Delfin arranged sales. The Council would provide $430,000, sales would contribute to a rolling fund and profit would be shared with the Council. Delfin proved the worth of its involvement even before the project's launch, when flooding rain washed away the landscaping. 'Delfin whipped out their crews and put all the trees and shrubs back in place.' (Michael Findlay)

Mark Peel questioned a plan to solve Elizabeth's 'problem' by removing the poor, asking, 'Who will get to stay in Elizabeth and who will have to leave?', but in Rosewood project's first year, when more than 400 people joined a waiting list to buy the renovated double units, 90% of them were public or private renters.[201]

The first work in Woodford Road illustrated the Trust's habit of offering practical help at Elizabeth, with land provided by St Stephens Church in part payment for the Trust upgrading the church building.[202] In other ways Rosewood was a break in tradition, as it involved both federal and private sectors. One of the first acts of South Australia's incoming Liberal housing minister in 1994 was to sign an agreement with Delfin to extend Elizabeth North's 'upgrade' following 'the proven Rosewood experience'. The Trust's responsibility for designing, managing and redeveloping its own stock was significantly (and permanently) lessened. The change was reinforced by the state's parlous economic situation, and by a new government determined to cut public debt.[203] In 1997 the Project Manager, Trust employee Mike Findlay, reported an expenditure of $10 million on infrastructure and the sale of 500 homes; more than 30% of them to Trust tenants or applicants. 'Rosewood is now considered a growing new community'.[204] However, in 1998 the General Manager reported that only 301 settlements had been achieved. Delfin's market research indicated 'general acceptance of the upgraded housing product', helped by affordability and HomeStart mortgages, but the return per house of $12,418 was 'well below the budgeted return of $21,394'. Delfin decided against developing the project's southern section, leaving the Trust to finish it with other partners.[205]

Later renewals turned attention to central Elizabeth (Windsor Green) and Peachey Belt, where the Trust owned 56% of housing, most built before 1960.

Rosewood Village official opening, November 1992. The federal minister Brian Howe and state minister Kym Mayes (seventh and ninth from left) join Delfin, Elizabeth Council and Housing Trust representatives, including Project Manager Mike Findlay (seventh from right).

The Trust and the City of Playford completed planning for Davoren Park in 1998–99, including Swallowcliffe Village with a shopping centre, primary school, community centre and an Aboriginal Elders Village. In 2002 a further agreement with the City of Playford identified Elizabeth Park as another renewal area. A feasibility study was approved for a demonstration project in 2005.

> The Masterplan features a range of improvements to public areas, including elements such as gateway and suburb identification treatments, a landscaped boulevard along Innes Street, pedestrian linkages, open space redevelopment, traffic calming/management and street tree planting. Public housing will be reduced from 214 mainly double units to 145 dwellings.[206]

Premier Mike Rann announced additional regeneration in the Peachey Belt district of Playford North in 2006. Over the next 15 years the suburbs of Andrews Farm,

Davoren Park North, Davoren Park South, Munno Para West and Smithfield Plains, together with 300 hectares of vacant government owned land, would be 'the focus of a whole of Government urban renewal initiative through the Playford North Regeneration Project' ('Playford Alive'). Around 13,000 people lived there, but by 2020 there were to be 40,000 people and 8,000 new homes. Long-time resident Betty Alberton was appointed chair of the Playford Alive Community Reference Group.[207]

And so regeneration continued, underscored by evidence of persisting disadvantage. Based on the 2006 census, Adelaide's lowest ranking suburbs – rated on the number of Trust tenants, low-income families and unemployed – were those on the northern margins, and Davoren Park was one of the poorest.[208] Betty Alberton said that with the Playford Alive redevelopment, 'things are looking up again, because really it's a good community and underneath it's a really strong community'. As for Elizabeth as a whole:

> We've got a lovely town centre now and some beautiful gardens, we've got the good and the bad. Now we're a swinging seat federally – just before the last election we had three visits from John Howard. They have started to build industry in Elizabeth West, for example, a Japanese car place, a big warehouse on Peachey Road. If they had done that 40 years ago, the unemployment wouldn't have happened.[209]

In Helen Fulcher's view,

> One of the real strengths of the Trust has been the work in community renewal, and while people certainly celebrate the enormous change that's happened in The Parks, in the Westwood Project ... I had a lot of involvement and felt that we'd done really good, sustainable changes in places like Salisbury North prior to that. And that's probably one of the examples I think most highly of ... If we really see ourselves as major stakeholders in the community, then ... we need to plan in very respectful ways with ... local government but also the community with whom we're working, because it's essentially their community. One of the strengths of the Salisbury North community renewal was actually the process, when a group of local citizens, so not simply Trust tenants, self-selected to be the third voice, essentially, we invested in some capacity-building to make sure that their voice could be as strong as possible.

Further renewal was announced with the $19.5 million Northway project at Elizabeth Park expected to deliver 228 new homes, as well as improved public spaces and retained public housing. Purchasers started to build their first homes in 2010 in the first stage release of small allotments.[210]

Salisbury North/Hawksbury Park

The Trust collaborated with the City of Salisbury in a ten-year renewal of almost 1,400 Trust properties at Salisbury North. This began in 1998.[211]

> The project has developed a focus on the provision of affordable homes for sale encouraging appropriate display homes to facilitate this in conjunction with an Easybuild house and land package initiative targeting first home owners and with linkages to HomeStart loan packages.[212]

In 2001 the Royal Australian Planning Institute commended the project's community consultation. Rock musician Jimmy Barnes, who grew up nearby, performed to a home crowd at a concert celebrating 10 years of redevelopment, with Mayor Tony Zappia praising the Salisbury North Urban Renewal Project.

> The area has been regenerated, creating a sustainable community, a better environment and improved standards of housing. This is a great opportunity to raise money for a worthy cause and for residents to ... show just how proud they are.[213]

Rock musician Jimmy Barnes and local students celebrating urban renewal at Salisbury North.

One hundred and eighty million dollars had been spent, and a further $16 million committed by the government to the fifth and final stage.[214]

Salisbury North Primary School served 'an area with a high Housing Trust occupancy and a very high level of transience'. Urban improvement was 'having a huge impact on the local community. The school ... has worked with the redevelopment group on community issues'. As families relocated due to demolitions, enrolments declined, but then stabilised. Many families chose to drive their children back to the school. Migrants housed by the Trust boosted the number of students from two classes in 2005 to 12 in 2007. 'The New Arrivals Program has been through a rapid increase ... as Anglicare settles more families in the northern suburbs, due to more affordable rental opportunities'.[215]

Mapleton Grove (Kilburn) and Wandana (Windsor Gardens-Gilles Plains)
To the north of Adelaide, Mapleton Grove was a five-year renewal involving 275 houses. In 2005–06 contamination was found and remediated while final land division proceeded.[216]

The City of Port Adelaide Enfield approved a $35 million urban regeneration at Windsor Gardens-Gilles Plains in 2000, known as Wandana. The project demolished 160 double units built in 1950 using 'Proleta' (gypsum panels clad with asbestos sheeting). Intended as temporary housing, they were kept for 50 years. Land was cleared for subdivision and 230 replacement houses – a 40% increase – with one third retained for public and community housing.

John Girardi remembered residents of the long-established community at Windsor Gardens 'mourned the dismantling of their community while the reaction in the main from within the more transient and less functional Gilles Plains community ranged from ambivalence to "just get me out of here"'. Windsor Gardens residents met each fortnight in the local MP's electorate office, where they consoled each other, and housing staff in attendance reassured them about their rehousing options. Gilles Plains Community Connect Group also brought residents and staff together to build networks. Members met at the Wandana Community Centre, which gained an award in 2005 as Outstanding Learner Provider Organisation, under the management of Rilla Walshe.[217]

The Wandana project was also a demonstration of sustainable and affordable housing that illustrated the intent of renewals in the Trust's later years. Builders were required to install solar hot water systems, adopt a five-star energy rating and plumb rainwater tanks into the house, anticipating similar requirements introduced generally in South Australia in 2006. House prices were $140,000 to $350,000. Such prices were rare in a suburb less than 10 kilometres from the CBD, and they were not subsidised, rather they were influenced by market prices and the use of small lots of land, small houses and efficient designs.

The Trust also looked into private rental schemes 'to subsidise NGOs with a capital subsidy upfront to make it viable for them over the long term'. Crucially, the project was self-funded by the improvements and the sale of land for private homes.[218] However, slowing land sales extended the completion date to 2008.[219]

Westwood (The Parks)

> 'The Parks' suffered from a poor reputation, with high levels of crime, including drug trafficking, prostitution and other illegal activities ... Yet surprisingly the vast majority of the 2500 tenants relocated due to the Westwood project have sought to be rehoused within or as near to 'The Parks' as possible. What is it about this community which beckons its own to stay when others have seen it as undesirable? (John Girardi, 2010)

The Parks Urban Renewal Project (Westwood) was the last major joint venture run with the private sector. It was scheduled to run over 15 years. This was also the most challenging redevelopment, spanning five suburbs, six square kilometres and thousands of houses. The Parks was, in 1997, South Australia's largest and most notorious Housing Trust estate. The industrial and residential area in north-western Adelaide includes parts of Pennington and Kilkenny, and the suburbs of Athol Park, Mansfield Park, Regency Park, Woodville North, Angle Park, Ferryden Park and Woodville Gardens, and is collectively known as The Parks, after the community centre that opened in 1979. Trust construction in 1938, followed by the mass production of double units, had produced an estate of more than 3,000 Trust homes.

In building this enormous estate, the Trust also created a massive fixed investment that depended on local employment. Closure of many of the factories that had warranted development in the first place had dire effects. Local unemployment reached 30% in 1991. This dropped slowly to a post-recession low of 18% in 1999. Workers living in The Parks were often unable to find alternative employment because new workplaces required higher technical skills, and many were hampered by language difficulties. In 1971 an already high 26% of residents were born overseas; but the greater proportion were English speaking. By 1996 over 44% were foreign born, with Vietnamese the largest group (nearly 18%).[220] By the 2000s many newcomers were African.

The consequences of economic restructuring were similar to those at Elizabeth, but The Parks lacked the benefits of that town's design and support. There were also backwards connections between employment and public housing. A survey in 1996 found that mobility was a major problem for unemployed residents and that petrol costs limited the area in which they searched for jobs. People's willingness to move to get work was also constrained by their anxiety about securing a suitable transfer within the public housing system.[221]

In his detailed study, Neldner described how the Trust, having built 'a stereotypical residential area of double units scandalously under-resourced in social and recreational infrastructure, began the long process of rebuilding the community in the late 1970s'. This early renewal was a model for others in the 1980s, and involved 'selective demolition and refurbishment of its ubiquitous double units providing a range of alternative housing types for both single-parent families and elderly residents'. More than 400 houses, units and flats had been built or refurbished by the early 1990s.

Then there was a decisive change in approach, driven by the rise in public debt. In 1994 the state government announced a major 15-year redevelopment of The Parks to replace most of the public housing. Investigation of renewal options for Angle Park, Ferryden Park, Mansfield Park and Woodville Gardens and Athol Park began in 1994 following Board approval of the asset management plan.

In 1995 Pioneer Projects Australia Pty Ltd (later known as Urban Pacific Pty Ltd) was chosen as development partner, with Sue Crafter appointed as the company's 'public face'.[222] The State Bank crash meant that such joint developments were approached more cautiously. A legal framework, known as alliance contracting, with risk management provisions and escape clauses, was adopted. The Trust's Ian Hill was appointed Project Director in 1997.[223] Urban Pacific was, from 1998, wholly owned by Macquarie Bank, which confirmed its commitment to the project.[224] After delays caused by legal concerns and the bank takeover, the Westwood Consortium (Urban Pacific, Charles Sturt Council, Port Adelaide Enfield Council and the state government) launched The Parks Urban Renewal Project in February 1999. This involved 2,940 houses and plans to decrease the concentration of public housing by 23%. The first tenants were transferred and houses demolished for a display village (of purchase homes) opened in 2000.[225]

Private sale display homes at Westwood. (Photo Susan Marsden)

Simon Neldner argued that this solution to a precinct of jobless tenants involved 'removal, relocation and repackaging'. Having established the estate to support the profits of industrial capital, the government would now dismantle it to help renew profitability for property capital, in the form of Pioneer Projects and the Housing Trust. Neldner did not fault Trust staff, 'many of whom have been asked to sell flawed or unpalatable policies in difficult circumstances'. His comment has broader resonance for the experience of Trust employees in a context of diminishing state support for public housing, and he noted their attempts to add 'a few scraps of social justice into a leaner and meaner public policy'.[226]

Parks residents, having campaigned for facilities such as the Community Centre, merited an active involvement in the future. What would happen as the Trust demolished large tracts of housing?[227] A researcher working with local school children saw how the developer welcomed their suggestions about new parks, but their influence was limited. 'Some children learned through their research at school that their current dwellings were listed for demolition. Hardly empowering!' Like their parents, they were 'positioned as responders ... to witness and provide advice about a suburb that was being improved for ... someone else's children'.[228]

The Parks redevelopment site, looking west (Westwood).

Some in the Trust were anxious about the agreement, whether financial benchmarks would be met or standards lowered, although in 2005 the project was awarded the Planning Institute of Australia (SA) Urban Design Award: Plans & Ideas/Build (over $30,000). Westwood was described as Australia's largest renewal project, redeveloping 2,350 of 2,950 Trust properties. State Cabinet approved changes to accelerate the Westwood Project, and transferred $15 million to the Trust.[229] The Agreement was again amended in May 2006, and the City of Charles Sturt endorsed the master plan for precinct 6 (Athol Park–Woodville North). This final northern section of Westwood was expected to be the most financially successful, as this was usually the stage at which redevelopment projects came into profit.[230] In 2009 Westwood Consortium began to release stage three, centred on a large nature strip between Gateshead Street and Ely Street, called Central Park. Prices for new homes in Central Park ranged from $307,000 for a villa to $420,000 for a super villa, and refurbished houses were offered in Mansfield Park and Woodville Gardens from $242,000.[231]

For and against urban renewal

Renewal projects were driven by economic as well as social imperatives. Observing the change in approach imposed on the Trust by the withdrawal of public funding, Neldner wrote that redevelopment proposals now had to 'satisfy the litmus test of financial viability and market attractiveness'.[232] Ogden's review of the program lists among the benefits of the Gilles Plains renewal, for example, 'Diversity of price points for home ownership ($140,000 to $350,000)' and 'Home ownership which is well located, energy & water efficient and adaptable'.[233] Neldner warned that with the private sector negotiating from a position of strength, 'the ability of the Trust to equitably balance its social and commercial responsibilities may be an increasingly difficult, if not impossible task'.[234]

The Trust advised staff that renewal should integrate research, theory, community feedback and policy analysis. Renewal had its origins in the social policy areas of housing assistance, estate renewal to address locational disadvantage, and community empowerment. Debates 'centre on the relative merits of people versus place interventions and ... assets versus needs'. The Trust noted Arthurson's criticism that the effectiveness of social mix strategies was poor, and selling public housing to facilitate mix would deplete stock. She was urging a more rigorous evaluation of renewal.[235] Reorganisation to promote a whole-of-government approach, as when DHS was formed, could reduce coordination of services to redevelopment areas. She wrote that resources were important, not government structures. Social problems were merely dispersed by renewal. The problems of large estates might instead be solved by improving them for existing residents.[236]

Fincher's assessment of policies to address locational disadvantage concluded with a similar cautionary note.

> [D]isadvantage is not spatially confined, though it is spatially expressed. Its major policy implication is that measures to redress social inequities in

> places are best implanted within all government policies and programs, at their very core.[237]

Returning from the UK in 1999, the Trust's General Manager reported that the most successful regeneration programs were those with 'a major political commitment, eg, the Glasgow Alliance', with agreed targets 'on employment generation, education, training, public safety and housing'. He told the Board that the European Community, now a major source of funds for regeneration, required funds to be spent on developing community skills in renewal areas to enable residents to manage project committees.[238]

An imbalance of power between developers and renewal communities could also affect results. Neldner described many forms of public consultation during the Westwood redevelopment, but project objectives were stated at the outset, prior to any consultation. Residents formed The Parks Voice Redevelopment Action Group, but had no chance to debate alternative models. 'There would be no negotiations over the extent of the redevelopment, the number of tenants to be re-housed, or the establishment of a publicly accountable, democratically elected renewal authority'.[239] In 1998 the Trust developed a pool of trained neighbourhood development officers 'to initiate and implement [redevelopment] projects, develop communication strategies and advocate on the community's behalf'.[240]

Economic objectives that limited consultation and shaped results were equally apparent in redevelopment that did not include the Trust. Holdfast Bay (Glenelg) and Newport (Port Adelaide) were built on public land by private developers. 'Losing Port Adelaide's Heritage in a Tide of Development', reported *Stateline* (ABC-TV) in 2004: on the heels of public outrage about Holdfast Shores the government was signing off on a billion dollar redevelopment of Port Adelaide. Many hectares of housing was to be built around the old port's riverfront. 'But like Holdfast Shores, the plans are already facing rough seas, with residents and heritage groups seething at the prospect of multi-storey apartments in one of the State's most historical areas'. The Land Management Corporation spokesman responded,

> If we were unable to have buildings of that height, it would reduce both the economic benefits that would accrue to the State – the number of jobs that would be created and the financial returns not only to the Government but to the development partner as well.[241]

While underway, renewal has decidedly negative effects. Residents in Mitchell Park said they had no influence on decisions that affected their quality of life, and that benefits took years to become apparent. Neldner's study found the same at The Parks, and a photograph captioned 'Burnt out and boarded up' showed vacant double units in Ferryden Park damaged by vandals. 'While a private security service was employed, the residents who remained felt like hostages in their own homes'.[242] Downie noted that such a large project inevitably ran into criticism, particularly from tenants who lived in houses slated for demolition in the later stages, as properties were not maintained to the usual standards once they were marked for demolition. He said that the Board and the Minister believed that the Westwood project 'should be speeded up and after some tense negotiations with Macquarie Bank (Urban Pacific), it was agreed to shorten the project to eleven years'.[243]

In 2005 the Trust reported that tenants were being relocated more quickly as vacancies occurred in the project's earlier stages, with tenants of longest standing being given first choice of relocation in the project area.[244] Joy Riley observed that each agreement was different, and depended on when they became a tenant, and that this was not fair to long-term residents who were relocated. At Mansfield Park, she and her husband had 'some very good neighbours', but also suffered

> every drop kick, low life [who] have been put in the area as most of the houses will eventually go ... My husband and I are chair and secretary of The Parks Regional Advisory Board. Our group is trying to bring about change – the Housing Trust (and its staff) don't like change.

Looking north in 2007 from The Parks Community Centre, one could observe the dust and barrenness of a big development site near a few beleaguered double units. Clearance can breed resentment as a familiar landscape is transformed, feelings exacerbated by another unavoidable event: relocation. The Trust made great efforts to meet tenant preferences and found that most were happier in their new homes. Less attention was given to the destruction of old community networks and facilities.

The Parks Community Centre was itself placed under threat. Port Adelaide Enfield Council ran the fitness centre, library and theatres on behalf of the government, but under cost-cutting measures announced in the 2010 state budget, the government announced that all funding would be halted. The whole centre was to be closed and replaced with new government offices but community facilities would not be replaced and most of the site was to be sold for further housing.[245] One of many protestors responded, 'The Parks area has been revitalised and hundreds of new families have/and soon will be moving into the area. The Centre should be revitalised to cater for this – not demolished![246] Many other South Australians protested against the decision, persuading Premier Rann to announce that the centre would not be sold although its future was to depend on a review into community needs in the western suburbs.[247]

Renewal diversified estates and their tenants, but was that 'an acceptable (or equitable) trade-off for significantly reduced levels of public housing'?[248] Housing Minister Oswald claimed that Rosewood, for example, did 'not mean a total reduction of available Trust accommodation, but a more even spread, as we will replace those homes by building elsewhere'. His main emphasis was on reducing the concentration of public housing and adding value to private homes. He said that the Rosewood model was welcomed by owners, including tenant-purchasers, and 'there will be ... a general improvement of the surroundings'.[249]

Parks Community Centre protest outside Parliament House 28 September 2010. (Photo Susan Marsden)

The same concern about losses of public housing was raised in Neldner's study, and by Trust staff visited by the author at The Parks. Ogden, who played a major role in renewal programs, confirmed the loss of

> around 1700 houses through the Westwood project, breaking a concentration of about 60 per cent down to about 24 per cent of public housing, but it's being funded by the loss of that housing by using that asset to fund the improvements ... in the social, physical, environmental and economic changes occurring in those areas.[250]

An opposite view was expressed in the 2001 Triennial Review. This found that the Trust had carried too large a share of regeneration's infrastructure and community development costs compared to local and federal government, and urged that old properties be replaced rather than upgraded.

Regeneration achieved physical and financial goals, but social benefits were harder to measure.[251] Residents also required social and employment opportunities. The Trust increasingly emphasised training and employment in renewals, and appointed officers to address the fundamental issue underlying local poverty: 'long term and intergenerational unemployment'.[252] In 1994 an apprenticeship training project was run at Mitchell Park. Thirty unemployed apprentices joined an accelerated training program to construct 24 homes, units and townhouses at McInerney Place.[253] Relieving joblessness was a priority of the Salisbury North Improvement Study, and in 1998 a pilot program helped 20 long-term unemployed tenants into the building industry. Those who completed pre-vocational training were offered traineeships in jobs, or group training with contractors involved in the renewal, and participants gained preferred sub-contractor status.[254]

Susie Herzberg recalled the Board's enthusiasm for incorporating employment and training in regeneration projects and the challenge of writing contracts for tenderers that would help create local skills. Westwood's scale offered scope to employ tenants in redeveloping their own area. To build community capacity, facilities such as a tool library were introduced, and skills development included an aged-care course. Forty-two people gained employment and a further 52 took part in training during 2005, and Westwood Urban Renewal Fund later engaged an economic development manager.[255] A Community Planning and Renewal Unit was set up in 2005 to develop strategies that encouraged community cohesion and participation to ensure that residents gained lasting benefits from renewals. The unit had a state-wide ambit, but its first priority was the five suburbs known as The Parks.[256]

What did residents think? In 1998 the Trust commissioned the University of South Australia to survey 108 households on how they perceived renewal in Mitchell Park. They found a high level of satisfaction, with 82% of residents surveyed intending to stay, although they were doubtful that the improved streetscapes would be maintained. Rosewood's residents said that redevelopment had created a friendlier and more attractive place, but they were also uncertain about its long-term sustainability.[257]

Mitchell Park residents wanted more frequent bus and train services, regretted the exodus of services from neighbourhood centres, which restricted opportunities for local contact, and requested a new community centre. The Trust was willing to make such improvements, but reported that as 'a majority of new and long-term residents feel adequately integrated into the Mitchell Park community ... the ... renewal can be seen to be successful'.[258] John Girardi gave credit to the existing Residents Group as 'an effective vehicle for caring for, supporting and communicating with existing members of their community and for welcoming new residents'. The group also acted 'in the absence of a 10 year Master Plan, for involving both existing and new residents in a meaningful way, in planning for the remaining future stages of the project'.

A survey of public housing estates in NSW, Queensland, South Australia and Western Australia presented in 2003 found wide support for reducing concentrations

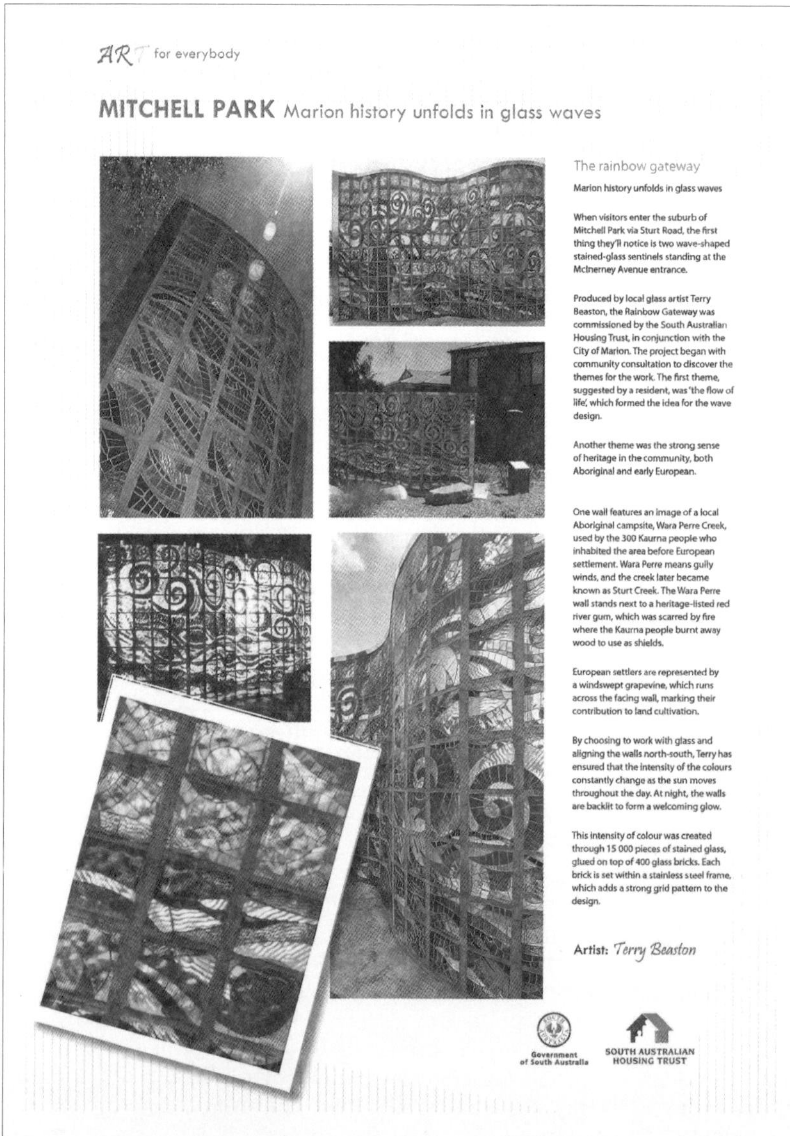

ART for everybody

MITCHELL PARK Marion history unfolds in glass waves

The rainbow gateway

Marion history unfolds in glass waves

When visitors enter the suburb of Mitchell Park via Sturt Road, the first thing they'll notice is two wave-shaped stained-glass sentinels standing at the McInerney Avenue entrance.

Produced by local glass artist Terry Beaston, the Rainbow Gateway was commissioned by the South Australian Housing Trust, in conjunction with the City of Marion. The project began with community consultation to discover the themes for the work. The first theme, suggested by a resident, was 'the flow of life', which formed the idea for the wave design.

Another theme was the strong sense of heritage in the community, both Aboriginal and early European.

One wall features an image of a local Aboriginal campsite, Wara Perre Creek, used by the 300 Kaurna people who inhabited the area before European settlement. Wara Perre means gully winds, and the creek later became known as Sturt Creek. The Wara Perre wall stands next to a heritage-listed red river gum, which was scarred by fire where the Kaurna people burnt away wood to use as shields.

European settlers are represented by a windswept grapevine, which runs across the facing wall, marking their contribution to land cultivation.

By choosing to work with glass and aligning the walls north-south, Terry has ensured that the intensity of the colours constantly change as the sun moves throughout the day. At night, the walls are backlit to form a welcoming glow.

This intensity of colour was created through 15 000 pieces of stained glass, glued on top of 400 glass bricks. Each brick is set within a stainless steel frame, which adds a strong grid pattern to the design.

Artist: Terry Beaston

Government of South Australia

SOUTH AUSTRALIAN HOUSING TRUST

Artwork to mark Mitchell Park's new McInerney Avenue entrance began with community consultation. Marion's history is expressed in the glass walls commissioned from local artist Terry Beaston.

and developing a better social mix. Tenants reported a significant reduction in stigma, but there was little evidence of greater social cohesion.[259]

Stretton wrote in 2005 'that "welfare" and "market" houses should ideally be indistinguishable from each other, and that more and less expensive houses can mix quite comfortably'. He continued, 'Will squalid, drugged and aggressive welfare tenants be dangerous to well-off neighbours? Offensive perhaps, but not as dangerous as they are to neighbours as poor as themselves', as better-off households are better defended. He concluded that 'neither poverty nor policy should be allowed to segregate the poorest 20 or 30 per cent of households from the rest'. With sensitive management, a 'single public supplier might mix home-buyers, rental purchasers, paying tenants and subsidised tenants'. He had once helped to contrive such mixtures through the Trust and found them better than income-segregated housing.[260] Stretton's opinion was reflected by Bernadette Kuhar after she moved to a 'completely mixed' neighbourhood: 'The area I moved from – in Plympton Park – still remains a "Housing Trust Ghetto" after 12 years'.

> Housing SA will try to relocate you to a home that meets your needs and will try to transfer any improvements you have made to the outside of your home and to transfer your curtains and floor coverings ... [and will] replace fittings that could not be relocated, changed or compensated.[261]

The Trust noted that 'the long term success of [renewal] projects is heavily dependent on tenant satisfaction with the relocation process and the way tenants are treated by Trust staff'. Elizabeth's regional manager surveyed people relocated in Rosewood and, as a result, acted to extend notice of transfer dates. Similar care was taken with single projects such as moving 78 tenants from Cambridge Flats at Elizabeth, a complex 'plagued with ongoing vandalism and maintenance issues' and marked for sale.[262] But Ogden had to allay public fears in 1997, stating that when 100 homes were bulldozed for Salisbury North redevelopment, 'Nobody will be forced out'.[263]

Mignon Schneider described the Trust as being 'very careful to consult with communities and relocate people in a sensitive way, employing relocation officers who worked with tenants. We also have generous relocation policies so that people will get their aviary or shed moved at our expense'. She acknowledged criticism

> for breaking up communities by moving people out, but it has always been a balancing act of renewing an area. There is a lovely story about a couple of old ladies who were neighbours for years and didn't want to be parted, so when we had to relocate them we found two houses next door to each other. We have a beautiful photo of them up on the wall in Riverside.[264]

Sue Crafter stressed the benefits of a large investment in social infrastructure, despite rising house prices in The Parks.[265] Westwood's new houses demonstrated a rise in value unprecedented in The Parks. In 2007 the *Australian Financial*

Review recorded Ferryden Park's median house price of $331,500 – a rise over one year of 16.3% – with a ten year trend forecast at 19.3%. By contrast, in Unley, the suburb with Adelaide's highest median price ($760,000), the ten year trend forecast was 14.6%.[266]

Kilner concluded that regeneration could alter Adelaide's classic urban geography with its concentrations of poor households in the western and outer suburbs. Their number would not alter, rather their distribution, and they would gain better premises. He did ask whether those outcomes were incompatible with the welfare uses of public housing, and the contraction of stock. There was also the effect of changes in the allocation of Trust housing. From the year 2000, allocations were formally limited to high needs applicants. A report on the effects of such targeting commended the Trust's community development projects.

> But it is a large step from applauding some successful low-key local initiatives to the claim that community capacity-building offers a major solution to the social disadvantage with which public housing estates are associated and which targeted allocations may exacerbate. Targeted allocations are based, after all, on assessments of supposed need or deficiency, not on assessment of capacity.[267]

'Building communities' was a principal objective of the government's 'Strategic Plan' released in March 2004. A year later, the 'Housing Plan for South Australia' reaffirmed the commitment to regeneration.[268] Board members stressed 'that urban renewal is instigated because a community is in high need ... urban renewal and community renewal are not programs but processes that are undertaken in response to community need'.[269]

From Mansfield Park, Bryan Atkinson wrote that, at the age of 76, 'I don't look forward to spending the remaining time I have on this earth in constantly arguing with the Trust in order to bring about "The Sustainable Community" the Minister keeps referring to in his press releases'. But the minister himself was acutely conscious of the problems.

> We used to understand ... that the relationship between affordable housing and the prosperity of the community, and also its capacity for it to function effectively as a community, is absolutely crucial ... liveable communities which are affordable to people are part and parcel of their prosperity, so we need to recapture that. The other element is how they function socially ... if you look at the existing Housing Trust estates, the ones that work best are where there's essentially a good mix of stock ... So you've got people of different abilities: people with more resources ... can support people with less capacity ... [and with] no one group essentially overwhelming the culture of a place ... In a perfect world for me every community would have fifteen per cent of affordable housing in it ... set aside for people on lower incomes; and ... indistinguishable from the housing around it in terms of style and design

Artist Margaret Worth aimed to make the redeveloped Osborne railway station 'playful and colourful to remove the sense of isolation'.

> so that we'd have well-integrated communities. Ideally those houses would be located near services and employment opportunities.[270]

Weatherill's aspirations informed the reorganisation of the whole housing system from 2006. In Downie's view, the Trust's 'role as a principal developer of new residential neighbourhoods and communities across metropolitan and regional South Australia appears to be over, with the responsibility being left up to the private sector'.[271] Sister Janet Mead regretted that 'other businesses have come in to take their place, which is a dreadful thing because it is a business; it isn't the Housing Trust. That means it's making a lot of money and people just can't afford it'.

Additional state funding *was* given to accelerate renewal. Westwood Renewal's conclusion was brought forward by three years to 2011, and Playford North and Elizabeth Park projects and Better Neighbourhoods Programs were continued. The Trust reported in 2007 that 'Success from existing programs can be evidenced by the proportion of first generation housing stock decreasing by 4% since 2000–01'.[272]

MP Nick Xenophon raised the fear expressed by many Trust tenants that they would be forced to make way for new developments, and after a public meeting held in 2007, Weatherill gave written assurances to people who questioned him about the security of their tenancy. He also said that about 90% of people were relocated within five kilometres of their original home, and the remainder usually chose to move to a new place.[273]

Leading into the Housing Trust's 75th year in 2011 were these renewals: Northway (Elizabeth Park), Playford Alive (Playford North), Hawksbury Park (Salisbury North) Westwood (The Parks), Woodville West (between Alma Terrace, Henderson Avenue and Emily Street), Inspire at Noarlunga Centre (off Goldsmith Drive), and Waymouth Street in Adelaide. Northway was described in 2010 as 'a resounding success with buyers'. Housing Minister Jennifer Rankine reported that

> Many of the people who bought land are from the local area and they are thrilled that they are able to stay in a neighbourhood they know and love ... This is a renewal scheme at the true community level. There is already a tremendous community spirit here and we hope to build on that by delivering a better neighbourhood for people to share.
>
> We've seen that this type of work can bring about a new feeling of wellbeing, along with positive economic change in the area.[274]

Meanwhile, over at Woodville West, regional manager John Girardi posed the question 'will the new Woodville West community that will emerge over the next few years ... enjoying its revised and improved street layout ... innovative housing and ... mixed tenure be as welcoming, inclusive and friendly to the little immigrant boy from the Middle East or Sudan or Burma, walking through its streets on his way to school ... as the Woodville West community was to me 50 years ago?'

Let the final words come from Betty Alberton, who welcomed the 'Rebirth of the Peachey Belt'.

> The Playford Alive Project is what we as a community have been waiting for, for a long time. I was here for the original 'Birth' and after watching over the years the ups and downs I am embracing this with open arms.
> This area has a lot to offer, and we are looking forward to a very positive future.[275]

Notes

1 S. Marsden, 'Constructing Playford's city: the South Australian Housing Trust and the transformation of Adelaide, 1936–1966' PhD thesis, Flinders University of SA, 1994, p. 539.
2 Rob Walker, 'Mitchell Park', <www.toorakcollege.vic.edu.au/warrickw/poetry/mitchell_park.htm> viewed June 2008; his website is at <www.users.bigpond.com/robwalker1/default.htm>.
3 DFC, SAHT Exhibition: 'Future', Migration Museum, Adelaide, 2006.
4 M. Peel, 'Urbanisation', in W. Prest, K. Round & C. Fort, eds, *The Wakefield companion to South Australian history*, Wakefield Press, Adelaide 2001, p. 565.
5 S. Marsden, *Business Charity and Sentiment*, Wakefield Press, Kent Town, 1986.
6 A. Marroncelli, 'The evolution of social mix in the South Australian Housing Trust', 1993, p. 46.
7 Marsden, 'Constructing Playford's city', p 449.
8 SAHT, Board minutes, 22 Feb 2000.
9 SAHT, Board minutes, 8 Dec 1987.
10 Arguments for and against urban consolidation are summarised in C. Forster, *Australian cities: continuity and change*, Oxford University Press, Oxford, 1995, pp. 131–134.
11 G. Seddon, 'Adelaide's alter-egos', C. Garnaut and K. Round, eds, *The Adelaide Parklands Symposium. A balancing act: past-present-future*, University of South Australia, Adelaide 2006, p. 194.
12 ABC, *Counterpoint*, Ideas and Australian cities (interview with Hugh Stretton by Michael Duffy), 29 May 2006, viewed Oct 2007.
13 Hutchesson, interview, 2007.
14 R. Parker, quoted in *HTN*, 2, 1, Feb 1991, p. 2.
15 Peel, 'Urbanisation', p 223.
16 Kilner, *Housing policy*, p. 247.
17 SA Parliament, G. J. Crafter, address to Estimates Committee, 16 Sept 1993. For ULT functions, see *Urban Land Trust Act 1985*.
18 NLA, TRC 3964, Professor Max Neutze, interviewed by S. Marsden, 9 Feb–8 Mar 2000.
19 SA, Housing and Urban Development (Administrative Arrangements) (South Australian Urban Projects Authority Dissolution) Regulations 1997.
20 Kilner, *Housing policy*, p. 316.
21 G. J. Crafter, Estimates Committee, 16 Sept 1993.
22 Adelaide City Council, Shared effort: Adelaide City Council and social housing in the city, 1986–1999, 1999, pp. 4–5; The number of SAHT tenants in the city increased from 612 in 1971 to 3,087 in 1991, but dropped to 3,008 by 1996, reflecting the curtailment of SAHT additions and rising property prices (B Badcock, 'Thirty years on: gentrification and class changeover in Adelaide's inner suburbs, 1966–96' *Urban Studies*, **38**, 9, 2001, p. 1565.)
23 Adelaide City Council, Plan Review 90–91, 'Plan Review issues', Social policy planning; Residential development strategy [Adelaide, 1990: NLA ephemera collection, Adelaide-Town Planning].
24 SAHT Board, Report: Information for weekly Minister's meeting, 1 Dec 2006.
25 P. Ogden (SAHT), 'A community for all ages – Building the future', Commonwealth Dept of Health & Ageing, National Speakers Series, Adelaide, 2 Dec 2005, pp. 1, 5 (including both quotations). Ogden gained two Australian Housing Institute awards in 2005 for Professional excellence in social housing and for Outstanding achievement in social housing. (SAHT, Annual Report, 2005–06, p. 13.)

26 Marsden, 'A history of Woodville, 1976–1986', 1987, p. 7.
27 Marsden, 'Constructing Playford's city', p. 535.
28 Kilner, *Housing policy*, p. 332–333.
29 Trust in focus 2005/06, p. 49.
30 Kilner, *Housing policy*, p. 332 (tables 6.8 and 6.9): between 1991 and 2001 there was a reduction of 12 houses in Adelaide's inner zone compared to 2,972 and 4,102 houses in the middle and outer zones; public stock rose from 8.9% to 10.7% in the inner zone, from 47.8% to 49% (middle zone), and dropped from 43.3% to 40.2% (outer zone).
31 SAHT, Board Minutes, 19 Dec 1995.
32 SAHT, Annual Report 1998–99, pp. 29–30.
33 SAHT, Annual Report 1986, p. 7; Chronology.
34 SAHT, Board minutes, 1 Feb 2000.
35 Miss Fay Rohrlach, interview, 26 Mar 2007.
36 During 1998 2,916 properties were modified to enable independent living for tenants with disabilities, at a cost of $1.63 million. As recorded in SAHT, Triennial Review 1997–2000 (p. 14), in 1998 there were an estimated 40,000 South Australians with profound disability aged 15–64: around 2,000 of them rented privately and 4,000 were boarders, compared to 7,000 in public housing. Over the six years 1993–94 to 1999–2000 the Trust had modified 13,500 properties for disabled people; and in 1999–2000 its Disability Housing Program leased 146 properties to 36 government and non-government agencies.
37 Reported in *Eastern Courier* 14 Feb 2007, which noted also that 14 boarding houses closed across the city in the three years leading up to 2005.
38 Mrs Barbara Schmidt, (Q) and in interview by telephone (7 Feb 2007).
39 Malcolm Downie, memoir, Sept 2007.
40 Ogden, 'A community for all ages', pp. 1–5.
41 ibid., pp. 6–7.
42 Stephanie Key, interview, 13 Feb 2008 (N).
43 'Twentieth-century allergy', or 'total allergy syndrome', is a condition attributed to hypersensitivity to a wide range of substances in the modern environment, including pesticides, pharmaceuticals, and chemicals used in the manufacture of plastics and epoxy resins.
44 1st Newsletter for the 'Housing Plan for SA', SA Government [Dec 2005].
45 SAHT exhibition poster c1997, including quotations (SAHT Memorabilia Collection).
46 Kilner, *Housing policy*, p. 315.
47 Patricia Sumerling, (Q), (E) 25 March 2007.
48 SAHT, Board minutes, 24 Feb 1987. The design and construct program was reintroduced in 1992 after a four year absence.
49 Kilner, *Housing policy*, pp. 289–290.
50 *HTN*, 2, 3, July 1991, p. 5.
51 Sister Janet Mead, interviewed for SLSA, 11 May 2010 (R) (SOHC/OH 934).
52 Kilner, thesis, p 369.
53 Ogden, 'A Community for All Ages', p. 1; Kilner, *Housing policy*, pp. 333–334, 337.
54 Glenice Bennett, Public Housing Customer Forum, 19 Dec 2006; and 'Life in a walk up flat' memoir attached to (Q).
55 *HTN*, 2, 3, July 1991, p. 7.
56 Housing SA, Factsheet 4. Asbestos: Information for Buyers of Housing Trust Homes, 01/07, <www.familiesandcommunities.sa.gov.au/>. Asbestos insulation was unsafe even if undisturbed as the fibres could be stirred up by vermin or wind and enter living areas through small openings in the ceiling.
57 A. Alcock, 'Health & safety in the non standard workplace' (Industrial Relations Society 2003 National Convention), <www.irssa.asn.au/Alcock_A_paper.doc> viewed Oct 2007.
58 'Asbestos Victims Association (SA) Newsletter', Sept 2006, <www.avasa.asn.au/files/Newsletter_September.pdf> viewed Oct 2007.
59 *Weekend Australian*, 20–21 Oct 2007 (statistics & quotation).
60 *ABC News*, 'Xenophon questions asbestos report responses' 26 June 2004, <www.abc.net.au/news/stories/2004/06/26/1141061.htm> viewed Oct 2007.
61 Current policy (2010) is to remove where the asbestos likely to cause a risk, that is, damaged,

and also when capital upgrade works are done. The only annual inspections are those for 'commercial' residential such as boarding houses, which are required to have Asbestos Registers under current legislation. (Note from Shirley Trebilcock, Sept 2010).

62 Downie, (E), 27 Dec 2007.

63 DFC, Triennial Review of the South Australian Housing Trust, Final report, Sept 2005, p. 8.

64 SAHT, Board Minutes, 26 April & 26 July 2005.

65 DFC intranet, 'Housing, Affordable Housing', 30 June 2006.

66 SA Parliament, *Hansard, Legislative Council*, 29 May 2007, p. 171.

67 DFC intranet, SAHT, 'Regional rental stock report', June 2006.

68 SAHT, Regional rental stock report, June 2006.

69 Weatherill, Speech notes, 3 Dec 2006.

70 SAHT, Board minutes, 28 Oct 1997.

71 Trebilcock, (E), 5 Oct 2007 (with attached chronological list of 'Environmentally sustainable SAHT activities and developments').

72 Trebilcock (list); SAHT, Board minutes, 28 Oct 1997 (includes list of dates).

73 2009 SA Women's Honour Roll, <www.officeforwomen.sa.gov.au/siteFiles/OFW/2009SAWomensHonourRoll.pdf> viewed 25 March 2010.

74 Crafter, Estimates Committee, 16 Sept 1993.

75 N. Allen & D. Cunliffe, 'Water recycling in South Australia: Overview from a public health perspective', *Public Health Bulletin*, 4, 2, July 2007, pp. 9, 10.

76 Susie Herzberg, recollections, Sept 2007.

77 SAHT, Board minutes 26 July 2005.

78 SAHT, Annual Report 2005/06, p. 13.

79 Office of Public Employment, SA Public Service Medal Winners, 2006: Murray Hutchesson, <www.cpe.sa.gov.au/PSMQueen2006/> viewed Oct 2007.

80 SAHT, Board minutes, 26 July 2005.

81 SAHT, Board minutes, 22 Mar 2005; Government of SA, Jay Weatherill, 'Housing Plan for South Australia, Two year report card', leaflet, May 2007.

82 Whyalla Eco-Renovation Information Centre (WERIC) brochure, , <www.housingtrust.sa.gov.au/resources/WERIC%20brochureoct04.pdf> viewed November 2007.

83 Mawson Lakes was built from 1997 on 620 hectares of disused grazing land in northern Adelaide as a joint venture between Delfin Lend Lease and the Land Management Corporation. 'Delfin ... has pushed for job creation, pursuing in-demand areas of growth such as their conference facilities ... [and] Mawson Lakes redevelopment also is intrinsically tied in with Technology Park Adelaide, which was Australia's first technology park when set up in 1982'. *Adelaide Review*, 24 April–4 May 2006.

84 SAHT, Annual Report 1998–99, p. 24.

85 DFC intranet, Tanya Plibersek, Minister for Housing, and Jennifer Rankine, Minister for Housing Joint News Release, 10 Dec 2009.

86 DHS, Ministerial, 21 Aug 2000, Archive, <www.health.sa.gov.au/> viewed July 2007.

87 Dennis Smith, interview/recollections, 6 December 2006.

88 Ombudsman Annual Report 2001–02, p. 9, and passim.

89 Ombudsman Annual Report 2004–05, Case study: South Australian Housing Trust, p 10.

90 *HTN*, 3, Christmas 1997, p. 2.

91 Betty Alberton, (Q) 19 Dec 2006.

92 M. Peel, 'The Forgotten Lessons of the Past: Housing, Security and Justice', Paper delivered at Shelter SA AGM, 20 Oct, 2004, pp. 2–3, <www.sheltersa.asn.au/Documents/Dr%20Mark%20Peel's%20AGM%20speech.pdf> viewed Mar 2008.

93 M. Peel, *Good Times, Hard Times: The past and the future in Elizabeth*, Melbourne University Press, Carlton, 1995, pp. 1–3. Peel's work (as for Hugh Stretton) also illustrates an activist tradition amongst historians, and how such writings have helped inform new policies.

94 NLA, TRC 4895, Interview with Hugh Stretton, 2002, transcript, p 100.

95 Mrs Betty Alberton, (E), 1 Nov 2006, and at Regional Advisory Board Forum, 19 Dec 2006.

96 Confirmed in Hasan's survey of 1997: V. Hasan, 'A critical review of the evolution of approaches to public housing provision in South Australia' B Planning thesis, University of South Australia, 1997, pp. 14–17, 23.

97 Fred Foord, (E), 10 Sept 2007.
98 Edwards, interview no 2, 18 Sept 1984, transcript, pp. 65, 100 (quotations).
99 Marsden, 'Constructing Playford's city', p. 532.
100 B. Badcock, 'Recently observed polarizing tendencies and Australian cities', *Australian Geographical Studies*, **35**, 3, 1997, pp. 243–249.
101 S. Baum & R. Hassan, 'Economic restructuring and spatial equity: a case study of Adelaide', *Journal of Sociology*, 1993, p. 165 (based on analysis of census data 1976 and 1986).
102 R. Fincher, 'Locational disadvantage: an appropriate policy response to urban inequities?', *Australian Geographer*, **22**, 2, November 1991, p. 132.
103 Kilner, *Housing policy*, pp. 332 (quotation), 333.
104 Forum of Regional Advisory Board, 19 Dec 2006.
105 DFC intranet, SAHT, 'Regional rental stock report', June 2006.
106 Julia Lester's ABC Radio program, 3 Aug 1990; S. Marsden, 'Constructing Playford's City', p. 427.
107 *HTN*, 1, 3, Feb 1990, p. 3.
108 D. J. Walmsley & H. C. Weinand, 'Is Australia becoming more unequal?' *Australian Geographer*, 28, 1, 1997, pp. 75–82.
109 Simon Neldner, (E) to S Marsden, 20 April 2007.
110 S. Neldner, 'Reversal of fortunes: the post-industrial challenge to work and social equality: a case study of "The Parks" community of Northwestern Adelaide', PhD thesis, University of Adelaide, 2001, p.284.
111 J. Spoehr, 'Tale of two cities', *Adelaide Review*, 29 Oct 2004, citing a new report 'Inequality in South Australia', by the University of Adelaide's Public Health Information Development Unit. The proportion of households living on less than $26,000 annually rose from 19% in 1996 to 24% in 2001. Between 1989 and 2001 the proportion of children aged under 16 living in low-income families rose from 31% to nearly 52%, representing an increase of around 68,000 children.
112 Spoehr, *Adelaide Review*, 29 Oct 2004.
113 *The Advertiser*, 18 Mar 2008: report on release of ABS, Adelaide 2006: a Social Atlas, 2008.
114 SAHT, Board minutes, 25 May 1993.
115 Phil Miller, (E) 5 July 2010.
116 McGregor Harrison Marketing, 'Tenants survey and consultation', stage 1, 18 Mar 1986, pp. 9, 15 (SAHT Triennial Review of Cost-rent formula, Appendix 1).
117 SAHT, Board minutes, 27 Jan 1987.
118 Kilner, *Housing policy*, p. 290.
119 *HTN*, 3, 3, June 1992, p. 1.
120 S. Scheiffers, 'Whyalla: the last 30 years', paper presented at State History Conference, Whyalla, May 2005, History Trust of SA <www.history.sa.gov.au/history/conference/Sue_Scheiffers.pdf>.
121 ibid.
122 At the 2006 census Whyalla had a population of 21,417, but the decline since 1981 was arrested in response to new industrial and housing development. Estimated population in 2010 was 23,028. (*Whyalla News*, 28 April 2010.)
123 DHS, South Australian Housing Trust Triennial Review 1997/98 – 1999/2000, DHS, Adelaide, 2001, p. 96 (including Table 38); Kilner, *Housing policy*, p. 331.
124 *ABC News Online*, 22 October 2002. The Trust's own offices in Whyalla had been damaged in an arson attack on several government offices in May, 1992. (*HTN*, 3, 3, June 1992, p. 11.)
125 SAHT, Board Minutes, 25 January 2005.
126 *ABC News Online*, 20 Feb 2002.
127 DFC intranet, Minister's Strategic Housing Advisory Committee, Berri Regional Consultation, 19 Aug 2008.
128 S. Baum, 'A typology of socio-economic advantage and disadvantage in Australia's large non-metropolitan cities, towns and regions', *Australian Geographer*, **37**, 2, July 2006, pp. 233–251.
129 SAHT, Board Minutes, 21 March 1995.
130 SAHT, Operational Policy Advisory Committee minutes, 21 May 2002.
131 ABC Radio, *SA Country Hour Summary*, 29 Nov 2005.
132 SAHT, Board Minutes, 21 March 1995.

133 Triennial Review 1997/98 – 1999/2000, pp. 92, 96.
134 'Lincoln Gardens ... Affordable, comfortable, convenient family living', SAHT brochure, c2005 (including quotation).
135 SAHT, Annual Report 2005–06, p. 25 (including quotations).
136 *Trust Talk Tenant Link* (TTTL) 13, June 2004, p. 4.
137 SAHT, Board minutes, 25 January 2005; SAHT, Annual Report 2005/06, p. 25 (including quotation).
138 DFC intranet, SAHT, 'Regional rental stock report', June 2006. (There were 2,378 DUs at Elizabeth, followed by 1,926 at Whyalla, 1,431 in the Port Adelaide region, and 1,136 at The Parks.)
139 SAHT, Board minutes 22 Feb 2000.
140 SAHT, Operational Policy Advisory Committee minutes, 21 May 2002.
141 SAHT, Annual Report 2005/6, p. 26.
142 *The Advertiser*, 14 Jun 2008.
143 Interview with Hugh Stretton, 8 October 2002, transcript, p. 100.
144 SAHT, Board minutes, 14 July 1987.
145 B. Badcock, 'The contrariness of Adelaide's property markets', in P Troy, ed, *Equity, environment, efficiency: ethics and economics in urban Australia*, MUP, Carlton, 2000, pp. 78–79.
146 SAHT, Board minutes 22 Feb 2000.
147 The Urban Land Trust Act was passed in 1981, and established SAULT. For a history of West Lakes and Delfin's role, see Marsden's two histories of Woodville (1977 and 1987).
148 See *BC & S*, p. 406.
149 SLSA, SRG 660/1/40, Edwards, 18 Sept 1984 – second interview, transcript, pp 18–19 rewritten by Edwards (attached pp. 2–3).
150 Golden Grove (Indenture Ratification) Act 1984 – schedule.
151 Hasan, pp. 24– 5.
152 Note from Shirley Trebilcock, Sept 2010.
153 SAHT, Board minutes, 27 January 1987.
154 SA Tenders & contracts, SAHT024, <www.tenders.sa.gov.au/contract/> viewed Aug 2007.
155 Kenny, *State of denial*, p. 12.
156 Badcock, 'The contrariness of Adelaide's property markets', pp. 78, 79 (quotation).
157 Kinsmen Pty Ltd, 'Seaford Joint Venture', c1991, p. 2 (SAHT Memorabilia Collection, Folder: Tour information originals).
158 SAHT, Board minutes, 12 May & 14 July 1987.
159 Hasan, p. 25.
160 Kinsmen Pty Ltd, 'Seaford Joint Venture', p. 2. The project manager Kinsmen Pty Ltd, was established in 1985 and formed the Seaford consortium with AV Jennings Ltd and Bank SA. SAHT interests in the joint venture were recorded in 1996 as: a 50% interest with SAULT to acquire and hold land for the venture; a 25% interest in the Seaford Joint Venture; and an investment consisting of vacant land valued at $6.7 million held for future development and $2.9 million under development. SAPD 1995/96, p. 622.
161 Marroncelli, p. 33 (who adds that the Seaford percentage range was in keeping with the Adelaide metropolitan average of around 11%, 'and emphasises that the SAHT, through integration coupled with moderate numbers, is attempting to achieve social mix in a way in which the stigma from highly visible and easily identifiable SAHT estates is removed).
162 Kinsmen property developments: Seaford Rise, viewed Dec 2007, <http://kinsmen.com.au/developMore.wt1?id=3494>. (Company history also supplied.)
163 Kinsmen Pty Ltd, 'Seaford Joint Venture', p. 4.
164 Quoted in Hasan, p. 26.
165 S. Marsden, 'Wonderful histories: The City of Onkaparinga', in G. Trott et al., *McLaren Vale: Trott's View*, Wakefield Press, Adelaide 2007, np.
166 State Library of SA OH 768/4, John (Jack) Holder, interviewed by S. Marsden, 13 Mar 2008.
167 Hasan, p. 28 (including quotation from Sarkissian, Forsyth and Heine study, 1990).
168 John Girardi (Housing SA regional manager) 'The new urban renewal development in Woodville West', Presentation given at the Housing Coalition (quarterly meeting of senior SA housing managers and directors), 16 Mar 2010 (supplied for this history by J Girardi).
169 Crafter, address to Estimates Committee, 1993.

170 SAHT, Board minutes, 1 Feb 2000.
171 SAPD 1995/96, p. 622; SAHT, Annual Report, 1992, p. 1; Hasan, p. 29.
172 SAHT, Board minutes, 1 Feb 2000.
173 Hasan, p. 30.
174 SAHT, Board minutes, 25 May 1993.
175 Hasan, pp. 30, 32–33; SAHT, Board minutes, 1 Feb 2000.
176 'Green Street', a Commonwealth initiative, promoted energy-efficient, higher-density housing.
177 Badcock, 'Thirty years on', p. 1569.
178 SAHT, Board minutes, 27 Jan & 24 Feb 1987.
179 SAHT, Board minutes, 28 Sept 1993; 24 Jan 1995.
180 *HTN*, 1, Sept 1997 (Capital Projects Bulletin).
181 Ogden, 'A community for all ages', p. 6.
182 *HTN*, 4, 3, Oct 1993, p. 1; Marsden, 'A history of Woodville, 1976–1986', p. 24.
183 ABC Radio, *Stateline*, The past comes back to poison us (including following quotation and further references to ABC 2003 report) 6 June 2003, <http://search.abc.net.au> viewed Nov 2006.
184 *The Advertiser*, 30 June 2007.
185 Badcock, 'Thirty years on', p. 1,571.
186 J. Connolly (SAHT), ' "Check-it" – a housing condition database', Paper presented at Hong Kong Housing Conference, May 1996, p. 5 (SAHT Memorabilia Collection).
187 Badcock's longitudinal study, 'Thirty years on', records completion of 'the circle of regeneration' on all four sides of the City of Adelaide by 2001, led by state government and in particular, Housing Trust projects; at the same time recording the curtailment of Trust activity in the early 1990s.
188 John Girardi, 16 Mar 2010.
189 *HTN*, 2, 3, July 1991, p. 1.
190 Kilner, *Housing policy*, pp. 374–375.
191 Forster, *Australian cities*, pp. 124–125.
192 Mignon Schneider, (E), 27 April 2007.
193 ibid.
194 Ogden, 'A community for all ages', 2005, pp. 5–6.
195 SAHT, Annual Report 2005–6, p. 25.
196 ibid., pp. 8–9.
197 ibid.
198 'Housing Trust Focus', in *HTN*, 10, Aug 1999; Paul Ogden, 'South Australian Housing Trust Urban Renewal', 22 Nov 2005 (including quotations), pp. 1–2, in DHS, Mitchell Park Urban Renewal Project, <www.housingtrust.com.au/resources/mitchell.pdf> viewed Nov 2006.
199 *TTTL*, 16, Dec 2005, p. 8.
200 *The Age*, 11 June 2008; *Independent Weekly*, 9–15 Feb 2008. There were fewer than 980 Mitsubishi workers at Tonsley Park in February 2008 when the parent company in Japan announced final closure of the factory.
201 SAHT, Board minutes 23 Feb 1993; Peel quoted in Marroncelli, p. 42; Marroncelli also noted that Rosewood encouraged owner-occupiers of the same background as SAHT tenants; and that 'Peel's criticisms of Rosewood Village are correct in essence but are unsympathetic to the efforts made to initiate social justice measures to avoid a deterioration of the already desperate socio-economic status of such areas' (p. 43).
202 SAHT, Board minutes, 25 May 1993.
203 *HTN*, 5, 1, Mar 1994, p. 1 (quoting Minister John Oswald); Neldner, p. 248.
204 *HTN*, 1, Sept 1997 (Capital Projects Bulletin).
205 SAHT, Board minutes, 24 Feb 1998.
206 SAHT, Annual Report 2005–6, p. 26.
207 *The Advertiser*, 9 Feb 2006; SAHT, Annual Report 2005–6, p. 26; 'Playford Alive', <www.playfordalive.com.au/playfordalive/> viewed Mar 2010. Partner agencies planned to 'comprehensively' regenerate the environment, 'including a holistic commitment to education, community development, human service delivery and training and employment'. Regeneration was to start

in 2007–08. Revenue raised from developing the land would fund construction of additional high need public housing, education and health facilities and services such as public transport.

208 *Eastern Courier*, 27 Feb 2008 (Report on Urban Research Program, Griffith University ranking of Australian suburbs).

209 Betty Alberton, Public Housing Customer Forum, 19 Dec 2006.

210 DFC intranet (Mar 2010), Community planning and renewal.

211 *HTN*, 8, Dec 1998, p. 1; SAHT, Annual Report 1998–99, p. 30. The Trust owned 37% of the houses, and aimed to reduce this to less than 20% by demolishing 500, selling 465, renovating 476 and building 75 new.

212 SAHT, Annual Report 2005–06, p. 24.

213 City of Salisbury, *Salisbury news and views*, 'Jimmy Barnes to rock Salisbury North', 31 Oct 2005, <http://cweb.salisbury.sa.gov.au/> viewed Nov 2006.

214 *ABC News*, 27 Nov 2005. Another 100 Trust homes would be upgraded, 100 renovated and sold, and other houses removed to make way for 170 allotments to be sold for private housing.

215 Salisbury North Primary School, context statement, May 2007, <www.decs.sa.gov.au/docs/files/communities/docman/1/Salisbury_North_R_7_School.doc> viewed July 2007.

216 SAHT, Annual Report 2005–06, p. 25.

217 *Words on Wandana* (community newsletter), Summer 2006, p. 1.

218 Ogden, 'A community for all ages' (all quotations), pp. 3–4.

219 SAHT, Annual Report 2005/6, p. 25.

220 Neldner, 'Reversal of fortunes', abstract, pp. 140–142, 155, 157, 186.

221 ibid., pp. 162, 164.

222 ibid., pp. 249–55.

223 Badcock, 'The contrariness of Adelaide's property market', pp. 79–80; *HTN*, 1, Sept 1997 (insert: Capital Projects Bulletin).

224 SAHT, Board minutes, 24 Mar 1998.

225 Neldner, 'Reversal of fortunes', abstract, pp. 249–255.

226 ibid., p. 269.

227 ibid., p. 247.

228 B. Comber, H. Nixon & L. Ashmore, 'Urban renewal from the inside out: Spatial and critical literacies in a low socioeconomic school community', University of SA, Paper presented in 2005, p. 4, <www.unisa.edu.au/hawkeinstitute/cslplc/documents/ComNixAshAERA05.pdf> viewed Mar 2008.

229 SAHT, Board minutes, 22 Mar 2005.

230 SAHT, Board minutes, 26 July 2005.

231 Central Park at Westwood, <www.westwoodsa.com.au/index.php?id=1> viewed Aug 2010.

232 Neldner, p. 249.

233 P. Ogden, The South Australian Housing Trust Urban Renewal Presentation – 22 Nov 2005, in DHS, 'Mitchell Park Urban Renewal Project', c2001, <www.housingtrust.com.au/resources/mitchell.pdf> viewed Nov 2006.

234 Neldner, 'Reversal of fortunes', abstract, p. 249.

235 DFC, SAHT – Research and Reports Resource Base, <www.familiesandcommunities.sa.gov.au> viewed Dec 2006; K. Arthurson, (1998) 'Redevelopment of public housing estates: the Australian experience', *Urban Policy and Research*, **16**, 1, 1998. See also Arthurson, 'Australian public housing and the diverse histories of social mix', *Journal of Urban History*, **34**, 3, 2008, which examines social mix through history by drawing on SA housing policy and Salisbury North housing estate as a case study of social mix in practice.

236 Summarised in Kilner, *Housing policy*, p. 335.

237 Fincher, p.134.

238 SAHT, Board minutes, 1 Jan 2000

239 Neldner, p. 253.

240 *HTN*, 5, June 1998, p. 5.

241 ABC, *Stateline*, 9 July 2004.

242 Neldner, p. 277.

243 Downie, (E), 27 Dec 2007.

244 SAHT, Board minutes, 22 Feb 2005.

245 *Weekly Times*, 16 Sept 2010; *Sunday Mail*, 26 Sept 2010.
246 Vicki Hyde of Angle Park, response to report in *Sunday Mail*, 26 Sept 2010; *ABC News*, 28 Sept 2010.
247 *The Advertiser*, 6 Oct 2010.
248 Neldner, p. 248.
249 Minister's announcement, quoted *HTN*, 5, 1, Mar 1994, p. 1.
250 P. Ogden, 'South Australian Housing Trust Urban Renewal', 22 Nov 2005, in DHS, 'Mitchell Park Urban Renewal Project', <www.housingtrust.com.au/resources/mitchell.pdf> viewed Nov 2006.
251 This review of critiques draws in part on Kilner's survey, in *Housing policy*, pp. 335–337.
252 Ogden, 'A Community for All Ages', p. 2.
253 Ogden, 'South Australian Housing Trust Urban Renewal', 22 Nov 2005.
254 *HTN*, 7, Oct 1998, p. 1.
255 SAHT, Annual Report 2005–6, p. 24; SAHT Board minutes 26 April 2005.
256 DFC intranet, DFC Annual Report 2005–06; Community planning and renewal (Mar 2010).
257 Kilner, *Housing policy*, p. 336.
258 SAHT & Social Policy Research Group, University of SA, 'Community perceptions of social outcomes of urban renewal: Mitchell Park', brochure, c2000.
259 B. Randolph & M. Wood, 'The Benefits of Tenure Diversification', Australian Housing & Urban Research Institute Paper, Melbourne, 2003. See also Spiller Gibbons Swan Pty Ltd, 'Public housing renewal in Australia' (for SAHT estate renewal, see p. 20), Australian Housing Research Fund, project no 212, Nov 2000, <www.fahcsia.gov.au/sa/housing/pubs/housing/public_housing_estate_renewal/Documents/Final%20Report.pdf> viewed June 2010.
260 Stretton, *Australia Fair*, pp. 129–130.
261 Housing SA, Fact sheet 40. Relocation: external improvements and internal fittings, June 2006.
262 SAHT, Board minutes, 28 Feb 1995 (including quotations).
263 *News Review* (Messenger Press), 6 Aug 1997.
264 Mignon Schneider, (E), 27 April 2007.
265 Kilner, *Housing policy*, p. 336.
266 *Weekend Australian Financial Review*, 28 Dec 2007, p. S10.
267 A. Parkin & L. Hardcastle, 'The impact of targeting housing assistance', Final report, DFC & Southern Research Centre, Australian Housing and Urban Research Institute, Adelaide, Nov 2004, p. 98, <www.socsci.flinders.edu.au/spis/staff/Impact.pdf> viewed Dec 2007.
268 Ogden, 'A community for all ages', p. 7.
269 SAHT, Board minutes 26 July 2005.
270 Interview with Jay Weatherill 11 Jan 2007.
271 Downie, (E), 23 Oct 2007.
272 DFC intranet, SAHT Triennial Review: Progress on Recommendations – April 2007.
273 SA Parliament, *Hansard, Legislative Council*, 29 May 2007, p.174.
274 DFC intranet (Mar 2010), Community planning and renewal, quoting Minister Jennifer Rankine.
275 Betty Alberton, (E), 19 July 2010.

CHAPTER FOUR

Using modern means, 2006–2011

Social housing is continuing to reinvent itself in response to the social and economic needs of the times. In the past seventy years, the social housing sector has supplied homes or access to private rental, for hundreds of thousands of people, providing security and stability to communities throughout the state. (Jay Weatherill, 2006)[1]

Michael Duffy: And what happened to the Trust?
Hugh Stretton: It's still there. It's changed its form a good deal and the functions that it does do have been very badly treated by government in the last 30 years ... above all, by state governments but under constraints and compulsions that come from Canberra. It's easy to go crook at the state government but if you find out how Canberra is changing the rules, above all the financial rules under which they can operate, you really should blame Canberra for a good deal of it. (ABC, 2006)[2]

We've lost an icon of South Australia, like we lost John Martins. (Marlene Littlewood, Public Housing Customer Forum, December 2006)

Introduction

An exhibition *Our Contribution, Past, Present and Future* fêted the Housing Trust's 70th anniversary in December 2006. In that time the Trust had built 122,000 dwellings, 19% of all homes built in South Australia, and retained more than 45,000.[3] Yet, for reasons unvoiced, but in every mind, this anniversary gathering at the exhibition opening was modest in size and muted in mood. Guest speaker Hugh Stretton pointedly dwelt on the achievements of an earlier age, but Housing Minister Jay Weatherill segued from the Trust's origins to his new housing system, introduced earlier in that very year.

People might not realise, but the Trust began its existence as a marriage between private enterprise and government. It provided affordable housing for workers ... a demand which the private sector couldn't meet on its own ... And now seventy years later we want to recapture the ideals of the past to create affordable housing for South Australians ... Once again, we are working with the private sector.[4]

South Australian Housing Trust's 70th anniversary and exhibition, Migration Museum, 3 December 2006. Housing SA's Helen Fulcher introduces Neil Bonsor, a tenant from Gawler Road, Two Wells, who was also celebrating his 70th birthday, with Minister Jay Weatherill and Hugh Stretton (right). Photo Susan Marsden.

But that was no longer a Housing Trust role. A new Affordable Housing Trust was encouraging 'more affordable homes for workers and those on low incomes'. The old Trust was confirmed as a provider of high-needs social housing, with both trusts subsumed in a new operational agency in the Department for Families and Communities.

Twenty years of reform and restructuring had culminated in the Housing Trust's repositioning as one part of a new DFC departmental entity: Housing SA. The division was established in July 2006 and brought together the housing services of three of the four state authorities: South Australian Housing Trust, Aboriginal Housing Authority, and South Australian Community Housing Authority (the fourth, HomeStart Finance, was left as it was). As Weatherill explained, this reorganisation was intended

> to clean up the fragmentation in South Australia's efforts to deal with the growing crisis in housing affordability, and to have structures all pointing in the same direction – developing creative ways, and new forms of partnership

> between government, the non-government sector, and the private sector, to restore our once-enviable reputation for providing affordable housing.[5]

The changes were implemented over time, but from mid-2006, the South Australian Housing Trust, in the form developed over the past 70 years, ceased to exist. Institutional repositioning involved 'using modern means', a phrase often invoked by Weatherill, who told radio listeners that 'We're looking at using modern means with things we have at our disposal as a state government to try to increase the supply of affordable housing because we accept there is a massive problem ... especially in growing towns like Port Lincoln'.[6] His main strategy was the 2005 Housing Plan, which adopted the Trust's urban renewal program as a key purpose and was designed to strengthen neighbourhoods by better linking them to services, accelerating redevelopment of public estates, extending collaboration, and developing self-funding capital programs.

The Minister's 'Report card' on the Housing Plan in 2007 ticked most of those boxes, with an extra $15 million provided to accelerate regeneration at The Parks, Salisbury North and Playford North.[7] But the two-year report made no mention of the South Australian Housing Trust which had vanished in its 70th year.

Or had it?

Jay's revolution[8]

> I had some trepidation with approaching these reforms because it could be characterised as essentially slaying this massive South Australian icon. But if I sat in this job and just presided over the slow demise of the Housing Trust, which is really what's been happening over a period of time, then that would have been irresponsible. So what I've been trying to do is to capture some of the original ... mechanism by which the Housing Trust was able to be successful. The essence for me was ... increasing the supply of affordable housing to low income earners, it was understanding that that could give you a surplus ... The Housing Trust was always a business, it always created a surplus ... to then take and use elsewhere. What I'm trying to do is use modern means to do it. (Weatherill interview, 2007)

When Premier Mike Rann led Labor to its strongest win at the March 2006 state election, Jay Weatherill moved swiftly to take control of housing services, as foreshadowed in the Housing Plan. On 2 May 2006, one year after its release, the Minister announced major changes to public housing. He told Parliament the streamlining of housing and disability services would 'leave more money for better services', although – he said – there would be no changes for the 47,000 tenants, nor any job losses. 'While each agency has been dedicated to providing support, there have been overlaps, gaps and confusion.' Within DFC, two overarching bodies – Housing SA and Disability Services SA – would replace a plethora of agencies and boards. The new Housing SA division would be a single entry point for all government housing services and supply all public and community rental housing. A single waiting list would be created for people requiring disability services such as accommodation and respite. The South Australian Housing Trust (SAHT) would be retained with a renewed role as a 'high-needs' housing provider; and a new Affordable Housing Trust would provide housing for low-income workers and families. He said the new body would 'recapture the early ambitions of the Housing Trust'.[9]

In Sue Vardon's recollection, Weatherill came in with a clear view about what he wanted done in housing, and believed that the bureaucracy was not listening to him. Both the Minister and the Chief Executive knew that the Trust was 'seriously bankrupt, and nobody had been able to work out a funding model to save it'. Part of the problem lay much earlier, when health and welfare agencies were amalgamated to create DHS. Vardon had argued against amalgamation, predicting that welfare would lose resources to health. 'When it finally happened, moneys which had been belonging to community services disappeared. The housing money disappeared, too. Part of the trouble that Jay and I had was to try and recapture the money that had been stolen.' By the time Vardon returned to head a new DFC, the Housing Trust, although a State icon, 'was continuing without any real understanding that there was an iceberg coming up to crash into it – if you can crash an icon into an iceberg!'

Weatherill summoned the four general managers of each housing agency and their four chairs to advise them of his decision to change the regulations and the Act to remove the boards, and said that their positions would be no longer required. In Malcolm Downie's words,

> The fact that the meeting occurred was no real surprise to any of us as the Minister had been talking with the Boards for over 18 months and had made it clear that his preference was to have less Boards. The timing was a surprise, but obviously the Government determined that having got back into office for a second term, now was the time to do it.[10]

Vardon and Downie viewed ministerial control as a crucial motivation for the changes – although they differed in their opinions of the outcomes. When Vardon took up the role of DFC chief executive in early 2005, she assumed oversight of seven different agencies. She said,

> I came back to Jay [Weatherill's] vision, really. He didn't want all these different agencies, they were all uncontrollable, they didn't know that they were responsible to the Treasurer; they didn't even know they were government agencies, you know, they pretended they weren't. They were wholly government agencies. And Jay wanted them to understand that he was the Minister. That suited my fundamental philosophy [as a public servant] that the minister is in charge.

Minister Jay Weatherill (second from right) presenting a cheque in 2006 to Flinders Medical Centre staff and General Manager, Michael Szwarcbord (far right) for upgrading the Neonatal Unit. The donation was raised by auctioning a new house built on land donated by the Trust in Salisbury North.

Downie said that executive staff had worked hard with the Board to put the balance sheet on a stable footing, but that 'forces within State Government had long since decided that it couldn't continue to run public housing services through agencies managed by Boards'. The transfer of the Trust into Families and Communities following the split of the Department of Human Services became the catalyst, as there were now four housing agencies and four disability organisations controlling the lion's share of the new Department's budget and staffing resources. Four new divisions were created: Families SA, Housing SA, Disability SA and later Communities SA, to better connect and manage services previously provided by the separate organisations.

In Weatherill's own words, 'we created the Housing SA idea ... to bring together all of our housing effort'. Instead of being managed by a board, activities would now be managed by the Housing SA manager who answered to DFC's Chief Executive. From 3 July the Aboriginal Housing Authority, SAHT, and the South Australian Community Housing Authority were combined as one board (SAHT) with all operations carried out by Housing SA. Within Housing SA, two new units replacing the former boards were titled Aboriginal Housing Services and the Office for Community Housing (representing registered community housing

Sue Vardon, when Chief Executive, Department for Families and Communities.

organisations). The SAHT Board retained ownership and management of the state's housing assets.

Vardon said that when the new job of heading Housing SA became available, Helen Fulcher was selected 'because she was seen to be someone who could hear what the Minister wanted'. Returning to South Australia as the first general manager of Housing Services, Fulcher was acutely aware of the challenges in making 'a system that's financially fragile work better'. She found it important to have 'a Minister with real courage and great will to make decisions, including the hard policy decisions ... that's something that we're very fortunate to have with Jay Weatherill'.[11] Vardon expressed similar views, stating in 2006, 'we have been privileged to work for a Minister with a clear vision and a creative mind who understands the complexities of our work and encourages us to do better. The fact that you support our people in the Parliament and publicly is appreciated'.[12]

Vardon reported that DFC had devoted the past year to bringing together its 'disparate parts' in governance changes driven by the Minister's strategic agenda, 'Connecting to the Future', and South Australia's Strategic Plan. 'At all times we have been concerned about improving services to the citizens of this State'. Access to services had become complex. 'We are now tackling this complexity.' The reforms had created three new service arms within DFC.

> This is a start. The next challenge is to integrate those agencies so that citizens don't have to travel around from place to place. Often people who need

> our help have little resources to negotiate with governments, and we have to make ourselves more accessible to them.[13]

Weatherill's ambitions to reinvigorate the housing system were part of a wider set of Labor government driven public sector reforms. Vardon and her deputy chief executive Peter Smith and Director of Strategy and Research, Elizabeth Wilson, shaped the restructuring in the Department. Smith was responsible for implementing the housing plan. His position was plain; in his words, 'The reforms are not just in Housing. There is a keenness to have a more effective Government, which is also more responsive in the Community Sector'.[14]

On 15 November 2006 the Minister introduced a Bill for an Act to amend the South Australian Housing Trust Act, the South Australian Co-operative and Community Housing Act, the Housing and Urban Development (Administrative Arrangements) Act, the Residential Tenancies Act, the Housing Improvement Act and the Development Act.[15]

Working for Housing SA

> The Trust as it was, is now gone, with social housing now integrated in a bigger organisation with a more holistic charter. For those associated with the old Trust there are regrets over the loss of what was an effective body, together with an acknowledgment that the demands of society now require an effective whole of government approach. There is also consolation to be had from knowing that many good people who were developed in the old organisation are part of the new, and will apply their talents and experience in taking that forward. (Don Lee, 2007)[16]

Restructuring brought the state's housing agencies together, building on 'the positive contribution' made by their staff.[17] Associate Professor Michele Slatter was already acquainted with senior Trust staff through her research and work with housing groups, but she was struck by the friendliness and family atmosphere when she joined the Board in 2004.

> I also noticed the pride and commitment demonstrated by many staff at all levels in what they did and where they worked. I hadn't met the 'bricks and mortar' staff in my previous connections and found them equally impressive with a vast amount of expertise and a willingness to innovate.[18]

Mignon Schneider described her position, 'Corporate Planner Operational Policy and Planning', as an amalgam of responsibilities (due to departmental reforms from 2006) of Business and Customer Services with Human Resources and Budgeting for Housing SA. Her section was also responsible for corporate continuity and risk management. She had 15 staff. She said that the 'carefree days of the public service are gone and too much work is now expected of too few staff'. There was more pressure on public servants and 'no time to think'. Levels of professionalism and accountability had increased and there was an emphasis on productivity and efficiency. The public service was required to do a lot more with a lot less.

As a manager, Mignon ran from meeting to meeting and took work home every weekend with emails coming in all the time. There were other pressures. 'Managers are chosen for their people skills and they are required to be very diplomatic in their dealings with staff members.' There was a big increase in the number of female managers. She said, 'Feminised management incorporates a tension between meeting high managerial standards and always being available to staff. A manager needs to be tough, but must treat staff with dignity and respect'. There were checks to prevent discrimination and harassment in the workplace and heavy scrutiny through regular staff surveys.[19]

The pressures could only increase as the restructure was put into effect. Downie said,

> For many staff in the Housing Trust, particularly those who had served under Alex Ramsay, this must have seemed like the final nail. People such as Jean Matysek, our legal advisor who had been providing advice to the Trust initially through Finlaysons since the late 1970s and then as a consultant, decided to call it a day.

The disappearance of the Housing Trust from public view, but the retention of the familiar services, meant that public response to the change was muted. Fred Foord said, 'it has not been very widely advertised and really I only am aware of it because I meet former colleagues ... at our 25 year club lunches'. But he spoke for many employees in suggesting that

> the Trust has not been fairly treated, it did an excellent job for many years and eventually its whole economy was undermined not by inefficiencies but by the social and political needs to subsidise low income tenants. I regret that the excellent organisation for which I worked for almost thirty years no longer exists.

Staff reactions ran the gamut of emotions. Helen Fulcher said that many were sad that 'people who were outside the Trust didn't necessarily understand that we did already provide a wide range of services through to homelessness and crisis accommodation'. Weatherill himself described the staff's response as one reflecting their consideration for customers.

> They also are painfully aware of the changes so that they know what's happened to the Housing Trust. So at one level they reflect the same concerns that everyone else has, that they're desperate to see something happen and they're frustrated that people keep coming in ... Category 3 people that don't

Reunion of long-serving Housing Trust staff, Adelaide, 21 November 2008. Top (from left): Mary Macdonald, Simon Worthington-Eyre, Nick Warming and Mary Rinaldi. Bottom (from left): Nick Warming, Rob Sharrad, Peter Chiappetta and Vassie Fitzgerald. (Photos Mary Macdonald)

> have any special needs, are being offered a ten- or fifteen-year waiting list for affordable housing, otherwise they're in the private rental market paying extraordinary amounts of their income in rent. And that's pretty soul-destroying for people in the Housing Trust to not be able to offer anything to those people. So I think generally they're supportive. There'd be some people that would be traditionalists who would say, 'Well, look: this is the best way of doing things and we should just be pouring more money into it,' and I think that's a respectable point of view; not really one that we would argue with, it's just a question of whether those resources are available.

The South Australian Housing Trust had included both the Board and the agency. From 3 July Housing SA was assigned responsibility for delivering all public rental services, including those of the Trust, Aboriginal Housing, and Special Needs Housing. The SAHT operated through Housing SA under a service level agreement between the Board and the Department. This meant that although the SAHT continued as a Board (and legal entity), all staff, those in the SAHT as well as from the dissolved AHA and SACHA, worked in Housing SA, and all services were delivered under that name. The Department for Families and Communities provided all corporate services, and so the divisions within Housing SA were those that were specifically concerned with housing.

The impact of this change on working conditions was small, as SAHT and SACHA staff were already DFC employees, although they were expected to work harder. Vardon said that 'the Housing Trust was overly-administered, in Jay's view and certainly in my view. There were very many staff'. The reduction in the public sector workforce generally also had a discernible effect. For example, the Trust had outsourced responsive maintenance and some programmed works to private companies since the mid-1990s, work that had previously been managed by in-house maintenance field staff. The management of the Maintenance (Telephone) Centre had been outsourced since 1991 through UnitingCare Wesley Port Adelaide, trading as 'Comskil'. From 1997–98 Housing SA was engaging private contractors and two private companies, John Hindmarsh and Programmed Facility Management, as metropolitan works managers.

Shirley Trebilcock, who became Manager, Maintenance in July 2006, recalled the Trust's 'big team of architects and a big team of engineers' in the past, compared with having just one architect and two engineers in her section as most of that work was outsourced. The architect, Rodney Barrington, developed design guidelines that were placed on Housing SA's website so that builders could refer to them. 'Then he has oversight of most of the projects that come through Housing to make sure that they're compliant. So his role is not so much a doer, it's more providing professional advice.'

In 2005–06, the Housing Trust reviewed its maintenance contracting arrangements to look at streamlining works into larger and fewer multi-trade head contracts. However, in response to South Australia's Sustainable Budget Commission report of September 2010 the government decided to extend its centralised

Facilities Management model to all agencies. This would bring maintenance and minor works on Housing Trust properties under the same central management, with anticipated savings of $31.5 million over three years. In Shirley Trebilcock's words, 'The details are still not determined, but this will most likely mean that the Housing Trust's direct relationship with trade contractors will cease and the new relationship will be through DTEI [Department for Transport, Energy and Infrastructure] and the FM Contractor'.

On the other hand, the merging of responsibility for Aboriginal, community and public housing in the Trust did restore some of the wide-ranging roles of former Housing Trust employees after 2006. Community housing was one growth area because of the focus on partnerships to provide more non-government housing.

What was fundamentally at issue in 2006? As a statutory authority, Mignon Schneider said that the Trust had determined its own policy and planning, and it had been 'dissected, beaten and split asunder'. Formerly a tight insular group, the Trust had lost its identity and the sense of a common goal. The SAHT logo was abruptly removed, even from office walls. The loss of history made her sad. 'The SAHT had felt like a family and now it feels like a family member has died. New staff to Housing SA don't know the Trust tenants and do not have or understand the Trust's core values.'[20] Few staff members joined the 70th celebration at the end of 2006. Malcolm Downie didn't have the heart to attend. 'For me', he said, 'the Housing Trust was the staff who worked in it (who always did the extra bit to assist vulnerable people seeking housing assistance) and as they weren't there any more I couldn't see much cause for celebration'.[21]

Michele Slatter made similar observations as a Board member between 2004 and 2007.

> After July 1 2006 when the Trust staff was effectively disbanded and transferred across to DFC it became much more difficult to locate expertise and to have confidence in accountability and planning processes. Housing expertise became diffused within a more generic public service and the whole sense of the Trust was gone.
>
> Reformers see this as a good thing: I think there is a real 'baby and bathwater' problem and it seems exceptionally wasteful to dilute commitment and knowledge like that to establish a model whose reputation is far from the best [NSW].[22]

Slatter noted the effect on staff of a further narrowing of purpose to welfare housing and the selling of stock, the lack of political support (especially from Treasury) and the 'low status in public service, so, hard to recruit stars'. The focus on 'difficult' tenants by regional staff 'is corrosive and develops a negative culture'; and the lack of training empathy or maturity could compound this. 'Especially when the very new role of public housing has not been taken into account and explained by/to government or management'.

Peter Smith worked with Weatherill on the new legislation, and had the task of implementing the changeover to Housing SA, and informing staff and community groups, a matter of many PowerPoint presentations. Vardon described Smith as 'the one who drove the housing stuff. Disability and housing were his areas ... His role is still not fully appreciated by the staff'.[23]

On the contrary, while most of them accepted the need for change, many were bruised by Smith's approach. Shirley Trebilcock said 'it was done in a way that wasn't all that consultative. The Housing Trust traditionally has been quite an open organisation and you actually heard what was going on', but in 2006 staff were simply told of the change, and that 'hurt a lot of people. There were some really good people who moved on. It was not so much what was done; but more about how it was done'. Until 2006 many employees still talked about the previous big restructure of 1990–91, but recalled that experience differently, having been well-advised and given training: 'it took six months or more to put all the staff through this new model. So it does come back to my point that the people knew what was happening then but in 2006 there was less consultation'. Yet she found that staff remained passionate about their work and many stayed on well past 25 years. Sister Janet Mead made a similar observation: 'there are still some people from the old guard that we knew in 1985–1995 who really have the great spirit. It was the best housing trust in Australia ... They call it Housing SA, but I can't really get into the habit of calling them that'.[24]

Senior housing staff from July 2006 included Peter Smith; Malcolm Downie, as General Manager Asset Services; Helen Fulcher, General Manager of Housing Services; Sue Crafter, General Manager, Housing Policy and Strategy; Dennis Huxley, General Manager, Corporate Services; and Phil Fagan-Schmidt, General Manager of SAHT and SAAHT (South Australian Affordable Housing Trust).[25] Downie initially accepted a transfer to Asset Services to ensure the division was sufficiently resourced following amalgamation of the aboriginal, community and public housing newbuild and maintenance programs, but he subsequently negotiated a transfer out of DFC to the role of Deputy Chief Executive at the Government Reform Commission, where he completed his contract because he couldn't support the directions that Housing SA was taking.

> There was a belief that the private sector would enter the arena of housing low income people if the Housing Trust was [not] such a big player in the residential rental market. I don't believe the private sector will ever adequately provide the necessary accommodation and support that is so important to keep our vulnerable customers out of homelessness. There are many thousands of vulnerable people and families on the waiting list for public housing, living in less than ideal situations provided by the private sector – so how can the sell down be justified? While the Board had originally put forward the strategy to sell properties to retire the debt and free up recurrent funds currently used for debt repayments, their emphasis was on selling the minimum number necessary and properties that weren't suited to the needs of tenants with high needs.[26]

Malcolm Downie, when General Manager of the Housing Trust.

Like Downie, Helen Fulcher had long connections with the Trust that dated from the 1980s when she was involved, as a Kensington and Norwood councillor, in a proposal to build a complex for aged people. She joined the Trust in 1994, where she was employed (for the first but by no means the last time) on reviewing a restructure. She was Acting General Manager during 2002 while Greg Black was on secondment, and then became chief executive of Housing New Zealand, before returning to Housing SA in July 2006. She described having the full range of housing services in New Zealand as valuable experience to bring back to South Australia.

Amalgamation of services to create Housing SA required both a realignment of staff as well as a widening of their responsibilities. The change took some years to effect. Indeed, as warned in DFC's 2006 annual report, 'full implementation of Housing SA is dependent upon the housing system being able to provide further housing support options that redress current supply shortages'. This in turn depended on improved levels of Commonwealth support. Extra help was provided, but there was no guarantee this would continue – an uncertainty highlighted by the lack of electoral support for returning Labor at the federal election in August 2010. A minority Labor government was formed under Prime Minister Julia Gillard in September, but only with the support of rural-based independent MPs.

In the intervening period there was incremental change in Housing SA. A new service delivery model was introduced in 2008, and the Minister's Strategic Housing Advisory Committee was asked to seek feedback. Barossa and Gawler region representatives responded that 'the reduction in housing numbers is such a problem that it overrides other considerations', and that 'Housing SA seems to be understaffed to provide the service being demanded of them'.[27] Under the new model of regional services, housing teams provided support to tenants, and helped customers plan for their future housing, including purchase. Housing officers worked across purchase, rental and Aboriginal housing and no longer had dedicated areas or tenants – now the responsibility of the regional teams. A new assessment process identified those in greatest need and responded quickly with a suitable housing option.[28]

While the Riverside headquarters in Adelaide were being refurbished, some of the Urban Strategy and Asset Investment staff moved temporarily to 153 Wakefield Street. Adelaide regional office also moved (in 2005) to premises at 120 Flinders Street; other metropolitan offices were at Elizabeth, Gawler, Marion, Modbury, Noarlunga, Port Adelaide, Salisbury and The Parks Community Centre. In the country there were regional offices in Alice Springs (Northern Territory), Anangu Pitjantjatjara Yankunytjatjara Umuwa Office, Berri, Ceduna, Coober Pedy, Mount Gambier, Murray Bridge, Port Augusta, Port Lincoln, Port Pirie and Whyalla. Mount Gambier was a new office built as a 'one stop shop' for all DFC services and single case management (as done in Victoria). This was a pilot intended for adoption in metropolitan offices.

The year 2008 brought further upheaval for staff, as the main drivers of institutional change – Weatherill, Vardon, Smith and Fulcher – all departed. DFC was responsible to two ministers: Jay Weatherill and Jennifer Rankine (Minister for the Status of Women). After a Cabinet reshuffle in July 2008 Rankine was appointed in Weatherill's place as Minister for Housing as well as Minister for Families and Communities, the Northern Suburbs, Ageing, and Disability. The new minister saw the main benefits in holding these several portfolios, as 'having

Phil Fagan-Schmidt, Executive Director, Housing SA, in 2010. (Photo Susan Marsden)

these agencies work collaboratively to address critical needs such as disability housing, and children in care'.[29]

Helen Fulcher moved in 2008, at the same time as Weatherill, from Housing SA to head the Environment Protection Authority, and Vardon retired in August 2008 and was followed as Chief Executive by Joslene Mazel. After three years at DFC as Deputy Chief Executive Housing and Disability, Peter Smith moved to Adelaide City Council as Chief Executive from October 2008.[30]

After these departures the impetus for change slowed, but continuity – not only with the Housing Plan, but also with the earlier system – was maintained by the appointment of Phil Fagan-Schmidt to the re-titled position of Executive Director, Housing SA, in January 2009 (the position of Deputy Chief Executive of DFC housing was abolished after Smith's departure). Fagan-Schmidt's experience dated from the 1980s when he worked on his thesis with Greg Black at the Emergency Housing Office (EHO). He then worked at the EHO with Robyn Morriset, again with Black in the Office of Housing, and as a housing adviser. Some years later he was recruited into the Department of Human Services, returning to housing when Sue Vardon was appointed to DFC. He established the Affordable Housing Innovations Unit.

That background meant that Fagan-Schmidt appreciated the 'terrific corporate knowledge and history and expertise in a large group of people' at the Trust, who were now required to work in areas of ambiguity. He said,

> it's simple to talk about owning houses, looking after houses and renting houses because the business has a precision. When you're talking about public policy concepts like intervening in markets, working with partners, using legal legislative policy and practice to achieve outcomes, it can be ... more nebulous.

Change itself was difficult for some staff, 'for others, the explanation of where we're heading can be difficult to understand, it's not an easy, clear story'. The Trust had developed a strong skill base in a narrow set of disciplines. Fagan-Schmidt added,

> We're seeing the Trust evolve into public policy and interventions in market rather than being a sole single monopoly provider, and that will take time. But it wouldn't take much tracking of the leadership of the Trust over the last five or 10 years to see there's been an enormous injection of new people [and the development of] a wider set of skill bases.

Looking back from retirement, Vardon said that no public briefing on the housing reforms ever stated what was in her view fundamental to them:

> The thing that was very obvious to Jay and I was 'Who was the customer?' Now [to the Housing Trust], the customer was the tenant; the customer was not the unhoused person. And we wanted to shift the notion of the 'customer'.[31]

THIS SECTION TO BE COMPLETED BY AGENCY STAFF (UNLESS REFERRING ONLY) AND/OR HOUSING SA STAFF

HOUSING NEEDS ISSUES

1. Please tick (✔) which of the following needs criteria apply to the customer's household

HOMELESS/AT RISK

- [ ] Homeless
- [ ] Life threatening situation at home
- [ ] Inadequately housed
- [ ] Persistent harassment
- [ ] Natural disaster eg fire, flood
- [ ] Domestic/family violence
- [ ] Victim of major crime
- [x] Living in transitional or crisis accommodation

If you ticked any of the above, please provide details and attach documentation to verify

IS CURRENTLY RESIDING IN SUPPORTED TRANSITIONAL ACCOMMODATION FOR WOMEN WHO ARE HOMELESS WITH A MENTAL HEALTH DIAGNOSIS.

ACCESS BARRIERS (HOUSING APPLICANTS ONLY)

(reasons why customer is unable to access/maintain private housing)

- [x] Long term health issues
- [x] ~~Lack~~ of financial skills/resources
- [ ] Long term disability issues
- [ ] Cultural or social issues
- [x] ~~Discrimination~~ in private rental
- [ ] Lack of social skills
- [ ] Exiting institutional care

If you ticked any of the above, please provide details and attach documentation to verify

IS CURRENTLY A FULL TIME STUDENT IN RECEIPT OF NEWSTART. HAS A HISTORY OF DRUG USE & MENTAL ILLNESS WHICH HAVE IMPACTED ON HER ABILITY TO OBTAIN INDEPENDENT HOUSING.

OTHER ISSUES (HOUSING APPLICANTS ONLY)

- [ ] Disability Support Pension recipient
- [ ] Refugees in Aust less than 2 years
- [ ] Totally & Permanently Incapacitated Pension recipient
- [ ] People exiting Direct Lease housing

If you ticked any of the above, please attach documentation to verify

If there are any EXCEPTIONAL CIRCUMSTANCES not listed above, please provide details and attach documentation to verify

IS CURRENTLY HOMELESS & MAY ONLY STAY AT CATHERINE HOUSE FOR A PERIOD OF UP TO 6 MONTHS.

TENANCY ISSUES (HOUSING TRUST OR ABORIGINAL HOUSING TENANTS ONLY)

(reasons why customer is unable to access/maintain private housing)

- [ ] Unresolvable neighbour dispute
- [ ] Health reasons
- [ ] Overcrowding
- [ ] Disability reasons
- [ ] Needs to be closer to supports
- [ ] Under occupancy

If you ticked any of the above, please provide details and attach documentation to verify

Housed and unhoused

> The 'changes' minister Jay Weatherill has announced regarding Housing SA (*The Advertiser*, 3/5/06) amount to nothing more than moving the deckchairs on the Titanic.
> It is clear that there is no real good news for those on huge waiting lists. The letter I received even admits no improvement for those on this waiting list.
> For those disadvantaged or disabled, the option of private rental is simply impossible in these expensive times.
> The good news he should be announcing is a decision to build many more Trust-type homes/units and reverse the shocking decline in public housing. (Jeremy Woods, tenant at Warradale, 2006)[32]

Formal restatement of the Housing Trust's role as a provider of rental homes for 'high-needs' customers merely confirmed the practice of the past decade. By mid-2006 the percentage of all tenants receiving rental subsidies had reached 84.89%, and the percentage of new tenants receiving subsidies was 94.8%. Over the year 68% of new tenants allocated to housing were category 1 or category 2.[33]

Lyndie Marsden became one of them. Living with severe cancer, she had the required support letter from her oncologist as the first step in applying to the Trust for herself and her two daughters. Having left their family home in Kilcoy (Queensland) for Adelaide, she said, 'My plan was to work, get a mortgage and buy, but I'm no longer in a position to do that'. The attraction of public rather than private rental was not only financial. 'It's the security, the stability, having something that's virtually yours. If I had a place with the girls it would be ours – as close as I can have now.' In September 2007, six months after her application was accepted, her urgent need was confirmed, and Lyndie Marsden moved into one of the Trust's renovated cottages at Mile End.[34]

Weatherill reported in 2007 that Housing SA was establishing a single waiting list, re-assessing people on existing lists to ensure 'a consistent approach to prioritisation'. Work was also underway to align the Disability SA single waiting list to housing allocation and planning processes managed by Housing SA.[35] Applications overall were in decline, but this was partly the result of changes in eligibility, including application review rules that removed those who did not renew contact about their application after 12 months. Category 1 applications continued to rise due to declining housing opportunities.[36] Many were recent immigrants, including more arrivals from African countries whose usual difficulties with finding homes (including language differences and lack of knowledge about services) were compounded by having large families and the general housing shortage. In 2006–07 approximately 3,300 of 22,000 public housing applicants had linguistically diverse backgrounds, but only 10% could be housed; most of the others were given help to rent privately.[37]

Speaking in Parliament, Hon. D. G. E. Hood spelled out another dilemma: to cut debt the Trust was 'disposing of 18 per cent of its stock – some 8,000 houses ... To deal with the reduced stock, the housing trust has redefined its eligibility criteria and ... demand has fallen from 13,892 applicants for housing in 1997 to just 6,184 applications in 2007'. This represented a 55% decrease in demand, far exceeding the 30% decline in supply since 1992. In June 2007, there were 22,339 applications for the 44,220 houses. Hood concluded by asking the Minister:

1. Is Housing SA now actively discouraging new applicants for public housing?
2. If this is the case, why should state and commonwealth funds not also be structured to bypass Housing SA where possible and be provided directly to the community housing organisations that appear to operate more efficiently at less cost?[38]

One argument used by ministers to justify this sell-down of stock was that South Australia had more public housing than the national average, and so received less than the state's proper share of Commonwealth Rent Assistance (CRA) funds for people on Centrelink benefits or low incomes renting privately.[39] As the amount of public housing fell, more CRA did flow to the state but, as Downie observed, 'we are not seeing private landlords providing more housing for low income tenants'. Private rental vacancy rates were at an all-time low by 2007, and he cited research by Judith Yates that found that half the lowest priced rental stock was occupied by higher-income earners. He said, 'The private sector continues to be very discerning about who it rents its properties to and with less of a safety net in the public sector, there may inevitably be more low income and vulnerable people inappropriately housed'. Local government and social service representatives from Gawler reported on discrimination by real estate agents against single mothers, Aboriginal people and large families. A shortage of private rental led to bidding wars, and there was a discrepancy between the amount of rent assistance offered and the actual rent charged by landlords.[40]

Lyndie Marsden's rent in 2007 for a small home unit in the eastern suburbs of Adelaide was $195 per week, consuming almost two-thirds of her disability support pension of $600 a fortnight (which included $104 rent assistance). Her pension was reduced by that amount (rent assistance) with her move into public rental, but the rent dropped to $200 per fortnight. At the time of Lyndie's move, private weekly rentals of less than $200 were already few. Only 38 suburbs offered properties with a median weekly rental of $200 or less; two years later such rentals were available in 11 suburbs only. Elizabeth Vale was the cheapest at $178.[41]

For Lyndie Marsden the other change for the better in her move to public rental was being able to stay in the one place. Before then she had had to shift with her daughters from one private unit to the next, in all, 'four times in three years. It's exhausting. The last move almost killed me'. In fast-growing semi-rural districts such as the Barossa and Gawler region, frequent moves by renters was also due to their need to follow seasonal jobs like grape picking.

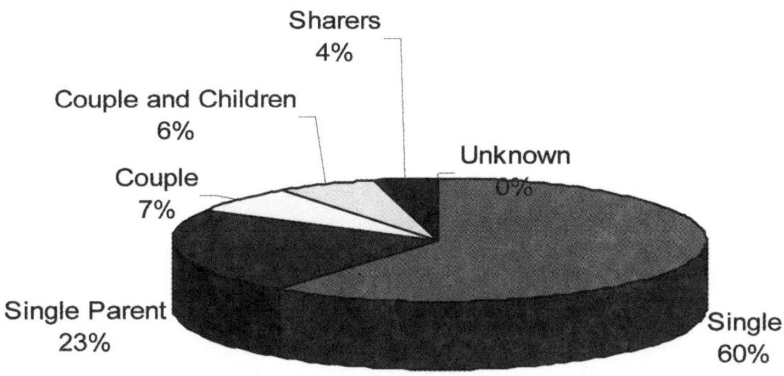

The majority of new public and Aboriginal housing tenancies were single people, as shown in Housing in focus 2007–08.

Unemployment was low because of the Barossa wine industry, but workers were paid only the basic $14.35 per hour, and had no permanent accommodation. The Barossa could not get enough workers for that reason, and also because of poor public transport.

Public services and public housing were concentrated in Gawler, low-cost boarding houses and hostels were being bulldozed for more profitable developments, and there were many substandard private rental places. Low-income tenants with multiple difficulties were congregating in poorly constructed private flats and causing wider problems. People were living in tents, cars and caravans in many towns, and young people were 'couch surfing' (a form of homelessness not recognised by Housing SA). De-institutionalisation had forced those with a disability, mental health or drug and alcohol problems, into unsuitable accommodation, there were bed blockages in hospitals and in respite facilities because there was nowhere to move people, and there was no local emergency or transitional housing to be had.[42]

Some 25% of social housing customers in Australia have a disability. Under Commonwealth State Territory Disability Agreements (CSTDA) dating from 1991 responsibility for housing remained with the states, with some funding from the Commonwealth. A Senate Inquiry reported in 2007 that CSTDA funding had not reduced unmet need for accommodation and support services. Many submissions asked what would happen to a son or daughter with disability when their parent carers died. Additional funding was provided, but the states still grappled with rising need for special housing.[43]

Responsibility for those customers involved more than rental subsidy or building modifications. Some new tenants, ill-equipped or disinclined to regulate their behaviour, continued to disrupt the lives of their neighbours. In Patricia Sumerling's words,

> For many years, we used to know everyone and looked out for each other's property when going away ... However, in more recent times, there is no doubt the types of tenants are changing ... we have had some run ins with newer tenants who do not do the right thing, by giving consideration to their neighbours. Some of these people could learn a lot from our more recent next door neighbours who come from the Sudan ... They are a simply lovely family and if we all had neighbours like them, no-one would be complaining.[44]

When Alison Murchie moved into Elliot Lodge, a group of 90 walk-up flats in Gilberton, many tenants were paying full rent. Twenty years later she said that less than 10% did so, 'and that's reflected in the standard of the flats. A lot of people have no living skills, no respect and lack the ability to look after their property. But that's a reflection of society, not the Housing Trust'. Once, she might have been able to buy her own house. 'Its too late now, I've retired and have no money. I live with the consequences. The vast majority are lovely – it's really difficult at times'. Elliot Lodge is in an upmarket suburb and she found that people's attitudes changed when they learned she was a Trust tenant, although

Elizabeth/Gawler Regional Advisory Board members and friends at the annual Christmas pageant, Munno Para, published in Trust Talk Tenant Link, *Issue 17, June 2006.*

'Walkerville has the highest ratio of Housing Trust tenants of any council area'. She was proud to be a Trust tenant, and recalled with pleasure growing up in a Trust house in Clearview.

> There was no stigma. We were all working class. That was one of the reasons I applied for a Housing Trust house. To this day I support social housing. But it fell apart when it changed from social housing to welfare housing ... Now you feel you have to apologise about being a Housing Trust tenant. The media are not interested in good news stories about the Trust.[45]

Some places were rarely out of the news. A suburban newspaper reported in 2007 that the change from public to welfare housing was 'personified in the conflicts between neighbours at Stow Court, Fullarton' that had caused complaints and police callouts for many years. In this group of 106 flats, elderly tenants were mixed with people with 'mental health problems, disabilities, drug addiction and violent behaviour'. The local MP said that the problem was having tenants 'who should be living in Glenside and they're not getting any outpatient services ... The long-term tenants are being asked to live in a drop-in centre and their sense of pride is being lost'.[46]

Weatherill agreed on 'essentially this clash of the new and the old Housing Trust'. The old tenants, now pensioners, had been working people housed under a different set of policies and paying market rents.

> So they've made this place their home and they're now seeing a large proportion of the new tenants being people who are the most vulnerable people who might have a range of challenges that might also cause trouble for the neighbourhood. So there are these two Housing Trusts occurring side-by-side.[47]

Drawing on her experience as a former employee and as a long-standing tenant, Barbara Holt said that ordinary families who were good Trust householders could also become 'welfare prone'. There was a danger of returning to the old 'stigma thinking' that would not benefit tenants or government as debt built up. A more equitable balance had existed under the old system, with those who could paying full rent, and reduced rent being supported rent only until the tenants found employment. 'SA will now become the same as other states. If you live in "state housing" you have to learn to be "poor" = The stigma'.[48]

Her views were echoed by Housing SA's Phil Fagan-Schmidt, who suggested that the narrowing of public housing into 'a focus on social housing for a minority of the population runs the risk of marginalising the groups that you're trying to encourage back into economy, employment, training, participation ...'; hence the broadening of scope to encourage a wider range of affordable housing in South Australia.[49]

The Housing Trust's reputation still compared favourably with public housing interstate. David Jackson, who works for DFC, was told by a friend who moved from Victoria, that, unlike Victoria and New South Wales, 'where acquiring a Housing Commission house is considered a blight, it was a matter of pride and success when you got a Housing Trust house. It was completely different being in Housing Trust in South Australia.'

But for the population at large, attention was fixed on bad tenants, fanned by a bad press. Helen Fulcher said that she was saddened that talkback radio characterised all Trust tenants as 'careless as citizens'. High-needs customers were only a proportion of tenants. 'We often do an injustice to tenants who are quite proud people in their own homes. Just on the radio the other day there was a suggestion that Trust tenants are people who drink and smoke to excess, and it's a very melodramatic picture to paint'. The Trust and its advisory committees had always struggled with how to get a more respectful media portrayal of tenants.

One Housing Trust home at Parafield Gardens stood at the centre of a notorious child neglect case reported in 2008. On another occasion the Minister explained that, like any other landlord, Housing SA did not have the power simply to evict and must seek permission to do so from the Residential Tenancies Tribunal, but he also oversaw stringent changes to deal with the problem. Housing SA developed memoranda of understanding (MOUs) with SA Police, Mental Health and Families SA to assist in managing challenging tenancies. The MOU agreed in 2006 with SA Police was to work together to evict drug dealers and disruptive tenants, and more than 400 cases were jointly examined in the first six months.[50]

In 2007 another MOU was signed between the Minister for Housing and the Minister for Mental Health, 'to guide the development and management of collaborative working practices to improve accessible and sustainable housing outcomes for people with mental illness'. The MOU formalised working relationships between the agencies including through 'early intervention and prevention when managing tenancy issues'. Case management or tenancy support plans would be developed for each customer, and the housing organisations would contact Mental Health Services when difficulties occurred with a tenant who had support needs. The MOU emphasised respect for 'the right of tenants and their neighbours to live in peace, comfort and privacy'.[51]

That right was often tested. In 2007 Weatherill told *Messenger* readers of a new 'three-strike' policy leading to eviction for tenants who repeatedly misbehaved.[52] The Trust's 2008–09 annual report recorded 185 cases of severe and repeated disruption managed by the Disruptive Management Team. Only 15 of those tenants were evicted, but in 2010 Cabinet approved a plan allowing more flexibility to remove them. All new tenants would be placed on one to 10 year contracts after a six-month probation. The changes would bring public housing into line with private rental and community housing, and would reduce the long waiting list, but were not retrospective. The acting minister said that 'tenure will not be automatic, but based on behaviour, debt and need'. This meant less security for tenants and brought an end to an era when they gained a Trust home for life. The usually forthright Tony Elmers cautiously welcomed the change, saying that 'unfortunately not everyone does the right thing'.[53]

In 1985 the first Regional Advisory Board was established in Marion, whose members celebrated their 20th year in 2006 with housing and other officials. Left to right: Mayor of Marion, Felicity-Ann Lewis, with RAB chair Marlene Littlewood and an original member, Elsie Burrows.

If any views were sought from other tenant representatives, they were not quoted, although they would not have been easy to get. Changes as important as fixed-term contracts would have once been discussed by Regional Advisory Board members, but the boards and their Public Housing Customer Forum were no longer in operation. Nor were those tenant representatives closely consulted on the service reforms of 2006. Meeting in December 2006, Forum members accepted the Minister's point that communication was difficult under the previous setup of four separate boards, but (in Murchie's words), 'We weren't told why this desperate need for change'. Betty Alberton concurred, writing later that the private sector would never be able to replace government in providing good affordable housing for people on low incomes with the support some of them needed.

> I believe that a Government run housing sector or Community housing for low-income people is definitely the way to go. SAHT was the best-run public housing organization in the country (my opinion). But I feel that they have

lost their way with the changes that they have put in place over the past few years.[54]

Forum members saw that the changes were confusing tenants and staff, and increasing staff turnover. They wrote, 'Since these changes have been put in place we are concerned for the future of Public Housing and tenants/customers are becoming more and more confused, disillusioned and frustrated'.[55] Their observations were echoed by Downie, who noted that for the first time since the National Customer Survey began (in 1996), 'SA did not come out on top and Housing SA ran second in the 2007 survey results'.[56]

Even before 2006 RABs were losing support from 'certain elements within the SA Housing Trust', although not all staff felt this way and the Trust still provided financial support. RAB members and Forum representatives knew that reform was needed, hoped for 'an injection of new younger blood', and were looking at how to expand. Changes to the Trust's client base meant that representation should widen, 'but without the support from the organisation [we] felt that we were fighting a losing battle'.

One final aim was realised. The Public Housing Customer Forum had pushed to get a 'one stop shop' informing public, private or community housing renters. In January 2007 the independent Tenant's Information and Advocacy Service was opened. Forum member Marlene Littlewood hoped this would mean staff, rather than just an answering machine, were available to answer the 'phone. 'Some people take a lot to make that critical phone call and then get an answering machine and don't call back.' Anglicare supplied the service, and in 2009–10 it fielded 2,850 telephone enquiries, and advocated for nearly 400 people to landlords and at Residential Tenancies Tribunal and Housing Appeal hearings.[57]

In 2008 Minister Weatherill hosted a ceremony at Parliament House to acknowledge the contribution of 32 housing volunteers active in these customer representation groups. They were the five RABs (Adelaide City, Modbury, Marion, The Parks, Salisbury and Elizabeth/Gawler region) and Salisbury North Urban Improvement Project Reference Group. Several guests had been housing volunteers for more than 15 years, and gave time also for other voluntary services. Judy Croucher, a volunteer with Salisbury North Improvement Group, had worked voluntarily for 70 hours a month for 50 years, and was at the time a management committee member, minute taker, tool bank coordinator and a member of the northern region's Neighbourhood Watch. The same 'dedicated group of volunteers' were thanked by Helen Fulcher, but her praise prefaced a dismissal. Housing SA had farewelled regional advisory boards to make way for a participation model based on those used in Domiciliary Care, and in Glasgow, UK. The advisory board structure would be replaced with 'a forum approach that enables more timely and flexible customer participation'. This approach was intended to solicit feedback from a wider range of customers. Volunteers would be sought when the participation strategy was completed.[58]

Members of The Parks Advisory Committee established in August 2006 to ensure community involvement in the Westwood Urban Renewal Project, including future use of The Parks Community Centre.

Weatherill explained that the new focus groups (appointed by him) would more fairly represent public tenants, private renters and the homeless. At an Opposition news conference, Bryan Atkinson from The Parks Advisory Board said in reply, 'We're the only democratically appointed people, if the Minister is allowed to appoint puppets then he will just pull their strings like he always does'. RAB members, he said, did an important job in keeping an eye on disruptive tenants and overcrowded properties.[59]

Forum member, Betty Alberton, suggested that the old form of tenant participation 'had most probably run its course and was in need of a revamp', but that 'H-SA should have waited until they had a new scheme in place before they scrapped the old scheme. I think it will be much harder to get a new idea going now'. Two years after Fulcher's announcement, she wrote, 'I do hope the new "Community Champions Scheme" is successful because some form of tenant participation is needed'.[60]

As the Forum and Marion, Elizabeth and Gawler RABs were incorporated, they continued to exist but no longer met, having lost their funding. By 2010, Forum members were discussing the need to come together once again.[61] Looking back, they wrote,

> After 20+ years of voluntary service to both tenants and the Housing Trust funding was discontinued and all Boards were disbanded leaving a huge void

The Seasons at Wandana development offered homes for less than $170,000 to low income purchasers and received a 2008 Urban Development Institute of Australia award in the Affordable housing category.

> within the Trust community (tenants and staff) as there was no other means of consultation in place. We were bitterly disappointed with this decision and perhaps a little angry also.
>
> There were several attempts to develop a model for community particiation none of which were accepted; finally someone was commissioned to work full time on the project. Having a person work full time enabled a consultation and planning process and we did have input into this, but it was made quite clear to us that the organisation had no interest in what went before. We felt that to develop a new model there needed to be an understanding of how and why it all began and what the benefits were to both tenants and the Trust
>
> It is our understanding that much of the innovations are unable to proceed due to 'Funding cuts'. The 'Community Engagement' project is now being piloted in both the Modbury and Elizabeth regions.[62]

During its transitional phase in 2006–07 the Trust Board pointed out that if the citizen's voice was not accounted for at Playford North, the matter could escalate to 'a political risk'.[63] As Betty Alberton recalls, the importance of community consultation was well recognised, with equal project partners being denoted as Land Management Corporation, DFC, City of Playford and the community

through the Community Reference Group (chaired by her). An 'Imagine Peachey' information trailer was driven to shopping centres, and a well-attended community Fun Day was held in November. 'The trailer and fun day is community run and organized by volunteers with the assistance of the partners.'[64] Many other popular activities in old and new housing areas throughout South Australia were supported through Community Project Grant funding provided by the South Australian Housing Trust.

Playford Alive included one form of public partnership; affordable housing involved others. The Minister's Strategic Housing Advisory Committee held regional consultations during 2008 to discuss the crisis for low and middle income South Australians caused by the continuing deterioration in housing affordability and the worsening economic situation. What was being done?

Alternative approaches to affordable housing[65]

> The Housing Trust always had a very strong relationship with the private sector. This isn't a new idea; indeed, it wasn't established by a Labor government, it was established by a conservative government and there was no notion that there would be a government public works program that would be building these houses; it was essentially a relationship with the private

ladder

Multi-unit projects planned to reintroduce affordable housing and supported accommodation into the urban centres of Adelaide and Port Adelaide included the UNO Apartments in Waymouth Street (above) which is by far the tallest building ever constructed by the Housing Trust, Ifould Street Apartment (bottom left), and the Ladder Foyer that would provide units for homeless youth within Port Adelaide's historic Black Diamond Hotel.

> sector. So I'm trying to look at the modern tools that we have to see whether we can achieve some of the things that the Housing Trust in the past had to achieve by direct procurement of affordable housing opportunities. (Weatherill interview, 2007)

The 10-year Housing Plan aimed to halve the numbers of people in housing stress; encourage more affordable housing; and increase community-based housing options for people with a disability. The plan established the Affordable Housing Innovations Program with a 'potential' investment pool of $93 million. Although the Housing Trust had never ceased doing so, the Minister said, 'Once again, we are working with the private sector'. The new Affordable Housing Trust would be 'given the freedom to pursue innovation in new affordable housing supply in concert with private and community partners'. Again, as in the original Trust, this would be 'guided by a Board including people with substantial industry experience who will provide ideas and links to industry. I will be asking Affordable Housing Trust Board to build ... capacity to deliver around 1,000 new affordable housing opportunities per year'.[66]

Weatherill continued, 'The next step along the continuum – that is the affordable housing offering – is something that in the current environment we will only be able to expand if we form partnerships'. The Equity Start Program was introduced as part of the Housing Plan to encourage affordable ownership. Equity Start was a special home loan made available to social housing tenants through HomeStart Finance. Revenue from houses sold was paid into the Affordable Housing Innovations Fund. Subsidies were funded by Cabinet and by the SAHT, as tenants could also purchase houses from the private market, and when they did so the Trust was required to transfer an amount equivalent to the capital value of the rental property (less sale costs) to the Innovations Fund. This amount must be made up by further sales of Trust stock. By July 2006 this amount was $26,051,000.[67] Around 1,000 tenants took up the purchase offer and the proceeds were reinvested in the fund.

The Affordable Housing Innovations Fund was established in 2005, administered by the Affordable Housing Innovations Unit that was set up in DFC well before the new board was constituted (in 2006). Phil Fagan-Schmidt, who was appointed Director, understood Weatherill's intent 'to widen the role of housing into an economic agenda'. He described the unit's work in three parts: negotiating for policy change at national level; creating state legislation for inclusionary zoning and putting it into practice; and trialling a different way of supplying housing through the new Innovations Fund. This strategy to grow affordable housing supply is also reflected in the government's 30-year plan for Greater Adelaide that was released in 2010. 'For example, the plan says we have to build 38,700 new affordable housing opportunities or units in the next 30 years, so it gives us quite clear and specific targets and responsibilities.'[68]

Innovation funds were used to trial new partnerships with non-government groups, and the unit set to work with groups that had placed bids for funded

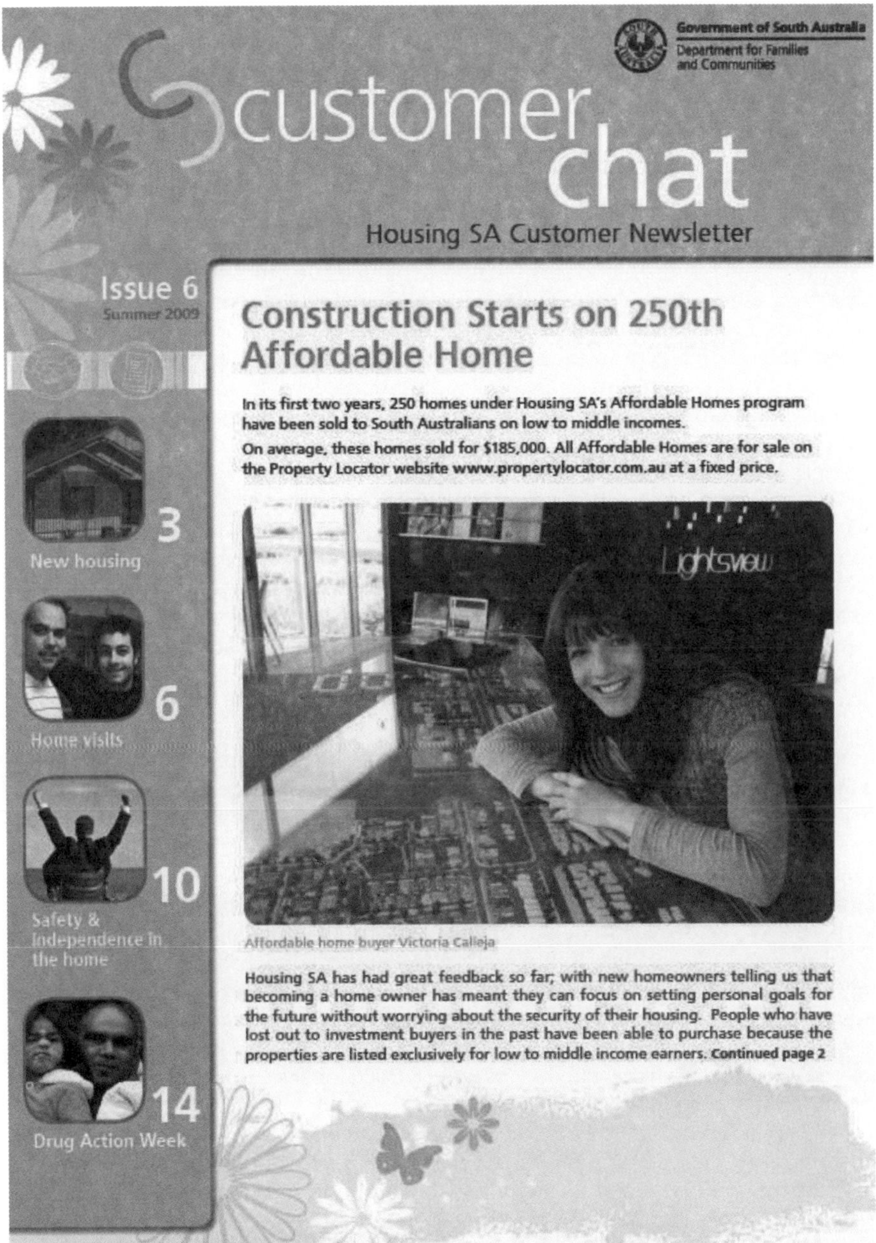

Government of South Australia
Department for Families and Communities

customer chat

Housing SA Customer Newsletter

Issue 6
Summer 2009

Construction Starts on 250th Affordable Home

In its first two years, 250 homes under Housing SA's Affordable Homes program have been sold to South Australians on low to middle incomes.

On average, these homes sold for $185,000. All Affordable Homes are for sale on the Property Locator website www.propertylocator.com.au at a fixed price.

Affordable home buyer Victoria Calleja

Housing SA has had great feedback so far; with new homeowners telling us that becoming a home owner has meant they can focus on setting personal goals for the future without worrying about the security of their housing. People who have lost out to investment buyers in the past have been able to purchase because the properties are listed exclusively for low to middle income earners. **Continued page 2**

3 New housing

6 Home visits

10 Safety & Independence in the home

14 Drug Action Week

Front page news, Customer Chat, *Summer 2009.*

projects. The first call for expressions of interest closed in December 2005, and by mid-2006 there were 11 capital projects underway. Partner organisations were committed to constructing 137 houses in metropolitan and country areas, and a 14 bedroom residential facility, with the fund supplying 46.5% of the cost.[69] Around 20 groups became involved in partnerships, Fagan-Schmidt describing them as organisations that were typically involved in such projects, 'many of them quite historic in South Australia', such as Adelaide Workmen's Homes, Adelaide Benevolent Society, James Brown Memorial Trust, Laura and Alfred West Cottage Homes (Anglicare) and the Lutheran Church. They usually raised half the funds for a project, and the unit provided the other half, Fagan-Schmidt observing 'innovation in new built form, in financing structures, in working with groups in different ways, in providing support services in different ways'. Just as in the UK, this represented a widening of housing providers, a process he compared to the change in public policy at national level from having a monopoly telecommunications provider (Telstra), to multiple providers. 'Our future is to not have a single provider but have more of a mixed economy.'

There were problems to address – apart from getting the money. The main challenge in moving from a monopoly provider as good as the Housing Trust was the 'patchy' performance of the new providers – some were very good and some were poor – and so it took too long to roll out some projects and required patience to build the new sector, and 'not expect that it's out there day one when government decides that they want to move into this'.

A 'Property Locator' website helped low income and first home buyers who also had access to HomeStart Finance (although purchasers who received student benefits were not eligible). There were sticks as well as carrots in the push to increase the supply of affordable housing. As Weatherill announced in 2007, under state planning laws affordable homes built in new developments would be offered exclusively to low and moderate income earners for 90 days, and 15% per cent of all new housing developments must be classed as affordable housing.[70] For example, when the state purchased the large Clipsal industrial site at Bowden, extended by purchase of the old Brompton Gasworks (2008–10) the Land Management Corporation began to plan a replacement 'mixed-use' village with 15% of residences to be supplied by affordable housing groups.[71]

Fagan-Schmidt and his staff were active in getting such housing included in new developments. He described this as 'creating social outcomes in economic markets'. Unlike the old Housing Trust, the unit was 'not the monopoly developer', but was a significant player using the new legislative powers. By 2010 legal agreements had been reached to supply 2,000 houses, more than the amount of new public housing.

The South Australian Affordable Housing Trust was 'guided by a Board including people with substantial industry experience who will provide ideas and links to industry'.[72] They would approve funding and advise the minister on housing opportunities.[73] Members met for the first time on 27 November 2006, before the Minister had publicly announced their names. They discussed the fund, industry trends, national reform, the 15% referral, and a proposed Rent to Buy program. They were told of negotiations by the Innovations Unit, including with the Wyatt Benevolent Institute, which had already provided assistance to Southern Junction Community Services for projects in Seaford Meadows. An 'eco-affordable' development was planned for Whitmore Square in Adelaide, as well as rental housing in stage 3 of the Northgate development in the northern suburbs.[74] At their meeting in the following March, members were told there was $66 million in the fund, of which $30 million had been committed.

It was not clear just how the role of the new Board differed from that of the Housing Trust; at the same meeting in March 2007 members requested some 'ad hoc discussions ... as the Board is new and has not totally defined "Affordable Housing"'. They also agreed that 'we need to differentiate: HomeStart = purchasing $ power – SAAHT = upping supply at achievable price'.[75] From later in that year, the SAAHT operated as a subcommittee of the Housing Trust, while the Affordable Housing Innovations Unit was 'mainstreamed', with inclusionary zoning placed in Housing SA's asset area, and the work with non-government organisations placed in the community housing area.

Weatherill's hope of reviving state and private sector support for low-cost housing was not unique to South Australia. Through the early 2000s government and non-government groups met to debate how to do the same. The Housing Industry Association initiated the National Summit on Housing Affordability in 2004. A meeting of ministers in 2005 adopted the Framework for National Action on Affordable Housing with a usefully broad definition of 'housing which is affordable for low and moderate income households across home ownership, private rental as well as public rental tenures'. Participants agreed there should be a 'sector development plan' for non-government providers.[76] The 2006 National Affordable Housing Forum released 'A call for action' in June 2007, in the leadup to the federal election.

Weatherill pushed for replacing the Commonwealth State Housing Agreement with an Affordable Housing Agreement. By early 2009, when the new national agreement began, Housing SA could report the start of construction of its 250th affordable home. Over the past two years these houses had been sold for an average $185,000. *Customer Chat* recorded 'great feedback' from satisfied purchasers. 'People who have lost out to investment buyers in the past have been able to purchase because the properties are listed exclusively for low to middle income earners.'[77]

By September 2009 South Australia's Affordable Housing Innovations Fund had committed $65 million for 42 leveraged rental projects (548 dwellings). Partner organisations had contributed equity of around $70 million in land, borrowings and philanthropic contributions. New Commonwealth funding through the National Rental Affordability Scheme, the National Partnership for Social Housing and the Nation Building-Economic Stimulus Plan was expected to boost growth of the sector.[78]

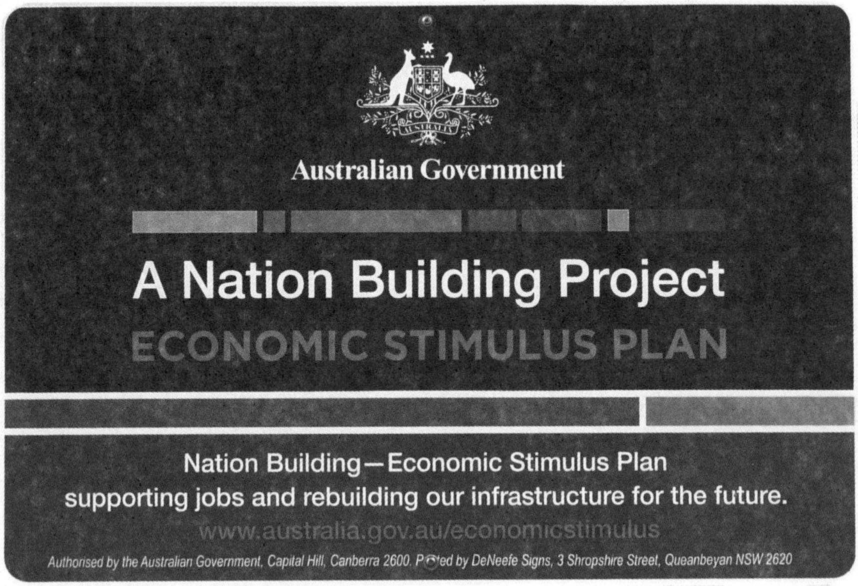

Nation building in South Australia

> In November, 2007, we heard from Prime Minister Kevin Rudd that he would pledge $150 million to ease the homeless crisis. We are told of the 100,000 out on the streets ... Now, Mr Rudd has pledged $1.2 billion over four years (*The Advertiser*, 22/12/08) to halve the number of homeless by 2020.
>
> It is not just money that is needed ... More affordable Housing Trust homes would be a start. These are being demolished for their land value and tenants wishing to buy them are being given outrageous valuations preventing them from ever getting a foot into a home of their own.
>
> More Trust rental properties would be a good start to getting people off the streets. Let's hope the Labor Government is not giving us another empty promise. (Yvonne Brand, letter to *The Advertiser* 24 December 2008)

Jay Weatherill understood that unhelpful national policies: declining financial support and new programs – such as first homeowners' grants and private rental assistance – had diminished affordability. 'One thing we identified in the State Housing Plan', he said, 'is that it will be difficult without a commonwealth partner to achieve our goals in affordable housing'.[79] In the Legislative Council debate on the new housing bill in 2007, Greens member Mark Parnell acknowledged

Weatherill's efforts to respond to national pressure. But Parnell advised that they wait for the outcome of the 2007 federal election before acting to dismantle the Trust. If Labor won there could be a change in the Commonwealth-state funding agreement, and the Party had talked about placing a greater emphasis on public housing.[80]

The Liberal coalition government under Prime Minister John Howard remained unsympathetic to state-supplied housing. Pre-figuring a new CSHA (due in 2008), the federal minister criticised the states for failing to increase the supply of social housing – noting that stock had fallen most precipitously in South Australia – while saying that he favoured instead allowing private developers to tender for Commonwealth housing funds.[81]

During the election campaign the ALP proposed the National Rental Affordability Scheme (NRAS) to package incentives for investment in and construction of social housing. In November 2007 Labor, led by Kevin Rudd, won government and implemented the scheme, aiming to increase the supply of affordable rental dwellings by 50,000 by 2012. The scheme was designed to pool resources from Commonwealth, state and local governments, financial institutions, investors and non-profit providers. Successful applicants could receive a 'national rental incentive' for each approved dwelling for a period of 10 years if it was rented to eligible low and moderate income households at 20% below market rates. The scheme began on 1 July 2008.[82] The first NRAS project in South Australia (12 new rental units at Hampstead Gardens) was opened in May 2009 and, by the end of the year, 961 incentives had been offered in South Australia, most for new dwellings in the inner suburbs and Adelaide city. Seventy per cent combined state capital with the Commonwealth's recurrent contribution.[83]

Labor had also promised funding for 'A Place to Call Home' to supply 600 dwellings as crisis accommodation for homeless people. This required matching state funds; each dwelling would be transferred to public stock after 12 months and the resident given tenancy. This scheme became part of the National Affordable Housing Agreement that succeeded the CSHA of 2003–08, as had been advocated by Weatherill. In the words of Phil Fagan-Schmidt,

> He wanted the Commonwealth-State Housing Agreement to be renegotiated to be a broad agreement that included affordable housing and high-needs housing, and he was incredibly influential and successful ... that's quite a coup if you think that the Commonwealth-State Housing Agreement was first drafted in 1945 and ran through till 2008, from memory.

The National Affordable Housing Agreement came into operation on 1 January 2009.

Australia's federal government can make specific purpose payments to foster the pursuit of national objectives in areas customarily administered by the states. The shock of the global financial crisis in 2008 brought urgent action by the Rudd government to mitigate the fallout of business failure and job losses. Under the 'Nation Building – Economic Stimulus Plan', $15.1 billion was offered for social infrastructure, including public housing and services for the homeless and Indigenous people, to be developed during a five-year partnership with the states. A series of ambitiously named schemes of similar purpose was started up between 2008 and 2010: the Nation Building – Economic Stimulus Plan; the National Affordable Housing Agreement; the National Partnership Agreement on Social Housing; the National Partnership Agreement on Homelessness; and the National Partnership on Remote Indigenous Housing. The Housing Affordability Fund was to reduce the planning and infrastructure costs of building new housing developments, while stimulus funding was intended to protect jobs during the global economic downturn.[84]

What followed was an unprecedented increase in Commonwealth funding for housing programs in South Australia: $291 million to build and upgrade remote Indigenous housing; $60 million for improved homelessness services; 3,800 new affordable rental homes; $30 million for new high-needs social housing; $404 million for construction of 1,350 new rental houses under the stimulus package; and $30 million for additional upgrading of social housing.[85]

The injection of such an exceptional amount of money addressed some gaps that the Trust had struggled with for years. One of them was reintroducing affordable housing into Adelaide's city centre. A $46.5 million development at 102 Waymouth Street to provide a mix of affordable rental and home ownership was funded under the stimulus plan. A total of 146 apartments in a 17-storey building adjacent to the historic Queens Theatre were planned for completion in 2012.[86]

Maintenance Manager Shirley Trebilcock described the Nation Building – Economic Stimulus Plan as 'fantastic'. Federal funding under the plan required 'a real combination of people in my team here as well as the Maintenance Operations staff, plus people in other parts of Housing in Urban Renewal and doing upgrades as well'. Some Rudd government infrastructure programs were criticised for being either too hasty or too slow, for cost over-runs, or for injuries inflicted by inexperienced contractors, but the well-established systems and skills of the public housing sector expedited success, especially in South Australia. Housing SA was quick off the mark: as Mychelle Curran reported to the Board, Commonwealth approval was finalised in December 2009 for all proposals submitted under the program, and by the end of the month 11 properties were complete and a further 223 were under construction.[87]

Shirley Trebilcock said that her staff identified properties that would have been sold because they were beyond their 'use-by date', or too costly to fix but were in well-located areas; these could now be upgraded. The federal government wanted to approve how they got the work out into the building industry: Housing SA had an existing list of around 70 pre-qualified building companies, and obtained agreement to invite more to join. 'We held a forum and talked to them about Nation Building and about what we were wanting to do, and we more than doubled the list of builders so it's been really quite good to help stimulate the industry'. Builders could indicate a preference for new construction, upgrade or both. Projects were divided into different sizes to share the workload – Trebilcock knew of a husband and wife team that could do one or two houses at a time, and of companies who could do 10 or 12. 'So we were able to actually spread the workload through different-size companies – small, medium and large – which has been quite a good thing, hopefully it's achieved what the Federal Government wanted us to achieve, not one or two companies picking up the work'. They tried to monitor project pricing and 'saw a bit of a creep, but not massive jumps'.

All of the building trades were very busy and some took on apprentices, and Trebilcock and her staff worked feverishly for 16 months: 'it's been really intense, just really pumping it out'. She found the reporting requirements were a challenge, as their systems were not automated and the timeframe was too short to train staff. 'So there's been an awful lot of manual intervention and trying to make things reconcile and balance.' Over 500 buildings were upgraded and, as one criterion was geographical spread, around 28% of them were in country locations. A cross-section of housing types was involved, and included double units converted into large family homes, whole groups of walk-up flats, enlarged cottage flats, and Aboriginal Housing properties. 'We had to do it quickly, so they've all been vacant properties. So tenants who are going into them are quite excited.' The federal government required housing to be supplied to people at risk of homelessness or priority 1 on the waiting list, 'and in some cases we've been able to relocate tenants into the upgraded houses to use the other house for other purposes'.

The other component was new construction done by Property Services. Although building partnerships had been developed with non-government groups under the state's own Affordable Housing Fund, when it came to getting houses quickly, Phil Fagan-Schmidt said that 'we chose to use our in-house [expertise]'. Under the stimulus plan, Housing SA decided to build all the houses itself 'because the rules were use it or lose it and we weren't prepared – with $400 million – to risk losing any of it, and that's proven to be a good choice. We're ahead of target. [The new construction was to finish in 2011]'.

In December 2009 Housing Minister Jennifer Rankine and her federal counterpart Tanya Plibersek announced $22.5 million in Housing Affordability and Nation Building funding for the regeneration of Woodville West. The seven-year project was to replace 180 double units dating from the 1940s with 425 new rental and purchase houses. The Commonwealth would also provide money to build or buy 40 dwellings in neighbouring suburbs for relocation. 'The Rudd Government is keen to see sensible and sustainable urban renewal projects – like this one in Woodville West – which create mixed communities.'[88] Rankine concluded that the 'nation building' funds had 'provided the largest building program for social housing in 20 years and allowed strategic planning for new developments like Woodville West as well as innovation in projects such as the UNO apartments'.[89]

When Joslene Mazel and Phil Fagan-Schmidt reported back from the 2010 Housing Ministers' Conference on the effect of the Nation Building Plan, they said that South Australia had completed 298 upgrades, was building 232 new homes and had completed 11.

Minister Jennifer Rankine (centre) with Barry Atherton, Housing SA Maintenance Coordinator (left) and Ann Prime, Principal, Salisbury High School at the Doorways 2 Construction collaboration at Smithfield Plains, 8 December 2010. (Photo Shirley Trebilcock)

> This will exceed the target for new houses by approximately 20 per cent, a reflection of all the hard work being done by Housing SA. South Australia also stood out as the *only* jurisdiction on track to meet its June 2010 target for the Remote Indigenous Housing Agreement with the Commonwealth Government.[90]

The Housing Trust lives[91]

> Basically, it comes down to our intent that we maintain a fully-fledged board that provides expertise and advice with regard to housing in this state. (Hon. T. J. Stephens, Legislative Council debate, 2007)[92]

Mary Marsland was the Trust's first female Chair, succeeding Jay Hogan in January 2006 and steering the Board through the 'uncharted waters' of the following years. Marsland, a senior public servant, was presiding member of the Construction Industry Training Board, and was also chair of the South Australian Heritage Council. She had only one or two meetings as SAHT Chair before the announcement of the reform agenda, which she described as a policy push by the minister and government, and not initiated by the Board. The Board 'resolved to effectively move into transition mode, support the reform, meet its statutory obligations but not be the public face of the reform program'.[93] As chair, Marsland became a significant transitional figure. In practical terms the Housing Trust continued, operating as Housing SA.[94] In formal terms the SAHT continued as a legal entity (owner of the housing stock, which was managed by Housing SA).

Ideas alone are not enough to realise social change. There must also be organisations to carry those ideas through time. 'Jay's revolution' was carried forward by Housing SA staff and by an enduring SAHT. The Board's role in maintaining corporate memory was enhanced as SAHT staff dispersed through DFC, resigned in response to the restructure, or joined the cohort of baby boomers deciding to retire. For example, oversight of the complex negotiations involved in large urban renewals spanned many years. Just before the restructure of 2006, Board members requested an update on the Glenside Development. They were told that the Trust had purchased part of the Glenside Hospital site on the corner of Greenhill and Fullarton Roads back in 1994, intending to construct 21 apartments in three multi-storey buildings. Local residents had strongly objected, and the Trust had since been caught up in compulsory conferences and in sessions of the Development Assessment Commission, the Supreme Court, and the Environment, Resources and Development Court. Nothing had yet been built. Board members urged discussing with the Land Management Corporation how to place encumbrances on land to ensure affordable and high-need housing could be constructed on similar strategic sites.[95]

The SAHT discussed a paper on corporate governance in early 2006 which noted that whatever board model was used, the government, and not Board members or senior executives, was ultimately accountable to the South Australian electorate. The writers noted,

> This is clearly demonstrated in public housing, where the government feels public reaction through the media and community groups. The corporate governance model, which best suits SAHT, should be considered in the light of the high profile of social housing, its $6 billion asset base, its complex financial arrangements, including contracts involving private investment, the CSHA requirements, SAHT's long history in SA and in particular the potential impact of social housing on the State Budget.[96]

Weatherill had proposed that an Affordable Housing Trust would replace the original Trust in June 2007. As amendments to the legislation were drafted and debated, SAHT Board minutes reveal the uncertainty, members asking, 'when the Board is dissolved who will be responsible for the signing off of Annual Accounts and Annual reports?'[97] Board member Michele Slatter recalled years of

> constant change, most markedly from mid-2006 onwards as it became clear that the Board would go or be radically reformed and the Trust would similarly disappear in all but name. This took us into uncharted waters as the Board continued to try and make sure its legal duties under the Act were fulfilled in an evolving environment.[98]

Affordable housing remained on the agenda for the time being: a presentation to the SAHT Board in August 2006 by Hugh Stretton Award winner Jarrod Gitsham described his findings from examining affordable home ownership opportunities in the USA.[99]

A 'transitional meeting' of the Board was held at Riverside on 20 March 2007. Members considered a list prepared by Mary Marsland and Dennis Huxley (Acting General Manager, Asset Services) to help define risks needing attention. Of main concern were customers, housing outcomes, financial viability, governance, and operational management. Under 'financial viability' the discussion touched on the lack of preventative and program maintenance, the running down of the stock, and what the Trust would get for selling an additional 8,000 homes – no more than land value?[100] (Cabinet had approved the additional sell off – called the Affordable Homes Program – as a financial viability strategy, with the proceeds used to pay off debt. The Trust was told that the program would eliminate all housing portfolio debt by 2012–13, ending the need to sell down further stock to fund operations.)[101]

Customer satisfaction was at risk, given the pressures of the housing system, especially for Aboriginal Housing. 'Special Groups – is taking up not only high needs ... refugees, people in far regional areas – who are we housing?' Board members said also that they had lost contact with 'people management'. Matters of recruitment and selection, training and leadership needed to be addressed. A strategic direction for information technology had not been considered for a long time.

The Board had been operating 'remotely' through a service level agreement for 15 months. 'We have been told to operate under a care and maintenance basis through a 3rd party and have had to let go of the strategic issues.' And yet members had been appointed for their expertise and had made suggestions on matters needing to be dealt with beyond their 'caretaker terms'. They decided to look again at the wording in the service level agreement as well as the letter of support they had given to the Minister for the reform program 'that did diminish our role around policy direction'.[102] Weatherill's draft legislative amendments went even further in proposing to abolish the Board, but for legal and administrative reasons the legislation did not go through as anticipated.

The Legislative Council's role in Parliament as a house of review was put to the test in a prolonged debate between March and May 2007 on the Statutes Amendment (Affordable Housing) Bill. Passage of the legislative changes can be tracked through Hansard. When the bill was first debated, the government proposed to change the governance structure from independent governance (the Trust Board) to accountable governance (the minister). But that did not gain the support of the majority of members in the Legislative Council. No-one raised any concern with the operation of the Trust Board and no-one, apart from the government itself, made a case for change. Government members argued that a key principle of the reforms was ministerial accountability. 'Effective governance arrangements are those that enhance the minister's powers to govern and ensure that there are no unnecessary barriers ... [and] unimpeded accountability between the chief executive and the minister.' Council members were not persuaded of 'the merits of an increased emphasis on accountable governance rather than independent governance'.[103]

'I found this a particularly difficult bill to deal with, largely because it invites support on the basis of its name. Who can be against more affordable housing?' asked Greens MLC Member Mark Parnell, opening debate in the Council on 29 March 2007. But, he continued, the bill represented a major shift in public policy: 'we are abandoning the traditional role, function and model of an independent housing trust, that is, a model that has served this state very well'. He was surprised by the lack of public debate about this. Having himself consulted Hugh Stretton, Parnell eloquently surveyed the Trust's historical successes and canvassed alternatives to a bill that would dismantle it. The SAHT had provided both 'housing of last resort' and housing for blue-collar workers. Public housing had been used as a driver for economic growth, and was closely integrated with wider economic and social planning. The model had been highly successful and financially sound, leading to cheaper housing in South Australia than anywhere else. Present challenges included a high level of debt, outdated stock, welfare dependent clients, an increase in single-person households, and a political culture focused on individual rather than community rights, including the targeting of Commonwealth resources to high-needs individuals, rather than to working communities by way of public housing.

Parnell noted that the South Australian government's response to these trends was to no longer support public housing for a broad range of people. He sympathised with Weatherill, who was 'stuck between a rock and a hard place', but questioned the bill's radical response to end the model of independent housing authorities, reduce stock and target the remainder to welfare clients. The latest proposal for further reductions was heading for a residual 20,000 homes, and many were being transferred to housing associations and cooperatives. 'It seems to me that the government is effectively outsourcing responsibility for providing low-cost housing to the private sector ... it is, effectively ... a move to privatisation'. Whilst Commonwealth funding changes might be driving the bill, the state could allocate more funds to public housing. 'The dominant ideology that is driving this debate, as I see it, is an obsession that all debt is bad.' Stretton had asked 'What's wrong with the government actively borrowing to obtain housing stock?' The Greens believed that an independent Trust could be kept. The Minister's intention to achieve more affordable housing was genuine, but if the bill went through, and the Trust came under direct government control, divestment of public housing stock would continue. Parnell acknowledged the extent of market failure in the provision of affordable housing, but said the bill did not address the problem. The proposed new model would mean a much reduced public capacity to respond to housing needs.

Parnell said that the 2004 National Summit on Housing Affordability had highlighted three main requirements: more (not less) investment in public housing; better planning laws; and smarter use of government resources. The Greens praised innovative elements of the bill, such as the use of covenants to drive affordable housing and increasing the role of cooperative and community housing. 'However', he said, 'We do not need to effectively demolish the South Australian Housing Trust to achieve those ends ... a decision to abandon a public housing model that has worked so successfully in South Australia for many decades should not be taken lightly'.[104]

In short, the Legislative Council did not support dismantling the SAHT Board. At the crucial subsequent reading of the bill in May 2007, Paul Holloway tabled amendments in line with the Council's views, saying that the government would 'retain the status quo as far as the Housing Trust is concerned'. He dismissed the Liberal Opposition's proposal for a new name: South Australian Housing Board, describing the SAHT name as 'iconic'. Australian Democrat Sandra Kanck, who had intended to vote against the bill, told members that during the Parliamentary break she'd voiced her concerns to Weatherill. 'My key issue was accountability, which I felt was very much missing in what the government was proposing, but I am now satisfied, and I thank the minister for his time and also for the work of his officer, Simon Blewett'. Mark Parnell and Nick Xenophon also voiced their support. Parnell said,

> We do not want to be too hung up on names but having the word 'trust' still in there, I think, is an important symbolic measure, and it reminds those administrators that they are acting in a trustee capacity on our behalf, as a community, in relation to public housing.

Xenophon said that the government had backed down on its initial position because the Opposition and crossbenchers had fought against it. He continued,

> not only does the name, the brand, the iconic nature of the words 'Housing Trust' ... mean a lot to South Australians, but I also think it is a continuing acknowledgment of the legacy of Sir Thomas Playford in setting up the Housing Trust. I think it is important that that continue to be acknowledged. I support the government's position. I see it as being a significant improvement to what was proposed previously ...

Holloway proposed amendments pertaining to the SAHT Board as currently structured. Most were accepted. Some of them broadened the role of the Trust.

South Australian Housing Trust Board members and the General Manager in June 2006, front from left: Julia Dance, Mary Marsland and Don Lee; rear: Malcolm Downie, Jan Connolly, Mary Patetsos, Michele Slatter and Graham Foreman.

For example, the government added a clause requiring the SAHT to establish 'consultative arrangements with groups and organisations with an interest in the housing sector, including ... [those] that represent the interests of tenants or the providers of community or Aboriginal housing'. The new governance structure established over the past year would provide a more streamlined service delivery though Housing SA 'but', Holloway said, 'in recognising the need to ensure appropriate means for citizen voice and representation, the proposed amendment provides an assurance that the South Australian Housing Trust will consult with groups and organisations'. Another amendment clarified that the committee the SAHT must establish to increase the supply of affordable housing was the South Australian Affordable Housing Trust board (already in place). The SAHT was also responsible under the South Australian Cooperative and Community Housing Act.

In other words, South Australia's upper house agreed to both trusts. *The Statutes Amendment (Affordable Housing) Act 2007* received assent in June 2007, and commenced on 1 July 2007. Far from disappearing, the SAHT Board continued. It encompassed the separate boards of the SAHT, the South Australian Community Housing Authority, and the Aboriginal Housing Authority; and there was the South Australian Affordable Housing Trust (SAAHT). As Downie recalled, 'It didn't all go to plan and the Minister still has a Housing Trust Board and an Affordable Housing Trust Board (which is a subset of the former) but under the legislation, can report separately to the Minister'.[105] The SAAHT Board, established as part of the legislation, could report to the minister, but many of its activities were under delegation to the SAHT, and the SAAHT operated as a subcommittee of the SAHT. From July 2007 the SAHT Board was responsible for 'overseeing the achievement of strategic housing outcomes across the housing continuum', while the SAAHT Board acted as a facilitator 'increasing the supply of affordable housing through partnerships with the non-profit and private sector housing industry', but the SAHT Board would make decisions on expenditure of the Affordable Housing Innovations Fund, doing so through delegation.[106]

In effect, the South Australian Housing Trust was restored to its original oversight of state-supported 'worker housing', as well as the supply of housing for the poor. The Board's additional governance roles included ensuring that Housing SA established strategic and operational plans aligned to government priorities, funds available and CSHA requirements; and assisted Housing SA to advise the Minister on housing strategies.[107]

Although the SAHT Board was maintained, Mary Marsland, Mary Patetsos and Julia Dance were the only members whose appointments continued after July 2007 – the latter's term ended later that year. (See also Appendix 2.) Marsland and Patetsos continued as members of both the SAHT and Affordable Housing Boards, and Marsland was chair of both boards. New members of the SAHT Board included former housing minister Greg Crafter, Ted Byrt, Carole Davidson and Kerrynne Liddle. Commercial developer, Theo Maras, Land Management Corporation representative Pam Martin, and Estelle Bowman were also invited to join the SAAHT Board.[108] As a standing committee of the SAHT, the Affordable Housing Board shared members, some of whom were also appointed by the Labor government to related committees. For example, former ALP minister Greg Crafter was on both boards, as was Mary Patetsos, who was also a member of the Premier's Social Inclusion Board as well as the Public Space Advisory Committee. Her husband Nick Bolkus, a former ALP Senator and minister, was Chair of the Playford North Steering Committee.[109]

The first official meeting of the new SAHT Board was held on 6 September 2007, chaired by Mary Marsland, and visited by Minister Weatherill, who told members they would need to unlock opportunities by leveraging the existing asset base, as no extra money was likely to be available for housing. Weatherill restated his vision for a system that was a continuum from high-needs housing to home ownership, with Housing SA focussing on high-needs and the Board generating new opportunities through innovative and affordable initiatives. He voiced his hopes for a future in which Treasury was 'comfortable' with the financial viability of the SAHT, and comfortable with it entering partnerships that included taking on debt to unlock the potential of the asset base. There would be a newer, smaller public housing stock, better distributed, better located and universally accessible to transport and services, and sensitive to certain disability groups; as well as a robust community housing sector that would supply 5% of stock.

The Minister advised the Board to set strategic policy direction and urged collaboration with other housing institutions, such as HomeStart and the Land Management Corporation, and to form partnerships through the SAAHT Board. Board priorities included developing new approaches and partnerships to increase the stock of affordable housing, setting policy to help deliver the 15% targets, and identifying potential demonstration projects.[110]

The Board canvassed the feasibility of being offered first option on any government land that became available, 'questioned the Minister on the Government's appetite for SAHT to resume a development role', and asked him to clarify its roles. The Minister reiterated that the Department would look after tenancy and other day-to-day operations, but 'he agreed there is a fine line'. While the Board should keep to strategic policy and remain financially focused, it might 'need to drill down if it is concerned about any operational procedures that may arise'.

What then, were the differences between Housing SA and the Housing Trust from that time? The general understanding – still prevalent in 2010 – that there was no longer a Housing Trust, was certainly not the case. The legislative changes of 1995 and 2006 brought the Trust under more direct ministerial control, but as a statutory body created by legislation, the Trust retained a body corporate (the Board), remained the owner of the assets of housing and land, and was the contracting body. It also retained important operational responsibilities as required by the Act. As the only surviving board from 2006, its responsibilities were broadened rather than narrowed.

Both Fagan-Schmidt and Trebilcock observed that the SAHT Board had become less operational and more strategic, but its responsibilities were large and included housing improvement, decisions on budgets, audit and contracts and, because the Trust formally owned huge resources, monitored its own performance. Triennial investigations were still required under the Act, and another was concluded in 2010. Notice of intention to declare a property sub-standard continued to be considered and, if the owner or agent gave 'an insufficient response', the Board could declare the property to be sub-standard.[111] These actions under the Housing Improvement Act were little changed since 1940, but the Act was comprehensively reviewed in 2010.

The legislative amendments introduced in 2006 gave certain powers (previously belonging to the Aboriginal Housing and Community Housing boards) to the SAHT and others to the Minister, who also gained additional responsibilities (for example, management of Aboriginal housing in remote communities). Under Section 17 of the Act, the SAHT used DFC staff for the provision of services. Hence, Housing SA was the operational arm of the SAHT, but its role was broader than the Trust's had been in 2006. Fagan-Schmidt headed 1,000 Housing SA staff, who carried out a diverse range of housing activities including managing around 45,000 rental dwellings.[112] Weatherill's plan for the state to assume wider responsibilities for housing was realised. Fagan-Schmidt said, 'Certainly the

breadth of Housing SA is wider in South Australia than in any other jurisdiction in the sense of what sits within the set of policy tools'.

If Housing SA had a broader role than the SAHT, the difference was blurred once the legislation of 2007 restored an expansive role to the Trust. Fagan-Schmidt witnessed Minister Weatherill challenging the Board to be more strategic, and to widen its ambit to encompass the whole housing market. The members appointed to the SAHT and the Affordable Housing Trust Board had impressive industry, legal and other connections. 'Certainly', he added,

> having had the privilege of attending Board meetings as a reporting officer, a great deal of the conversation is around how to position and modernise and transform our business into a future that is working in the market, beyond the owner and landlord of properties. That's a core part of our business, but it's about extending it wider.

There was a mismatch between the continuation, even resurgence, of the Housing Trust and the carefully cultivated public perception of its eclipse. Tenant representative Glenice Bennett spoke for many others in declaring at the time of the 70th anniversary, 'The foundation of Housing SA is the SAHT. I cannot for the life of me see why they had to change the name'.[113] Using modern means to restore the full range of state support for public and affordable purchase housing need not have involved substituting 'Housing SA' for the Housing Trust. In doing so the impression was given that this was an obsolete model better discarded. Sue Vardon, who remained convinced of the necessity for 'Jay's revolution', acknowledged that substituting 'Housing SA' for 'Housing Trust' was a matter of administrative neatness because at the time a plethora of agencies in DFC were being regrouped. She said,

> We thought, 'We'll disband the Housing Trust. We'll make Housing SA, Disability SA – and, by the way, Families SA, we might as well make it consistent while we're here – Domiciliary Care SA' – So Jay wanted this consistent pattern of government agencies across the board. So it wasn't that anyone was particularly *after* the Housing Trust, it was that there was a pattern of things happening, and the Housing Trust was going to get into the pattern.

As an outcome of administrative repositioning now done, the title 'Housing SA' might soon be replaced. By contrast, 'South Australian Housing Trust' has earned an enduring esteem. The broad social and economic roles played by the Board and staff have been restored, together with new forms of historical state–private sector partnership. Phil Fagan-Schmidt said in his interview that his organisation worked every day with developers, 'as Playford would have', to build the supply of affordable housing, and that, 'there is a great deal in history that we are learning from again but, equally, not being trapped by history'. For him the challenge was 'about an organisation that is 75 years old building forward, respecting the past but also modernising for the future'.

The Trust celebrates its 75th anniversary in 2011 when South Australians will also commemorate 175 years since the state's foundation. As an icon of social and economic development should the name of the South Australian Housing Trust be restored in full in that same year?

Notes

1 ABC, *Counterpoint*, interview with Hugh Stretton by Michael Duffy, 29 May 2006.
2 Jay Weatherill (Minister for Housing), Speech notes: 70th Anniversary of SAHT, Migration Museum, Adelaide, 3 Dec 2006 (supplied by Minister's office).
3 Ogden, 'A Community for All Ages', p. 1; DFC intranet, SAHT, Rental regional stock report, June 2006. The Trust's historical record was also acknowledged when the SAHT Memorabilia Collection was opened by the Minister at Riverside on 16 Nov 2005. Memorabilia exhibitions were also held during 2006 at regional offices.
4 Susan Marsden, personal observations at 70th anniversary celebration, and Minister's speech, 3 Dec 2006.
5 *The Adelaide Review*, May 2006.
6 ABC Radio, *News online*, West Coast SA, 'Hard choice', 8 May 2006 www.abc.net.au/eyre/stories/s1631906.htm> viewed November 2006.
7 'Housing Plan for South Australia, Two year report card', 2007, p. 2.
8 Phrase used by Sue Vardon during discussion before her interview on 24 March 2010.
9 *The Advertiser*, 3 May 2006. Note that in this chapter the abbreviation SAHT will often be used in the text to distinguish it from the new trust and reduce repetition of similar names.
10 Malcolm Downie, (E), 27 Dec 2007.
11 Helen Fulcher interview, 11 Jan 2007 (SLSA, OH 807/2).

12 Sue Vardon, Introduction, DFC, Annual Report 2005–06 (Sept 06).
13 Vardon, DFC, Annual Report 2005–06 (Sept 06).
14 DFC intranet, Peter Smith, DFC, addressing Community Housing Council of SA, at the Special Briefing of The South Australian Housing Review, Stage 2, Public Sector Reform in DFC, 12 May 2006.
15 SAPD, House of Assembly, 15 Nov 2006, p. 184.
16 Don Lee, Recollections, 17 Sept 2007.
17 DFC Reform: FAQs – Housing (DFC intranet, May 2006), p. 1; *The Advertiser*, 3 May 2006.
18 Associate Professor Michele Slatter, 23 Sept 2007 (Q).
19 Interview with Mignon Schneider by Anne Lord, 7 Feb 2007 (N).
20 Mignon Schneider, 7 Feb 2007 (N).
21 Downie, (E), 27 Dec 2007.
22 Slatter, 23 Sept 2007 (Q).
23 Sue Vardon, notes from discussion, 24 March 2010.
24 Sister Janet Mead, SLSA interview, 11 May 2010 (R).
25 SAHT, Minutes 25 July 2006.
26 Downie, (E), 27 Dec 2007.
27 DFC intranet, Minister's Strategic Housing Advisory Committee, Barossa & Gawler Regional Consultation Outcomes (22 July 2008), p. 9.
28 HSA, Regional Services Service Delivery Model (Planning Day presentation, 2008).
29 Housing Minister Jennifer Rankine, 18 Oct 2010 (E).
30 *The Independent Weekly*, 23 Sept 2008.
31 Sue Vardon, interview, 24 Mar 2010 (SLSA, OH 807/3).
32 Quoted in *The Advertiser*, 5 May 2006
33 SAHT, Board Minutes, 22 Aug 2006 (Performance indicators, July 2006).
34 Lyndie Marsden, interviewed by S. Marsden, 15 Feb 2007 and 17 July 2009 (N).
35 SAPD, Legislative Council, 29 May 2007.
36 SAHT, Board Minutes, 22 Aug 2006 (Performance indicators, July 2006).
37 M. Findlay, 'Social housing for diverse cultural groups', Conference paper, Melbourne 2009, p. 1.
38 SAPD, 5 Mar 2009 (Hood's source was the SAHT's Annual Report, 2007/08).
39 It should be noted that the sales program was also intended to divest the Trust of low demand and poor performing stock, and to encourage home ownership amongst sitting tenants.
40 DFC intranet, Minister's Strategic Housing Advisory Committee, Barossa & Gawler Regional Consultation Outcomes (22 July 2008), p. 3.
41 *The Advertiser*, 11 Jan 2010.
42 Minister's Strategic Housing Advisory Committee, Barossa & Gawler ... (22 July 2008), pp. 2–4.
43 C. Johnston, 'After the 2003–08 Commonwealth–State Housing Agreement', Shelter, NSW, 2007, p. 47; Australian Government, Disability Supported Accommodation Program Consultations Report (Jan 2008) <www.facs.gov.au/sa/disability/pubs/policy/Documents/supported_accom_consulatations/default.htm> viewed May 2010.
44 Patricia Sumerling (Q), (E), 25 March 2007.
45 Alison Murchie, Public Housing Customer Forum, 19 Dec 2006.
46 *Eastern Courier*, 11 April 2007 (quoting MP David Pisoni).
47 Weatherill interview, 11 Jan 2007.
48 Barbara Holt, 6 Dec 2006 (Q).
49 Philip Fagan-Schmidt interview, 2010.
50 *The Advertiser*, 26 Apr 2007.
51 'Memorandum of Understanding between the Minister for Housing (on behalf of HSA and the Office for Community Housing) and Minister for Mental Health and Substance Abuse (on behalf of SA Mental Health Services) for the coordinated delivery of mental health, support and housing services to enhance the wellbeing and improve housing outcomes for people with a mental illness', Jan 2007, preamble, p. 4; operational guidelines, p. 1.
52 *Weekly Times*, 11 April 2007.
53 *Sunday Mail*, 8 Aug 2010.
54 Betty Alberton, memoir, (E), 19 July 2010.
55 Memoir provided by Public Housing Customer Forum members, (E) 23 July 2010.

56 Downie, 27 Dec 2007. The 2007 National Social Housing Survey – SA Report, Jan 2008, p. 10, recorded that the proportion of tenants dissatisfied with SAHT services decreased from 12% to 8% between 2003 and 2005, a change reversed between 2005 and 2007 when the proportion dissatisfied with Housing SA increased significantly from 8% to 11%.
57 Marlene Littlewood, Public Housing Customer Forum, Dec 2006; Anglicare, 'About TIAS' <www.anglicare-sa.org.au/about-tias/> viewed Aug 2010.
58 HSA, *Customer Chat*, Winter 2008.
59 *ABC News* 30 June 2008.
60 B. Alberton, 19 July 2010.
61 Marlene Littlewood, (E), 30 July 2010.
62 Public Housing Customer Forum memoir, 23 July 2010.
63 Minutes of Transitional Meeting of SAHT Board, 20 March 2007.
64 B. Alberton, (E), 15 & 19 July 2010.
65 From a phrase in SAHT Annual report 2005/06, 'Developing alternative approaches to the supply of affordable rental accommodation'.
66 Weatherill, speech notes, Dec 2006.
67 SAHT, Board Minutes, 22 Aug 2006 (Corporate performance report, July 2006).
68 Fagan-Schmidt interview, 2010.
69 SAHT, Board Minutes, 22 Aug 2006 (Progress Report on Affordable Housing Innovations Fund).
70 *The Advertiser*, 14 Aug 2007.
71 Verbal information, André Stuyt, Place Manager – Bowden Urban Village, Land Management Corporation, 6 July 2010.
72 Minister's speech, 3 Dec 2006.
73 DFC, Housing: corporate information, 16 May 2005 <www.housing.sa.gov.au/affordable/Default.aspx?tabid=306> viewed June 2007.
74 SAHT, Board, Report: Information for weekly Minister's meeting, 1 Dec 2006.
75 SAAHT, Minutes, 13 Mar 2007.
76 Johnston, p. 28. See also K. Rudd, T. Plibersek and W. Swan, 'New directions for affordable housing: addressing the decline in housing affordability for Australian families', ALP, June 2007.
77 HSA, *Customer Chat*, Summer 2009.
78 P. Stojanovich, 'Affordable Housing Innovations Fund' in PGP Update, Nov 2009.
79 *Adelaide Review*, May 2006.
80 SAPD, Legislative Council, 29 March 2007, pp.
81 *The Australian*, 8 Oct 2007.
82 Johnston, p. 29; Australian Dept of Families, Housing, Community Services and Indigenous Affairs, 'National Rental Affordability Scheme' <www.fahcsia.gov.au/sa/housing/progserv/affordability/nras/Pages/default.aspx> viewed July 2010.
83 SAHT, Annual Report 2008/09, pp. 19–20; J. Shadiac, 'From the NRAS', in PGP Update, Nov 2009.
84 *The Age*, 30 Nov 2008; HSA, PGP Update, Nov 2009; DFC intranet, Plibersek and Rankine, Minister for Joint News Release, 10 Dec 2009; <www.coag.gov.au/coag_meeting_outcomes/2009-02-05/docs/20090205_nation_building_jobs.rtf>; <www.coag.gov.au/coag_meeting_outcomes/2008-11 29/docs/20081129_national_affordable_housing_factsheet.pdf>; <www.coag.gov.au/intergov_agreements/federal_financial_relations/docs/national_partnership/national_partnership_on_social_housing.rtf> viewed June 2010.
85 SAHT, Annual Report 2008/09, p. 6.
86 DFC intranet, '102 Waymouth Street – the future of housing in the CBD', Dec 2009.
87 SAHT Board Paper, Mychelle Curran (Director, Urban Strategy And Asset Investment), Property Services 2009/10 Second Quarter Report, 11 Feb 2010.
88 Plibersek and Rankine, Joint News Release, 10 Dec 2009.
89 Minister Jennifer Rankine (E), 18 Oct 2010.
90 DFC intranet, March 2010.
91 Quoted from Sue Vardon's interview (2010).
92 SAPD, Legislative Council, 29 May 2007, p. 169.
93 Mary Marsland, (E), 1 Sept 2007.

94 As expressed in Housing SA memos and reports.
95 SAHT, Minutes, 26 April 2006.
96 SAHT, Board, Planning Workshop, 10 April 2006.
97 SAHT, Minutes, 25 July 2006.
98 Michele Slatter, 23 Sept 2007 (Q).
99 SAHT, Board Minutes, 22 Aug 2006.
100 Minutes of Transitional Meeting of SAHT Board, 20 March 2007.
101 SAHT, Triennial Review: Progress on Recommendations – April 2007.
102 SAHT, Transitional meeting minutes, 20 March 2007.
103 SAPD, Legislative Council, 29 May 2007 p. 168.
104 ibid., pp. 1,828–1,830 (and including following paragraphs and quotations).
105 Malcolm Downie, (E), 27 Dec 2007.
106 SAHT, Annual Report, 2006–07, pp. 8–9.
107 DFC, Mychelle Curran, Presentation to Maintenance Executive Team, National Directions In Housing, SAHT, Board/Housing SA Priorities (PowerPoint presentation, Feb 2008).
108 J. Weatherill, 'Industry summit and new pilot project to tackle affordable housing', Media release, 2 July 2007.
109 Hon Rob Lucas, Liberal Member of Legislative Council, 'Rann appointments update' (based on Government Gazette, media reports and 'Government Boards and Committees' 30 June 2007, tabled in Parliament), 28 Aug 2008 <www.roblucas.com.au/news/default.asp?action=article&ID=232> viewed May 2010.
110 SAHT, Board minutes, 6 Sept 2007 (and following paragraphs).
111 HSA, Fact Sheet no 55, Key services of Housing Improvement Branch', 3/2010.
112 DFC/HSA Intranet, Rental Stock Report Dec 2009: this gives a total of 44,896 lettable dwellings (excluding properties under construction, undergoing major maintenance or redevelopment and for sale).
113 Glenice Bennett, Public Housing forum, Dec 2006 (she had been chair of the Adelaide RAB since its formation in 1990).

Appendix 1

Housing Trust stock built, purchased and leased, 1937–2011

Year Ending 30 June	Detached Houses Completed			Attached Houses Completed			Flats Completed		
	Metro	Country	Total	Metro	Country	Total	Metro	Country	Total
1938	–	–	0	84	–	84	–	–	–
1939	–	–	0	290	–	290	–	–	–
1940	–	–	0	244	–	244	–	–	–
1941	–	–	0	206	100	306	–	–	–
1942	–	–	0	138	66	204	–	–	–
1943	–	23	23	218	140	358	–	–	–
1944	–	1	1	210	142	352	–	–	–
1945	–	–	0	344	–	344	–	–	–
1946	9	3	12	276	20	296	–	–	–
1947	265	20	285	258	44	302	–	–	–
1948	446	56	502	458	56	514	–	–	–
1949	513	212	725	389	138	527	–	–	–
1950	795	394	1,189	445	148	593	–	–	–
1951	1,941	467	2,408	513	138	651	–	–	–
1952	1,900	448	2,348	660	110	770	–	–	–
1953	2,696	632	3,328	910	192	1,102	56	–	56
1954	2,101	369	2,470	778	215	993	92	–	92
1955	1,409	302	1,711	1,078	309	1,387	80	–	80
1956	1,213	455	1,668	1,128	306	1,434	36	–	36
1957	1,395	361	1,756	892	272	1,164	132	–	132
1958	1,462	325	1,787	720	300	1,020	161	–	161
1959	1,294	365	1,659	878	320	1,198	184	–	184
1960	1,295	451	1,746	688	434	1,122	167	–	167
1961	1,071	360	1,431	1,106	490	1,596	169	10	179
1962	1,011	427	1,438	1,166	408	1,574	120	–	120
1963	1,007	295	1,302	1,080	314	1,394	69	–	69
1964	1,515	265	1,780	728	214	942	55	–	55
1965	2,243	222	2,465	428	286	714	45	–	45
1966	2,060	406	2,466	162	426	588	53	–	53

Cottage Flats Completed			Houses Bought	Houses Leased	Total		Rental Stock
Metro	Country	Total	Total	Total	Yearly	Cumulative	
–	–	–	–	–	84	84	84
–	–	–	–	–	290	374	374
–	–	–	–	–	244	618	618
–	–	–	–	–	306	924	924
–	–	–	–	–	204	1,128	1,128
–	–	–	–	–	381	1,509	1,509
–	–	–	–	–	353	1,862	1,862
–	–	–	–	–	344	2,206	2,206
–	–	–	–	–	308	2,514	2,497
–	–	–	–	–	587	3,101	2,761
–	–	–	–	–	1,016	4,117	3,275
–	–	–	–	–	1,252	5,369	3,795
–	–	–	–	–	1,782	7,151	4,454
–	–	–	–	–	3,059	10,210	6,162
–	–	–	–	–	3,118	13,328	7,629
–	–	–	–	–	4,486	17,814	9,671
–	–	–	–	–	3,555	21,369	12,513
90	–	90	–	–	3,268	24,637	14,667
100	–	100	–	–	3,238	27,875	16,135
88	–	88	–	–	3,140	31,015	17,765
64	–	64	–	–	3,032	34,047	19,012
101	–	101	–	–	3,142	37,189	20,294
139	–	139	–	–	3,174	40,363	21,551
108	–	108	–	–	3,314	43,677	22,513
113	5	118	–	–	3,250	46,927	23,592
120	6	126	–	–	2,891	49,818	24,895
81	–	81	–	–	2,858	52,676	25,916
91	2	93	–	–	3,317	55,993	26,775
140	–	140	–	–	3,247	59,240	27,514

Year Ending 30 June	Detached Houses Completed			Attached Houses Completed			Flats Completed		
	Metro	Country	Total	Metro	Country	Total	Metro	Country	Total
1967	1,880	412	2,292	148	574	722	–	–	–
1968	1,104	415	1,519	264	481	745	17	–	17
1969	715	517	1,232	146	386	532	30	–	30
1970	771	528	1,299	57	246	303	45	–	45
1971	797	574	1,371	138	282	420	214	31	245
1972	816	580	1,396	166	332	498	68	–	68
1973	505	364	869	181	236	417	134	40	174
1974	507	305	812	111	170	281	75	67	142
1975	619	499	1,118	68	201	269	56	25	81
1976	860	646	1,506	359	271	630	84	–	84
1977	821	652	1,473	256	249	505	31	–	31
1978	1,286	466	1,752	57	64	121	150	18	168
1979	1,256	340	1,596	180	30	210	42	12	54
1980	707	231	938	62	58	120	61	–	61
1981	469	410	879	243	64	307	5	6	11
1982	363	346	709	128	39	167	9	25	34
1983	461	393	854	411	2	413	83	26	109
1984	545	417	962	507	42	549	15	–	15
1985	696	297	993	510	51	561	25	–	25
1986	677	334	1,011	751	50	801	46	–	46
1987	892	333	1,225	735	140	875	44	6	50
1988	565	173	738	413	160	573	40	8	48
1989	401	9	410	552	124	676	78	20	98
1990	354	5	359	597	30	627	80	–	80
1991	222	14	236	1,024	44	1,068	22	–	22
1992	120	9	129	696	49	745	114	–	114
1993	169	4	173	558	24	582	111	–	111
1994	274	19	293	467	35	502	–	–	–
1995	239	–	239	522	39	561	–	–	–
1996	293	–	293	86	4	90	–	–	–
1997	59	–	59	11	–	11	–	–	–
1998	23	–	23	11	–	11	–	–	–
1999	99	1	100	8	–	8	–	–	–

Cottage Flats Completed			Houses Bought	Houses Leased	Total		Rental Stock
Metro	Country	Total	Total	Total	Yearly	Cumulative	
200	14	214	–	–	3,228	62,468	28,691
82	12	94	–	–	2,375	64,843	29,891
92	12	104	–	–	1,898	66,741	31,202
53	12	65	–	–	1,712	68,453	31,869
169	8	177	–	–	2,213	70,666	33,250
231	8	239	–	–	2,201	72,867	34,253
114	44	158	167	–	1,785	74,652	35,025
86	18	104	428	–	1,767	76,419	35,387
103	18	121	246	–	1,835	78,254	36,414
38	18	56	284	–	2,560	80,814	37,473
99	36	135	257	–	2,401	83,215	38,601
172	27	199	274	–	2,514	85,729	39,757
64	4	68	303	–	2,231	87,960	41,559
239	53	292	442	6	1,859	89,819	42,763
204	21	225	740	91	2,253	92,072	44,603
227	83	310	526	13	1,759	93,831	46,263
451	117	568	529	3	2,476	96,307	48,466
577	208	785	531	1	2,843	99,150	50,914
375	146	521	912	2	3,014	102,164	53,281
369	236	605	644	–	3,107	105,271	56,028
379	151	530	180	1	2,861	108,132	58,884
320	109	429	152	–	1,940	110,072	60,655
266	64	330	516	–	2,030	112,102	62,339
226	31	257	437	–	1,760	113,862	61,954
90	15	105	100	–	1,531	115,393	62,675
38	16	54	70	–	1,112	116,505	63,022
27	6	33	142	–	1,041	117,546	63,014
–	–	–	125	–	,920	118,466	62,322
–	–	–	87	–	887	119,353	61,359
–	–	–	109	–	492	119,845	60,460
–	–	–	59	30	129	119,974	59,339
–	–	–	94	–	128	120,102	57,731
–	–	–	96	–	204	120,306	56,301

Year Ending 30 June	Detached Houses Completed			Attached Houses Completed			Flats Completed		
	Metro	Country	Total	Metro	Country	Total	Metro	Country	Total
2000	96	–	96	25	11	36	–	–	–
2001	112	7	119	34	–	34	–	–	–
2002	118	15	133	12	4	16	–	–	–
2003	240	4	244	8	–	8	–	–	–
2004	307	4	311	46	–	46	–	–	–
2005	318	1	319	82	–	82	–	–	–
2006	395	9	404	116	–	116	–	–	–
2007	304	26	330	120	2	122	–	–	–
2008[1]	249	10	259	57	–	57	–	–	–
2009[2]	123	17	140	44	2	46	17	–	17
Total	**49,468**	**16,245**	**65,713**	**27,442**	**10,084**	**37,526**	**3,115**	**294**	**3,409**

Note: Prior to the establishment of the independent Aboriginal Housing Authority (AHA) in the 1999–2000 financial year, properties managed by the Aboriginal Housing Unit (AHU) were included in Housing Trust Levels

Tenantable property definitions have changed since 2003–04 and a change in data is as a result of these changes.

1 316 houses were constructed through the Newbuild Program in 2007–08. Twenty-six of these were not retained by Housing SA for rental stock.

2 Includes Wandana development at Gilles Plains (24 dwellings constructed, nil retained by Housing SA). An additional six dwellings were not retained by Housing SA for rental stock.

Cottage Flats Completed			Houses Bought	Houses Leased	Total		Rental Stock
Metro	Country	Total	Total	Total	Yearly	Cumulative	
–	–	–	74	–	206	120,512	53,310
–	–	–	20	–	173	120,685	51,251
–	–	–	17	–	166	120,851	49,543
–	–	–	18	–	270	121,121	47,551
–	–	–	12	–	369	121,490	46,737
–	–	–	13	–	414	121,904	46,122
–	–	–	8	–	528	122,432	45,455
–	–	–	8	–	460	122,992	44,886
–	–	–	28	1	345	123,337	45,819
–	–	–	40	–	243	123,580	45,103
6,526	**1,500**	**8,026**	**8,688**	**148**	**123,580**	**n/a**	**n/a**

Appendix 2

Members of the Board and General Managers, 1987–2011

General Managers	Term
Mr Brian Russell Abbey	26/04/1990 – 02/01/1996
Hon Stephen Baker	26/07/2001 – 25/07/2004
Mr Michael Ainslie Brock	03/01/1996 – 22/04/1997
Mr Edward (Ted) Byrt	10/08/2007 – 30/09/2010
Ms Jan R. Connolly	03/01/2004 – 30/06/2007
Mr Greg Crafter	10/08/07 – current (term expires 13/01/2014)
Ms Julia Dance	02/09/2004 – 19/10/2007
Ms Carole Davidson	10/08/2007 – 30/09/2010
Mr J. Davidson	03/01/2002 – 28/04/2002
Mr Trevor Gordon Dunsford	22/05/1997 – 23/05/2001
Mr Robert Weir Fairweather	04/01/1984 – 10/1989
Mr Graham Foreman	26/07/2004 – 30/06/2007
Mrs Sheila Kennedy Hall	04/01/1984 – 02/01/1996
Ms Bronwyn Kay Halliday	03/01/1996 – 02/01/2001
Dr Mal Hemmerling	13/01/2011 – current (term expires 13/01/2014)
Ms Susie Elizabeth Herzberg	03/01/1996 – 02/01/2006
Mr Jay Hogan Deputy Chair Chair	03/01/1996 – 13/01/2006 03/01/1996 – 03/01/2002 03/01/1999 – 02/01/2006
Mr James Maitland Hullick	29/04/1993 – 29/04/1997
Mr Peter John Humphries, Chair	05/09/1991 – 08/03/1993
Mrs Elizabeth Johnston	04/01/1984 – 03/01/1988
Mr Gerasimos Karidis	03/05/1984 – 25/07/1991
Ms Stephanie Wendy Key	04/01/1984 – 02/01/1996
Ms Josephine King	13/01/2011 – current (term expires 13/01/2014)

General Managers	Term
Ms S.T. King	05/09/1991 – 02/01/1996
Ms Kerrynne Liddle	21/05/2009 – 30/09/2010
Mr Donald Ralph Lee	30/04/1997 – 30/06/2007
Mr Claude Long	13/01/2011 – current (term expires 13/01/2014)
Mr Paul Madden	03/01/2001 – 02/01/2004
Mr John Francis McGirr	26/04/1990 – 02/01/1996
Ms Carmel O'Loughlin	04/01/1988 – 06/1990
Ms Mary Marsland, Chair	14/01/2006 – 13/01/2011
Professor Rodney Bruce Oxenberry, Chair	29/04/1993 – 02/01/1999
Mr Ray F. Paley, Chair	04/01/1980 – 03/01/1988
Ms Mary Patetsos	03/01/2006 – current (term expires 13/01/2014)
Mr C. Robin Pleydell	26/04/1990 – 03/01/1992
Mr Donald Sarah	04/01/1984 – 12/1989
Ms M Slatter	26/07/2004 – 30/03/2007
Mr Hugh Stretton Deputy Chair	14/01/1971 – 31/03/1989 04/01/1973 – 31/03/1989
Mr Leon Turnbull Sykes, Chair	14/04/1988 – 12/1991
Dr Josephine Mary Tiddy	03/01/1996 – 02/01/2001
Ms Karen Thomas	03/01/2001 – 29/03/2004
Mr Russell John Thomson	09/04/1993 – 11/08/1994
Mr Chris White	27/06/2002 – 26/06/2004
General Managers	
Mr Paul B. Edwards	02/10/1978 – 21/09/1990
Mr Richard W. Parker	04/02/1991 – 10/1994
Ms Jan R. Connolly, General Manager: Housing Services	10/1994 – 03/1997
Mr Peter A. Jackson, General Manager: Property Management	10/1994 – 02/1999

General Managers	**Term**
Mr Greg Black	10/1996 – 09/2002
Mr Malcolm Downie	28/04/2003 – 03/07/2006
Mr Phil Fagan-Schmidt,	03/07/2006 – 29/12/2007
General Manager: SAHT & Affordable Housing Trust	03/07/2006 – 29/12/2007
General Manager: Affordable Housing & Sector Development (*title change*)	29/12/2007 – 25/09/2008
Executive leadership, Housing SA	
Mr Peter Smith, Deputy Chief Executive: Housing and Disability	23/02/2005 – 24/10/2008
Ms Helen Fulcher,	
General Manager: Housing Services	03/07/2006 – 1/07/2008
Executive Director: Housing Services (*title changed*)	01/07/2008 – 29/08/2008
Mr Phil Fagan-Schmidt Executive Director: Housing SA	25/09/2008 – current

Glossary

***Note**: these definitions are based on those provided by Housing SA and current in 2010.*

Accessible housing For people with a disability, including supported accommodation and home modifications.

Affordable Homes Program Advice for people who wish to buy an affordable house.

Aboriginal Rental Housing Program Public housing for Indigenous people, applying similar eligibility criteria and wait-listing as for mainstream public housing.

Community housing An alternative to public or private rental housing. Affordable and appropriate housing provided for low-income-earners and people with special needs. Community housing includes that provided by associations and cooperatives.

Emergency accommodation Temporary accommodation for anyone who urgently needs somewhere to live.

Housing associations Not-for-profit organisations that manage housing for people who need support. Housing cooperatives are managed by the tenants who must be willing to participate in the running of the cooperative, and so households with high needs are more likely to be in association housing. Although government eligibility criteria apply, community housing differs from public housing because the landlord is an association and not a government agency.

Private rental housing Accommodation owned and rented out by a private landlord. People finding it difficult to get into private rental, as well as people in private rental with low incomes or other special needs may be eligible for government support or financial assistance.

Private rental assistance Advice and help for people renting accommodation from a private landlord.

Public housing Government-provided rental housing (SAHT/HSA) for people on low to moderate incomes who may also have other needs. Eligibility criteria apply to favour households most in need, although most applicants join a waiting list. Rent is based on 25% of household income.

Public housing types:

Attached houses: Medium density (ground level or multi-storey), may have some private garden, may have separate title, strata title or be part of a larger title. Include attached houses, 1 or 2 storey maisonettes, medium density units, villa flats or town houses

Boarding houses: premises used for short, medium or long term accommodation. Several unrelated persons (generally more than 10) rent single or shared rooms. Residents are homeless or transient, those who are disadvantaged or those needing support services

Cottage Flats: Purpose built flats for the elderly, not separately titled, may have some private yard, generally no direct street access, usually only ground level. Include Cottage Flats and Bedsitter dwellings.

Double Units: Original SAHT rental dwellings constructed in pairs with party wall (or carport linked), on a single title or part of a larger title; have their own street access and private garden space (see also B,C&S)

Single Unit Brick: Detached brick dwelling that may have a separate strata title or be part of a larger title, have their own street access and private garden spaces. Include Rural Grant Houses.

Single Unit Timber: Detached timber dwelling that may have a separate strata title or be part of a larger title, have their own street access and private garden. Include Imported Dwellings (see B,C&S).

Walk Up Flats: Dwellings which are attached, have no private yard space, generally multi-storey configurations, may be strata titled.

Transitional accommodation For anyone in a period of transition - for example new arrivals in SA, young people leaving care, Aboriginal people travelling between remote communities, or people leaving prison.

Urban consolidation Development aiming to increase the number of dwellings in established urban areas to curb suburban sprawl, by building on vacant sites and large gardens (also called in-fill), or through demolition of old houses and construction of larger numbers of smaller houses in their place.

Abbreviations

ABC	Australian Broadcasting Corporation
ABS	Australian Bureau of Statistics
AHA	Aboriginal Housing Authority
ALP	Australian Labor Party (Labor)
B,C & S	*Business, Charity and Sentiment* (SAHT history, 1986)
BHP	Broken Hill Proprietary Ltd
BNP	Better Neighbourhoods Program
COAG	Coalition of Australian Governments
CRA	Commonwealth Rental Assistance
CSHA	Commonwealth State Housing Agreement
CSTDA	Commonwealth State Territory Disability Agreements
CSO	Community Service Obligation
DHS	Department of Human Services (SA)
DFC	Department for Families and Communities (SA)
(E)	email
EHO	Emergency Housing Office
ESD	Ecologically Sustainable Design (or Development)
ETSA	Electricity Trust of SA
GST	Goods and Services Tax
HIA	Housing Industry Association
HTN	Housing Trust News (staff newsletter)
HSA	Housing SA
MFP	Multi-Function Polis
NARS	National Rental Affordability Scheme
NLA	National Library of Australia
OPAC	Operational Policy Advisory Committee (SAHT)
PHA	Public Housing Authority
PRESS	Private Rental Establishment and Support Services
(Q)	History questionnaire sent to tenants, staff and board members
RAB	Regional Advisory Board
SAAHT	South Australian Affordable Housing Trust
SAAP	Supported Accomodation Assistance Program
SACHA	South Australian Community Housing Authority
SAHT	South Australian Housing Trust
SAPD	South Australian Parliamentary Debates (Hansard)
SAULT	South Australian Urban Land Trust
SHA	State Housing Authority
SLSA	State Library of South Australia
TTTL	*Trust Talk Tenant Link*
UPA	Urban Projects Authority

Bibliography

This bibliography adds to that published in *Business, Charity and Sentiment*, and so does not include sources cited in 1986. To help readers, this bibliography follows a similar format, as follows:

Official sources and Archives (excepting the following); SA Housing Trust/ Departmental sources; Books and articles; Unpublished papers, reports and theses; Newspapers; Internet and other; Interviews and written recollections When only one or two references are made to a source, details are provided only in the footnotes; and full details of individual interviews are also provided there.

Abbreviations: *see* Glossary

Official sources and archives

Australia. Industry Commission 'Public housing' Report no. 34, 11 Nov 1993, I & II.

ABS (2001) 2001 *Year Book Australia*, ABS, Canberra.

Australian Dept of Families, Housing, Community Services and Indigenous Affairs, National Rental Affordability Scheme, viewed July 2010.

Commonwealth of Australia, Senate Community Affairs reference Committee, A hand up not a hand out: renewing the fight against poverty, Report on poverty and financial hardship, Parliament House, Canberra, March 2004.

Planning Review '2020 vision: planning strategy for metropolitan Adelaide' SA Government, Adelaide, June 1992.

SA Parliament, *Hansard* (SAPD) See chapter notes for details.

SAHT, Triennial Reviews See chapter notes for details.

SA Dept of Housing and Urban Development 'Evaluation instrument 1996–1997. Building Better Cities South Australia' End of program report, July 1997.

SA Housing Trust/Housing SA/departmental sources

Note: a wide range of historical records, including Board minutes, staff newsletters, reports, plans and photographs, were consulted in the SAHT Memorabilia Collection, kept by Housing SA in the Riverside offices, Adelaide. For specific references to most SAHT/Housing SA, brochures, leaflets and media releases, *see* endnotes.

DFC/SAHT/Housing SA brochures, 2006–2010; Rental Stock Report (for details, see chapter notes).

Department for Families and Communities (see also endnotes)
Customer chat ('Connecting you to housing') no 1, November 2006 –
'Sue's news' Intranet newsletter from CEO, Sue Vardon, 2006–
Peter Smith 'Public sector reform in DFC', Powerpoint presentation, 2006
Annual report 2005–06.
S Marsden, R Carrigan, A Romanic & R Whitten, 'An overview of past and current practice. A brief history of State involvement in the care of children and young people in South Australia', Report commissioned by DFC, submitted to Commission of Inquiry (Children in State Care), Adelaide, Sept 2006.
DHS, *SAHT Act 1995*: National Competition Policy Review report [2000?]
Housing SA, 'Housing Plan for South Australia, Two year report card', 2007.
Ogden, Paul (SAHT) 'A Community for All Ages - Building the Future', Commonwealth Dept of Health & Ageing, National Speakers Series, Adelaide, 2 December 2005.
South Australian Affordable Housing Trust (SAAHT), Minutes, 13 March 2007.
SAHT, Annual reports 1986–2009; *Housing Trust in focus* 1986–2000 (supplement to Annual Report). Note: the SAHT was legislatively required to produce an Annual Report for the Minister
SAHT, Board Minutes 1986–2010; Board letters 1989–2006.
SAHT, Chronological history of the South Australian Housing Trust (1st edition based on chronology prepared for B,C&S by S Marsden and D Price, updates by Wendy Bromell), 2001, 2004; <www.housingtrust.sa.gov.au/resources/SAHT_Chronological_History.pdf>.
SAHT, 'Guidelines for writing support letters for early housing assistance', 2001.

SAHT/Housing SA Newsletters

staff

TrustTalk. Note: the DFC library holds issues to 1967, with a large gap from 1968–1996, and the set is incomplete. See also below.
Housing Trust News (HTN) 1989–94; 1997–2000.
'From my desk' (General Manager, Paul Edwards), no 5, March 1990
Blackchat, 1996–2002? Intranet staff newsletter, from Greg Black (General Manager)
'Fulchat' Intranet staff newsletter, from Helen Fulcher (General Manager), no 1, 26 July 2006–

customers

From the GM's desk, no 1 (May 1989), 1st state-wide issue of SAHT tenant newsletter, *Tenant link*.
Tenant link trust talk (merged 'TrustTalk' and 'Tenant link') June–Dec 1998; replaced by *Trust Talk Tenant Link* 1999–2006; replaced by *Customer Chat* May 2006–

Focus 2000 (a magazine for and by tenants), 1989–

Books and articles

Adelaide City Council (1999) *Shared effort: Adelaide City Council and social housing in the city, 1986–1999*, Adelaide City Council, Adelaide.

Allery, Linda, compiler (1996) *Elizabeth: from dusty plains to royal names*, City of Elizabeth, Gawler, SA.

Badcock, Blair 'Recently observed polarising tendencies and Australian cities' *Australian Geographical Studies*, 35, 3, November 1997.

Badcock, Blair 'Thirty years on: gentrification and class changeover in Adelaide's inner suburbs, 1966–96', *Urban Studies*, 38, 9, 2001.

Baum, S. 'A typology of socio–economic advantage and disadvantage in Australia's large non–metropolitan cities, towns and regions', *Australian Geographer*, 37, 2, July 2006.

Bosman, Caryl Jane 'Golden opportunities: the making of Golden grove, South Australia, 1975–2000', D Jones, ed., 20th century heritage: our recent cultural legacy, Australia ICOMOS national conference proceedings, Adelaide, 2002.

Burnley, I, Murphy, P and Fagan, R, *Immigration and Australian cities*, Federation Press, Sydney, 1997.

Coles, Rita, ed. (1997) The end of public housing? Discussion forum 1996, Urban Research Program, ANU, Canberra.

Dinzey–Flores, Z Z, 'Public housing, policy and design in Puerto Rico' *Journal of Urban History*, 33, 3, March 2007.

Donley, R J R, (2001) *Marion: a suburban city 1945–2000*, Peacock Publications, Adelaide.

Fincher, Ruth 'Locational disadvantage: an appropriate policy response to urban inequities?' *Australian Geographer*, 22, 2, November 1991.

Foard, G, Karmel, R, Collett, S and Hulmes, D, (1994) *Public housing in Australia,* Australian Institute of Health and Welfare, Canberra.

Gabriel, M and Jacobs, K, 'Opportunities and constraints in state housing policy: the example of Tasmania's "Affordable Housing Strategy"', *Urban Policy & Research*, 24, 4, December 2006.

Graham, B, (2005) *PEACH Housing Co–operative Inc., 1983–2005: our story*, 2nd ed., PEACH Housing Co–operative Inc., Adelaide.

Harloe, Michael, (1993) 'The social construction of social housing', Urban Research Program Working Paper no 34, ANU, Canberra.

Hassell in association with Graeme Hugo, (1996) *Immigrants and public housing*, Department of Immigration and Ethnic Affairs, Canberra.

Haughton, Graham, 'Searching for the sustainable city: competing philosophical rationales and processes of "ideological capture" in Adelaide, South Australia', *Urban Studies*, 36, 11, 1999.

Hugo, Graeme, 'SA's population policy', *Independent Weekly*, 9–15 February 2008.

Johnston, Craig, 'After the 2003–08 Commonwealth–State Housing Agreement: a background to some debates in national housing policy', Paper, Shelter NSW Incorporated, Nov 2007 <www.shelternsw.org.au/docs/rpt07postcsha-sb34.pdf>.

Jones, Michael, (1996) *The Australian welfare state: evaluating social policy 4th edition*, Allen & Unwin, Sydney.

Kemeny, Jim, (1995) *From public housing to the social market. Rental policy strategies in comparative perspective*, Routledge, London & New York.

Kenny, Chris, (1993) *State of denial*, Wakefield Press, Adelaide.

Kilner, David, (2002) *From dream to reality. A history of the Northern Suburbs Housing Co-operative Inc. 1981–2002*, Northern Suburbs Housing Co-operative Inc., Adelaide.

Kilner, David, (2005) *Housing policy in South Australia since white settlement*, Digitalprintaustralia.com, Adelaide.

McClelland, A, (2003) *A common purpose: ethical, practical and transformative directions for public and housing policy in Australia*, Swinburne University of Technology, Hawthorn, Vic.

Marsden, Susan and Parkin, Andrew, (1989) 'Hugh Stretton and the South Australian Housing Trust', in L Orchard & R Dare, eds, *Markets, morals and public policy*, Federation Press, Sydney.

Marsden, Susan, (1986) *Business, charity and sentiment: the South Australian Housing Trust 1936–1986*, Wakefield Press, Adelaide.

Marsden, Susan, 'Housing', in W Prest, K Round & C Fort, eds, *The Wakefield companion to South Australian history*, Wakefield Press, Adelaide 2001.

Murphy, Catherine, (2006) *Women housing women, 1980–2005: the first 25 years of the Women's Housing Association Inc*. Women's Housing Association Inc. Kilburn, SA.

National Shelter, (1994) *Public housing in Australia: issues and directions for change: a report*, National Shelter (Australia), Canberra.

Neilson, Lyndsay, (2005) 'Managing urban change. The need for diversity & choice in housing & urban development', 12th Annual F Oswald Barnett Oration, University of Melbourne, Carlton, Vic.

Neutze, Max, (1998) 'Housing and infrastructure for Indigenous Australians', Urban Research Program Working Paper no 65, ANU, Canberra.

Paris, Chris, [1996] 'Governments, communities and housing policies in Australia', AHURI, Working paper no. 8.

Paris, Chris, (1993) *Housing Australia*, Macmillan Australia, South Melbourne.

Peel, Mark, (1993) 'Making a place: women in the "Workers' City"', Urban Research Program Working Paper no 38, ANU, Canberra.

Peel, Mark, (1995) *Good times, hard times: the past and the future in Elizabeth*, MUP, Carlton, Vic.

Percival, R, Landt, J, & Fischer, S, (1998) 'The distributional impact of public rent subsidies in South Australia', April 1997 Discussion paper no. 26,

National Centre for Social and Economic Modelling, University of Canberra, Canberra.

Purdy, S and Kwak, N, 'Introduction: new perspectives on public housing histories in the Americas', *Journal of Urban History*, **33**, 3, March 2007.

Reeves, Paul, (2005) *An introduction to social housing*, 2nd edn, Elsevier Butterworth–Heinemnn, Oxford.

Self, Peter, (1995) 'The Australian Urban and Regional Development Review: what can it achieve?' Urban Research Program Working Paper no 46, ANU, Canberra.

Shelter SA, (2007) 'Become a member today!' Brochure, Shelter SA, Adelaide.

Stilwell, Frank, (1997) 'Globalisation and cities: an Australian political–economic perspective', Urban Research Program Working Paper no 59, ANU, Canberra.

Stretton, Hugh, (2005) *Australia Fair*, University of NSW Press, Sydney.

Troy, Patrick, ed., (2000) *A history of European housing in Australia*, Cambridge University Press, Cambridge.

SAHT, (1992) *Urban consolidation: a record of achievement in public housing*, SAHT, Adelaide.

Walmsley, D J and H C Weinand, 'Is Australia becoming more unequal?' *Australian Geographer*, **28**, 1, 1997.

Wood, G A, (2004) 'What is happening in Australian housing markets? Why policy makers should be concerned', 11th Annual F Oswald Barnett Oration, University of Melbourne, Carlton, Vic.

Wright, Bruce, (2000) *Cornerstone of the capital. A history of public housing in Canberra*, ACT Housing, Canberra.

Unpublished papers, reports and theses

Baker, Emma, 'Public housing tenant relocation: residential mobility, satisfaction, and the development of a tenant's spatial decision support system', PhD thesis, University of Adelaide, 2002 [online: Australian Digital Theses Program]

Cody, Sam, 'Tenants' verdict: South Australian tenants' experiences of the private rental market', Report [questionnaire conducted in 1999], Shelter SA, Adelaide [?2001].

Gael Fraser & Associates, 'West End boarding and rooming house strategy', Draft report to Adelaide City Council, May 1995.

Fraser, Gael, 'Community housing and urban renewal', Minor thesis, Master of Regional and Urban Planning, University of SA, 1999.

Girardi, John, (Housing SA) 'The new urban renewal development in Woodville West', Presentation given at the Housing Coalition (quarterly meeting of SA housing managers and directors), 16 March 2010.

Findlay, Michael (Housing SA), 'Social housing for diverse cultural groups', Paper presented at 6th National Housing Conference, Melbourne 2009.

Hasan, Vesna, 'A critical review of the evolution of approaches to public housing provision in South Australia', B Planning thesis, University of South Australia, 1997.

Hoth, Tammo, 'An examination of the social and physical outcomes of urban renewal, with reference to the "Mitchell Park" Urban Renewal Project', B Urban and Regional Planning thesis, University of South Australia, 2002.

Hughes, Melanie, 'Community development and public housing estates', Shelter NSW Co–op Ltd., Shelter Brief 24, Sydney, 2004.

Kilner, David, 'The evolution of South Australian urban housing policy 1836-1987', PhD thesis, University of Adelaide, 1988.

Marroncelli, A, 'The evolution of social mix in the South Australian Housing Trust', Grad. Dip. Regional and Urban Planning, University of SA, October 1993.

Marsden, Susan, 'A history of Woodville, 1976–1986', Adelaide 1987, unpublished typescript (City of Charles Sturt Library).

Marsden, Susan, 'Constructing Playford's city: the South Australian Housing Trust and the transformation of Adelaide, 1936-1966', PhD thesis, Flinders University, 1994.

McIntosh, Greg, 'Changing face of public housing', Research note no. 24, 1999–2000, Parliamentary Library, Commonwealth of Australia, Canberra.

Monro, Dugald, 'The Results of Federalism: an examination of housing and disability services', PhD Thesis, University of Sydney. Economics and Political Science, 2006.

Neldner, Simon, 'Reversal of fortunes: the post–industrial challenge to work and social equality: a case study of "The Parks" community of Northwestern Adelaide', PhD thesis, University of Adelaide, 2001.

Slatter, Michele and Beer, Andrew, 'Housing evictions in South Australia: a study of bailiff–assisted evictions', Flinders University and SAHT, Adelaide, 2003.

Thorp, Katherine, 'The benefits of inner city living for low income earners. A study of Housing Trust tenants in inner Adelaide', BA (Hons) thesis, University of Adelaide, 1990.

Victory, Jan, 'Social justice in the market place and the South Australian Housing Trust', B Social Work thesis, University of South Australia, 1993.

Weatherill, Jay, (Minister for Housing), Speech notes: 70th Anniversary of SAHT, Migration Museum, Adelaide, 3 Dec 2006.

Newspapers

Adelaide Review
The Advertiser (SA)
The Age (Victoria)
The Australian
Australian Financial Review
Australian Society

City Messenger (Messenger, Adelaide)
Eastern Courier (Messenger, Adelaide)
Independent Weekly (SA)
News Review (Messenger, Adelaide)
Sunday Mail (SA)
Sydney Morning Herald
Weekly Times (Messenger, Adelaide)
Whyalla News

Internet and other media

For most Internet references, see chapter notes, including for specific reference to from DFC/SAHT/HSA intranet and from *ABC News* and other programs, <www.abc.net.au/>.

ABS <www.abs.gov.au/ausstats/abs>

DFC Intranet, including DFC Reform, Housing – Staff Question and answers (May 2006) <http://in.dfc.sa.gov.au>; as well as: Housing; Aboriginal Housing; Affordable Housing; Housing SA; and SAHT, including: Our history (prepared by Beverley Morris for 70th anniversary exhibition, 2006 <www.housingtrust.sa.gov.au/text/text.asp?swId=1&pgId=11>), viewed 2006 & 2007.

(For further details of reports, media releases and papers accessed on the DFC Intranet, between 2006 and 2010, see chapter notes.)

Hayward, D, The reluctant landlords? A history of public housing in Australia [1995] 'The last throes of public housing? 1973–1995', viewed July 2007 <www.infoxchange.net.au/rhchome/iurhc/s0502.htm>.

Ministers – Premier and Ministers of South Australia, viewed 2006, 2007, 2010 <www.ministers.sa.gov.au>

NSW Dept of Housing, The History of Public Housing in New South Wales, viewed August 2006, <www.housing.nsw.gov.au/history.htm>.

Interviews and written recollections

These recollections were provided as written responses to staff or tenant/client interview questionnaires (Q), prepared by Susan Marsden (SM), helped by Anne Lord, with follow-up question-and-answers by telephone or email. Some interviews were recorded by Marsden in notes (N) and those digitally recorded are marked (R). (These interviews have been lodged in the State Library of SA.) Recollections supplied by email, mainly by staff (all in 2007) are marked (E). Further details are supplied in chapter notes. Interviews recorded for other histories were also consulted, and full details are given (including interviewer's name).

Mr John (Jack) Holder, former Noarlunga Councillor, interviewed for City of Onkaparinga and SLSA, 13 March 2008 (R) (SLSA, OH 768/4)

Mr David Jackson, personal communication, 12 Sept 2010.

Sister Janet Mead, interviewed for SLSA, 11 May 2010 (R) (SLSA, SOHC/OH 934)

Ms Stephanie Key, former Minister for Housing and former SAHT Board member, 13 February 2008 (N)

Hon Jay Weatherill, Minister for Housing, interviewed 11 Jan 2007 (R) (SLSA, OH 807/1).

Hon Jennifer Rankine, Minister for Housing, response to interview questions, 18 Oct 2010 (E).

Tenants and other customers.

Except where indicated all of the following people responsed to questionnaires between Nov 2006 and Feb 2007 (Q). Some gave further interviews in 2007, (E) or noted (N). Interviews marked (PHCF) were recorded by Marsden and Lord with Public Housing Customer Forum members at their meeting at Housing SA on 19 Dec 2006. Another memoir was provided by Forum members, compiled by chairperson Marlene Littlewood on 23 July 2010.

Mrs Betty Alberton – also interviewed (N) (PHCF); and (E) 15 & 19 July 2010
Mrs Joy Atkinson
Mr Bryan Atkinson
Mrs Michele Austen
Mr R.A. Bamblett
Ms Nancy Barber
Mrs Joan Beagley
Mrs Glenice Bennett – also interviewed (N) (PHCF)
Mr Paul Burger
Ms Sandra Chapple – and further interview (E)
Mr Peter Chigwidden
Ms Jenni–Lee Cotton
Miss Mary Cusack
Mr Graham George Daniels
Mr Ray Dunstall
Mr Michael J Elijah
Mr Tony Elmers, Tenants' Association – interviewed (N)
Mrs Josephine M Elphick
Mrs Ellen Greenslade
Mr Ronald Harding
Ms Joanne Holmes
Ms Bernadette Kuhar
Ms Marlene Littlewood – interviewed (N) only (PHCF); (E) 8 & 23 July 2010.
Dr Leith MacGillivray – and further recollections (E)
Miss Catherine McGlaughlin
Ms Lyndie Marsden – interviewed (N)
Ms KM [requested not to publish her full name]

Ms Suzanne Millard
Mr Phil Miller (E) 5 July 2010
Ms Alison Murchie – also interviewed (N) (PHCF)
Ms Elizabeth Ostermann – memoir written in response to Q (Dec 2006-Jan 2007)
Mrs Daphne Pettman
Mr William AG Pegram
Mrs Joy Kay Riley
Miss Fay Rohrlach – also interviewed (N)
Mr Dennis Smith
Mr John Strang – also interviewed (N) (PHCF)
Ms Patricia Sumerling (E) 25 March 2007
Ms Melva Wallace
Miss Zoi W. (pseudonym: name supplied).

Housing SA/SAHT present and past Board members and staff

Interviewed by or recollections provided to Susan Marsden (SM) unless otherwise indicated. Note: interviews lodged in the NLA and SLSA include transcripts.

Mr Jim Birch, former CEO, Department of Human Services, 9 May 2008 (N)
Mr Greg Black, Emergency Housing Office Manager, interviewed by SM for *Business, charity and sentiment*, 14 June 1982 (R) (SLSA, SRG 660/1/6)
Mr Greg Black, SAHT General Manager, interviewed by Vicki Lachlan for 'The Women's Housing Oral History project', 7 Aug 2003 (R) (SLSA, OH 669/2)
Ms Janet Combridge, Housing Advisor, Marion Region, 29 Jan 2007 (E)
Mr Malcolm Downie, former SAHT General Manager, 23 August, 23 Oct, 27 Dec 2007 (E) and (N)
Mr Paul Edwards, SAHT General Manager, interviewed for Business, charity and sentiment, 11 & 18 Sept 1984 (R) (SLSA, SRG 660/1/40)
Mr Phil Fagan-Schmidt, Housing SA Executive Director, interviewed 31 Mar 2010 (R) (SLSA, OH 807/5)
Mr Mike Findlay, Housing SA, Manager, Development Opportunities, 16 April 2009 (N)
Mr Fred Foord, former staff member (25 Year Club), 6 & 10 Sept 2007 (E)
Ms Helen Fulcher, Housing SA, General Manager Housing Services, 11 Jan 2007 (R) (SLSA, OH 807/2)
Dr Ian Halkett, SAHT officer, interviewed by Karen Burnes for The Women's Housing Oral History project, 7 Aug 2003 (R) (SLSA, OH 669/3)
Ms Carmel Hallion, Housing Manager, Modbury Region, 22 Jan 2007 (E)
Ms Wendy Hackel, Housing SA staff & former SAHT Librarian, 2 Nov 2006 (N)
Ms Susie Herzberg, former Board member, Aug & Sept 2007 (E)
Ms Barbara Holt, former staff member and current tenant (Q)

Mr Murray Hutchesson, Housing SA, Director, Technical Services, 16 Oct 2007 (N)

Mr Don Lee, former Board member, 9 Sept 2007 (E); 12 Sept 2007 (N)

Ms Tina Lloyd, former staff member, 2 June, 12 & 13 Sept 2007 (E), and further comment provided, 2010.

Ms Mary Marsland, Board member, 1 Sept 2007 (E)

Ms Helen Ottaway, Project Officer, Special Needs Housing Unit, 24 Feb 2007 (Q)

Mr Robert Rathbone, former staff member (25 Year Club), (Q) (and 'A short story of a maintenance inspector's experiences'), 10 Sept 2007

Ms Tracey Roissetter, Housing Manager, Murray Region, 29 Jan 2007 (E)

Mr Keith Rothe, former staff member (25 Year Club), 7 Sept 2007 (Q)

Ms Mignon Schneider, Housing SA, Manager, Business & Customer Services, 2 Nov 2006 (N); 7 Feb 2007 (N, recorded by Anne Lord)

Associate Professor Michele Slatter, former Board member, 23 Sept 2007 (Q)

Emeritus Professor Hugh Stretton, interviewed 4 & 8 Oct 2002 (R) (NLA, TRC 4895)

Ms Shirley Trebilcock, Housing SA, Manager Maintenance, 3 & 5 Oct 2007 (Q) (E); interviewed 26 Mar 2010 (R) (SLSA, OH 807/4); 2 Dec 2010 (E)

Ms Sue Vardon, former DFC Chief Executive, interviewed 24 Mar 2010 (R) (SLSA, OH 807/3).

Note also numerous media interviews, in particular with ministers and with general managers, e.g., ABC Radio transcripts (see chapter notes)

Index

T

X

Y

Z